Virtual Private Networking

ISBN 0-13-020335-1

90000

The Prentice Hall PTR
Internet Infrastructure Series

VIRTUAL PRIVATE NETWORKING
A View from the Trenches

Bruce Perlmutter

Prentice Hall PTR
Upper Saddle River, New Jersey 07458
www.phptr.com

Library of Congress Cataloging-in-Publication Data

Perlmutter, Bruce.
   Virtual private networking: a view from the trenches / Bruce Perlmutter, Jonathan Zarkower.
      p. cm.
   Includes index.
   ISBN 0–13–020335–1
   1. Extranets (Computer networks) I. Zarkower, Jonathan. II. Title.
   TK5105.875.E37 P47 1999
   650′.0285′46—dc21   99–047024

Acquisitions editor: *Mary Franz*
Editorial assistant: *Noreen Regina*
Cover designer: *Anthony Gemmellaro*
Cover design director: *Jerry Votta*
Manufacturing manager: *Maura Goldstaub*
Marketing manager: *Lisa Konzelmann*
Project coordinator: *Anne Trowbridge*
Compositor/Production services: *Pine Tree Composition, Inc.*

© 2000 by Prentice Hall PTR
Prentice-Hall, Inc.
Upper Saddle River, New Jersey 07458

Prentice Hall books are widely used by corporations and government agencies for training, marketing, and resale.

The publisher offers discounts on this book when ordered in bulk quantities. For more information contact:

> Corporate Sales Department
> Phone: 800–382–3419
> Fax: 201–236–7141
> E-mail: corpsales@prenhall.com

> Or write:

> Prentice Hall PTR
> Corp. Sales Dept.
> One Lake Street
> Upper Saddle River, New Jersey 07458

Printed in the United States of America
10 9 8 7 6 5 4 3 2 1

ISBN: 0–13–020335–1

Prentice-Hall International (UK) Limited, *London*
Prentice-Hall of Australia Pty. Limited, *Sydney*
Prentice-Hall Canada Inc., *Toronto*
Prentice-Hall Hispanoamericana, S.A., *Mexico*
Prentice-Hall of India Private Limited, *New Delhi*
Prentice-Hall of Japan, Inc., *Tokyo*
Prentice-Hall (Singapore) Pte Ltd., *Singapore*
Editora Prentice-Hall do Brasil, Ltda., *Rio de Janeiro*

Contents

Preface

*T*he first time Bruce and I met, in Autumn 1996, we got into an argument. It was about VPNs—Virtual Private Networks, that is. Specifically, we had slightly different opinions as to exactly what the term VPN *meant*. I was a Product Manager for Bay Networks at the time, and was heavily involved with the development and roll out of our early VPN solutions. Bruce, a Corporate Systems Engineer, and new to the company, had been selected (or was he forced by our marketing group—I can't recall!) to be a technical speaker at a quickly organized set of customer seminars on VPNs. One of the marketing types had protested to me about this "new guy" that was attempting to "derail the entire seminar." "He won't let us include some of the slides," complained the marketer, wringing her hands. "He says they're not accurate." I quickly sought out the culprit, with the goal of setting him straight. Two things about that argument were impressive. The first was Bruce's passion for the topic. That anyone would argue so vehemently about a subject so innocuous in the overall scheme of things meant *here is a guy that is a true professional, and also really cares about what he does.* It was either that or he had a major screw loose. I understood quickly, as I got to know him, that it was definitely the former. The second thing that impressed me was Bruce's depth of knowledge on the topic. At that time, not many people knew or cared about VPNs in the data communications world. Some did, but not many. The term "VPN" had been used for a long time in the telephony arena, but was really just coming into vogue among data networking professionals in 1996. Having come over to Bay Networks from Digital, however, Bruce was well informed. This wasn't all that surprising, considering DEC's early presence in the VPN field with its AltaVista Tunnel product. It was refreshing, though, to work with someone who not only could discuss a variety of technical topics, but also, like me, enjoyed a good argument. That initial argument was the beginning of a professional relationship that I have enjoyed as much as any in my career. Two years later, when I was trying to write this book and first realized that I was not going to be able to finish it without help, there was only one person I knew I could turn to. When I later realized that I was not going to be able to work on it much at all, I knew Bruce would carry the load, and would do so with pleasure. Now this book is his, and it is based largely on his ideas. I guess you could say that he ultimately won the argument! Way to go, Bruce!

—*Jonathan Zarkower, Summer 1999*

Motivations

This book was written for two reasons. One is that there are many books on VPNs today that, to us, read like articles you'd find in so many trade publications. This is not surprising, since most (not all, but most) of the VPN books out there are written by professional writers, *not* by anyone who actually works in the networking business or has actually built a network. That is why we are calling this book "A View from the Trenches." While our style may not match that of the other books, we hope that you find our *perspective* useful as well as refreshing. We have enjoyed reading all of the other VPN books (there were five or six the last we counted) out there, but we wanted to provide a slightly different angle that would *complement* the others, not compete with them.

The second reason was that the other books on VPNs tend to focus on the enterprise view. Many large enterprises are doing a fine job of "rolling their own" VPN. As it so happens, both of us have spent the majority of our time the last few years working with service providers. We believe that service providers are in a position to do a fantastic job of helping many of the Fortune 50,000 (small to mid-tier companies) deploy Virtual Private Networks. Alas, none of the VPN books that we've seen really addresses the topic of VPNs from the point of view of the service provider. We have therefore tried to sprinkle the book with liberal doses of information and ideas that address the reader who may be employed by the ever-increasing number of service providers out there. A side benefit to this—we hope—is that the enterprise reader will learn a little more about what is actually happening inside that mysterious "cloud" that appears in just about every network diagram we've ever seen.

Maximizing Your Experience

For best results, this book should be read linearly, not referenced like an encyclopedia. Frankly, we weren't out to write yet another piece of reference material. Not that we mind those—they can be incredibly useful—but why re-invent the wheel? We wanted to raise points that are not typically discussed in the more *encyclopedic* works and we think that our book does that. Our hope is that if you begin at the beginning of a chapter and read to the end, that you will emerge from that chapter feeling like an insider.

Another goal we set early on was to try not to make the content too "dry." As our friends and loved ones will tell you, both of us are slightly quirky people with slightly quirky senses of humor. We have been influenced by authors of other networking books (Radia Perlman come to mind first) that inject some of their own humor and personality so effectively without taking anything away from the actual content. If you find yourself supressing an occasional chuckle while reading this, and also learn a thing or two, we'll be happy.

Acknowledgments

There are countless people to thank, of course.

First thanks go to Mary Franz, our Acquisitions Editor, who combined patience, enthusiasm, insight, flexibility, and persistence in helping us bring this project home. No matter how late we were, Mary never became visibly angry and no matter how bad we thought the material was, Mary was always encouraging. She is just something else altogether. If Mary ever approaches you to write a book, there are two things you must do: 1) Do it; and 2) Let her develop your schedule, since you'll never in a million years meet the one you devise yourself!

Second thanks go to Rhonda Sheller, and Rebecca and Samantha Zarkower, whose willingness to "go it alone," sometimes at the worst of times, helped get this project off the ground in the first place. You know what we mean.

Third thanks go to all of the people at Bay Networks that we worked with on VPN-related projects too numerous to count. In particular, the folks in the Bay Networks (ex-Xylogics) Remote Access Systems Division (RASD), Corporate Systems Engineering, and everyone involved with the Contivity Extranet Switch were unknowing yet vital contributors to the experiences we drew from to write this book. There, now that we've thanked you, you can all go out and buy it!

Fourth thanks go to our parents, who always wanted the best for us and did everything in their power to help us get it. That goes for the rest of our families as well.

Fifth thanks go to all of the reviewers of this book. Your feedback was always fair and usually right on the mark. We really appreciate the comments coming from you, since all of you are highly respected networking professionals in your own right.

Sixth and final thanks go to the networking industry in general, which has provided us both with gainful employment since the early 1980s. Now that it is at the center of the second industrial revolution of the twentieth century, we look forward to many more years and in the meantime, thank our lucky stars!

CHAPTER

1

Introduction

If you have gone to the trouble of purchasing (or even borrowing) this book, the chances are pretty good that you've heard of Virtual Private Networking. The chances are also good that you are, or have been, pretty confused. Don't worry, you're not alone. The acronym *VPN* has been around for a long time, but the definition has changed several times. The good news—with the help of several hundred articles, countless papers, endless discussions, incessant trade show presentations, numerous seminar series, and yes, even a few books, the confusion seems to finally be melting away. We now know exactly six people (including the two of us) who actually know what a VPN is and can talk intelligently on the topic. Seriously though, we are not going to attempt to re-define VPNs. We will, however, articulate a definition of VPNs as well as a few guiding principles in this chapter.

Before we do so, however, we will cover some basic networking principles. We'll also include a brief look and background of the Internet, since its growth is one of central culprits responsible for creating the VPN "boom." Besides, we suspect that some of you VPN "newbies" may be new to networking or at least new to the Internet. The grizzled networking veterans among you are certainly free to skip over the sections that don't interest you.

Once we get finished defining VPNs, two important tasks need to be accomplished before you are taken headfirst into the mosh pit of actual subject matter. First, we'd like to familiarize you with some of the terminology we plan to use throughout the book. After all, if you don't understand what we mean, you can't expect to learn much. Worse, you could find yourself disagreeing with us when, in fact, we agree! Second, we are going to explain right up front what newfound knowledge we intend you to walk away with when you finally put this book down after reading it nonstop for three weeks and sleeping with it under your pillow. To that end, we'll lay out our goals for the book including the aspects we hope will make it different from others like it.

So pull up an EZ Chair and start reading!

Networking 101

Telecommunications and networking technology have been integral business enablers since the late 1960s. Over the last forty years, numerous waves of networking technology, and some might add, fads, have gained and lost prominence. In conjunction with the march of technology, some absolutely compelling applications have developed such that networking technology has become the *sine qua non* of whole business segments. There are plenty of books that can serve as good introductions to networking protocols and their historical evolution. Some of these are listed in our bibliography. For those who are interested, they are worth the read for the insight you will gain in understanding VPNs. In this book, we will give you just enough technical detail and background to understand the implications and tradeoffs of the concepts we develop. For those of you who are network experts, bear with us. This background will be short, and it is designed to make sure everyone is speaking the same language in an industry where jargon, buzzwords, and acronyms abound.

One thing before we begin: Despite covering some of the basics, we've decided *not* to include an actual networking primer in our book.

We thought long and hard on this one, but in the end decided that most readers have seen enough of concepts such the OSI model, CSMA/CD (that's Ethernet to you!), and basic bridging and routing to last a lifetime. There are many fine books on networking (many of which are offered by our equally fine publisher!), so if you need to bone up, our bibliography offers up several titles.

Having said that, we'd first like to propose a few insights about networking technology in general that will serve as background to our discussions of VPN technology that follows.

The Internet Protocol (IP) has won the protocol "battle." Almost all new applications are being developed or will be developed around *TCP/IP* (Transmission Control Protocol/Internet Protocol) and its many related protocols. Other networking protocols, such as IBM's *Systems Networking Architecture* (SNA), Digital Equipment Corporation's *DEC-Net*, Novell's *IPX/SPX*, and Banyan's *VINES* are for the most part regarded as "legacy" by most network managers. *Legacy* is a politically correct way to say that these protocols have had their day in the sun, are still widely deployed, but are fading into the networking horizon. On the other hand, the TCP/IP protocol suite is evolving very quickly, with new features and mechanisms being added almost daily (some of the newer VPN tunneling protocols covered in Chapter 4 are examples of this). Some of these enhancements are not widely deployed, and some may fall out of favor totally. Sometime in the next decade, the protocol suite will get what amounts to an engine change (IP Version 6) that is going provide job security (and insecurity!) for networking professionals for years to come.

Most enterprise networks are made up of a quilt of networking technologies, many of which are incompatible. It seemed like a good idea at the time. We didn't think it would last that long. The users were ready to revolt. The CFO's brother worked for the vendor. The expensive consultant suggested it. Our competitors were killing us. These are some of the reasons we hear behind this situation. Frankly, we think they are all valid! The corollary to this statement is that network management staffs are invariably overworked and stressed out. They need to keep up with the continued stream of user application demands, family alliances, and other competitive pressures, and do it in the extremely compressed period of time that has come to be referred to as *Internet time*.

Some networked applications have become *hygiene*. That's right, just like brushing your teeth in the morning, you just gotta do it. You get no extra credit for doing it especially well or creatively, but your friends and co-workers will sure let you know if you don't do it sufficiently. Further, there are increasingly standardized ways of implementing these applications, which include examples such as *Enterprise Resource Planning* (ERP), PC networking, and even remote access. This has increasingly opened the door to the outsourcing of these functions, that is to say, turning them almost entirely over to a third party.

An Enterprise Networking Model

Figure 1.1 shows a model of a major facility or headquarters of a typical medium-sized enterprise. We will use this model throughout the book to describe where specific VPN technology or supporting servers and management are situated. It will help explain how the new technology relates to existing installed technology. The model consists of a number of key components:

1. **Telecommunications Facilities:** These are various telecommunications services that literally connect the organization to the outside world. Chapter 2 takes a close look at each of these different types of networks, examines their characteristics, and gives hints as to how VPN technology can or will impact their deployment and use. The enterprise telecommunications facilities are "ground zero" for VPN technology. In fact, one of the chief goals of VPNs is to move one or more of these telecommunications facilities onto the Internet.

2. **Corporate Internet Connection:** It's a well-known fact that corporate Internet connectivity is growing by leaps and bounds. Organizations access the Internet for a variety of purposes including the ever-ubiquitous electronic mail (Email), online research, and increasingly, electronic commerce (E-commerce), which is an application used to facilitate actual business transactions over the Internet.

3. **The Corporate Data Center:** The corporate data center contains the "big iron" computing and data servers for the enterprise. In many large organizations the mainframe runs the company's "mission critical," or most important, applications. It is the growth of mainframe usage that, for the most part, drove the growth of SNA. Today, the SNA network can be found in the telecommunications facility, along with the many other types of internal networks in use. Other mission critical applications run on Unix-based servers

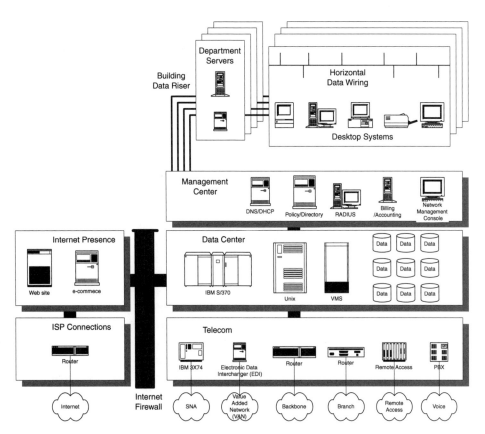

Figure 1.1 A Model of the Enterprise Computing Environment

or minicomputer platforms that, by the way, are also considered legacy (especially by those seeking to replace them!). These applications include corporate internal E-mail, file and print services, and custodial applications such as Enterprise Resource Planning (ERP), general ledger, payroll, and Manufacturing Resource Planning (MRP). Many of these applications entail network communication to other corporate offices, branches, or warehouses. As we'll see later, one of the main goals of a VPN is to provide secure and cost-effective access to these resources.

4. **The Corporate Internet Presence:** In addition to simply being connected to the Internet, many corporations are establishing their own presence on the Web. This presence typically includes corporate Web servers and file servers. These may have links to E-commerce systems to enable the enterprise to conduct busi-

ness on the Web. The design and implementation of many of these systems may be outsourced and/or packaged as part of more comprehensive VPN business deal. We will also examine how some E-commerce and Web technology can be seen as a competitor to VPNs.

5. **The Internet Firewall:** Central to connection of the Internet is the ability to let the good and useful traffic in and keep the bad traffic and users out. This is not a trivial task. A whole gamut of devices known as Internet firewalls have been developed to do this. Some firewalls even include VPN services. Generally speaking, VPNs will need to coexist and cooperate with a variety of Internet firewalls. Different VPN approaches will have different security issues to deal with. Many of these will be discussed in later chapters.

6. **The Enterprise Management Center:** In addition to network management consoles that host network performance, fault, topology, and configuration tools, the network management center hosts a number of other infrastructure servers. These include servers for naming, addressing, authorization, and a quickly developing area called "policy." Increasingly, this information is structured to mirror the organization of the enterprise and stored in directory servers based on the *Lightweight Directory Access Protocol* (LDAP). Finally, VPNs often require working with service providers. Monitoring service provider performance and the performance of the VPN, itself, introduces many new management challenges.

7. **Campus Infrastructure and Wiring:** All of the hubs, switches, routers, and wiring systems that connect all of the enterprise computing elements together represent the infrastructure. These network elements do not cross the public domain and only reach limited distances. They use very high-speed LAN technology that is inherently multiprotocol. Some key systems to consider are:

    ◆ The *data center system*, containing the highest speed switched connections, ties all of the servers of the data center together and connects it into campus and riser systems.

    ◆ The *campus systems* connect various buildings on a single campus together; communication typically stays on dedicated transmission systems over private property.

♦ The *building riser system* connects the various floors or departments into the infrastructure. These too, are often high-speed fiber optics-based switched services.

♦ *Horizontal wiring* connects the various desktop and end-user computing elements to the building riser. Often this is slower shared copper media, although this, too, is changing to higher speed switched infrastructure as more multimedia applications and powerful desktop appliances appear.

8. **Departmental Servers:** These include file and print servers used by a small group local to a floor or department. Often, these servers implement legacy protocols such as AppleTalk, IPX, or NetBEUI.

9. **End Users:** Finally, there are the end users themselves. In many companies it seems that the *WinTel* (*MS-Windows on Intel-based PCs*) architecture has won the heart of corporate Information Systems (IS). There are, however, other platforms to consider: UNIX desktops (especially in engineering environments), Macintosh, and IBM's OS/2, to name a few. It is the users who will gain the most from VPN technology, both from at the desktop and while away from the office.

An Abridged Evolution of the Internet

Before we tackle the Internet (with a capital I) we need to understand the concept of an *internet* (with a small i). An internet is what is created when we implement a network built around a set of networking standards that we will collectively (and simply) refer to as IP (Internet Protocol). This all sounds very recursive, but at the base is a very simple concept.

For our purposes, a *network* is defined as a homogeneous transmission system over which systems can communicate using simple rules. Networks exist on different levels. Two tin cans connected by a piece of string (Figure 1.2) constitutes a network, albeit a primitive one.

An Ethernet Local Area Network (LAN) connecting several computers (Figure 1.3) is a network. Two routers sending data packets back and forth over a long distance communications link (Figure 1.4) form a network. The same two routers can also be used to connect two Ethernet LANs using the same long distance link. This latter concept is a little closer to what we are getting at.

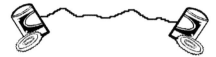

Figure 1.2 An Early Example of a Network

In real life, we need to enable communications that span multiple networks. An internet is what we get when we connect these multiple networks together using a common set of rules (known as a *protocol*), regardless of the physical or link infrastructure. The Internet Protocol (IP), for instance, rides on top of the string, the Ethernet, and/or the long distance lines, binding these disparate physical elements into a singular communications system.

Most of the networks we build inside our companies are, in fact, internets. Nowadays, to differentiate corporate internets from the public Internet, corporate networks used solely for one enterprise are often called *intranets*. Whew!

The original Internet started as a research project in packet switching by a U.S. government agency known as the Advanced Research Project Agency (ARPA). This network was called the ARPANET. The original goal of ARPANET was to support military applications. Of particular interest was developing the ability of the network to continue functioning despite major failures or outages, such as those that might occur during a war. During the 1970s the network grew and started to support many organizations within the U.S. Department of Defense.

While the ARPANET provided many of the technical foundations for today's Internet, the National Science Foundation (NSF) wanted to network a group of national supercomputer centers. That created the original seed of the Internet. As this network started to grow and new applications were developed for it, the NSF contracted to Merit Network

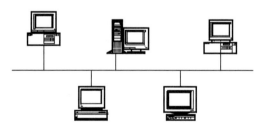

Figure 1.3 A LAN is a Network

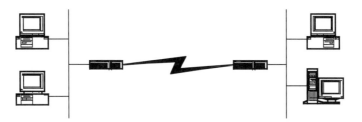

Figure 1.4 A Simple Internet

Inc., in partnership with IBM and MCI, to upgrade and operate the NSF backbone known as NSFNET. The original NSFNET operated over 56 Kbps connections; the new backbone ran trunks at 1.544 Mbps. Later, IBM and MCI would spin off a new independent non-profit organization known as Advanced Network and Services, or ANS, that would upgrade this backbone again to 45 Mbps trunks with routers based on IBM's RS6000 workstations.

In May 1993, the National Science Foundation fundamentally changed the character of the Internet when it decided to replace the existing infrastructure—the running of a backbone network—with high-speed network switching centers. Four Network Access Points, or NAPs, were located in San Francisco, Chicago, New York, and Washington DC. The NAPs are hubs where any nationwide commercial backbone provider may connect for purposes of forwarding traffic to and from other backbone providers. This activity is known as *peering.* In parallel with setting up the NAPs, a private provider of commercial high-speed Metropolitan Area Networks (or MANs) called MFS was also setting up high-speed switching centers called Metropolitan Area Ethernets (or MAEs). MFS was awarded the contract for the Washington, DC NAP known as MAE-EAST. Since then, MFS has built Internet switching centers around the United States that together with the NAPs and some additional government and commercial switching centers make up the heart of today's Internet. The MAE in San Jose is affectionately known as MAE-WEST.

One of the reasons why the Internet is so special is that it is where many of the protocols for today's intranets were developed. Another is that the Internet does not belong to any one company. Nowadays, the Internet is hierarchically structured, similar to the telecom transmission system. At the bottom of the food chain are smaller local Internet Service Providers or ISPs. Some say that these smaller ISPs are a dying breed, that larger carriers and nationwide providers will slowly drive these companies out of business. So far, this hasn't proven to be the case. This hardy group of Internet pioneers has stayed in business by offering good service and combining that with decent performance to their customer base. They have a cultural understanding of the Internet that the new deep-pocketed corporate players lack that often makes them more efficient.

So What Is a VPN Anyway?

We've already said that the industry definition of a VPN is fuzzy and varies depending on with whom you talk. Many of these definitions, while being "technically accurate," mislead people. They may offer a complete taxonomy of VPN technology, but they don't map to any commercialized product. Worse, they don't offer any guidance for implementation or selection of the VPN technology. In this book we will eschew all obfuscation (that means we'll avoid confusing terminology such as "eschew all obfuscation") and stick with a simple, straightforward working definition. We will fill out that definition with in-depth discussion and examples. We will describe the tradeoffs and positioning of the various approaches and the products that implement them.

Virtual Private Networks—A Basic Definition

Now comes the obligatory part of the book where we reach as far as we can into the depths of our combined knowledge and experience and shake the earth with our definition of the subject at hand. OK, maybe that's taking it a bit too far. We promise to try to contain ourselves going forward. So, for the remainder of this book, we will base our ideas and discussions around the following working definition:

> *A **VPN** is a communications network, built for the private use of the enterprise, over a shared public infrastructure. There are two primary applications covered by this definition: remote access connectivity and site-to-site connectivity (see Figure 1.5).*

For the most part, we're going to assume that the "shared public infrastructure" is the Internet, although the Internet is technically a subset of what is globally available. The crucial point, for purposes of the definition, is that the Internet is built on IP. Consistent with that, we will spend some time looking at VPN applications deployed over IP-based intranets—for example, intradepartmental communication between HR offices within a company.

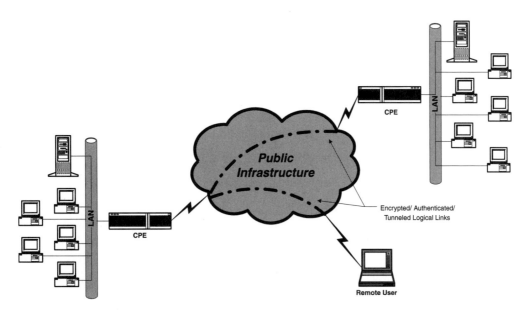

Figure 1.5 Internet-based Virtual Private Networking

Can the term "shared public infrastructure" also refer to networks not based on IP technology? Doesn't this term also refer to leased line or packet switched networks? Some will argue that a private leased line is, or at least can be, considered a VPN since leased line infrastructure eventually combines traffic from multiple customers for transmission over common long-haul facilities. Technically, these individuals are correct. The leased line infrastructure could classify as a VPN according to the strict definition. For the purpose of this book, however, we will be principally concerned with the phenomenon being driven by the maturity and ubiquity of the Internet to enable enterprises to substitute the shared infrastructure for more expensive or inconvenient private facilities.

Another area of controversy relative to VPN definition is Virtual Circuit (VC) based services such as X.25, Frame Relay, and ATM. Like leased lines, these packet and cell-switched services have the all of the characteristics required to meet our VPN definition. They combine traffic from many customers for transport over shared trunks and switches. Each customer "sees" only its private network. For a long time now, these services have been used as building blocks for building private Intranets. For the most part, though, they have been thought of as simple telecommunications services and *not* VPNs. Recently, ISPs, Competitive Local Exchange Carriers (CLECS), and other service providers have been combining Frame

Relay and ATM transport with management and provisioning services and calling them "VPN" service offerings. These networks also carry an added bonus. Because separation of data occurs at the link or circuit layer, as opposed to the network layer, a network layer firewall is typically not required to protect one Frame Relay or ATM customer's data network against possible encroachment from the "outside." Given all this, it's easy to see how the definition of VPNs has become muddled over time.

One of the defining features of the Internet is that it is based on the IP protocol suite. Since we are focusing on the use of the Internet as VPN transport, we are going to take the IP-centric view of VPNs. Above, we talked about how there was still a lot of legacy equipment in enterprises running non-IP protocols, especially Novell IPX and IBM's SNA. Some may not want to admit it, but these protocols are important to consider in the overall scheme of things. Although we will not ignore these protocols entirely, many of the methods discussed for handling these protocols in a VPN environment involve first encapsulating them within IP. From that point these legacy protocols become simply another IP application stream handled within the VPN.

Figure 1.5 shows the use of authenticated and encrypted logical links. Authentication and encryption are two of the techniques used to put the "private" in virtual private networking. Indeed, questions of authorization, authentication, and privacy have taken center spotlight in contemporary networking practice in general. Certainly, they are critical in implementing VPNs. Later chapters will discuss many of these various security mechanisms.

Another important technology often used in conjunction with authentication and encryption is *tunneling*. Simply put, tunneling is the encapsulation of one protocol packet inside of another. This is similar to putting a letter inside of an envelope. In the case of VPNs, the *envelope* applies the addressing, encryption, authentication, and compression; the VPN *services* that are applied to the original networking packet. Later, we discuss in depth how various protocols and products use each of these techniques.

Figure 1–6 also shows devices that are sometimes referred to as *CPE*. CPE stands for Customer Premises Equipment. CPE provides an interface between the *actual private* network and the *virtual private* network. As you'll see, there are a number of different models for how VPNs are implemented. Some of these models feature CPE in a leading role and some do not. The chosen implementation approach will be impacted, at least in part, by the cost, complexity, and management of the CPE. At

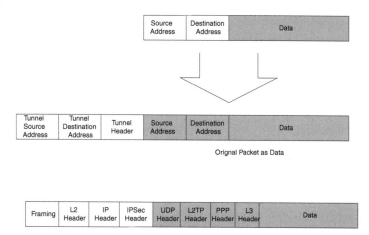

Figure 1.6 Encapsulating One Packet in Another to Implement Tunneling

one end of the spectrum, a service provider can put all of the complexity "inside the cloud." In this case, the CPE could simply be a standard router with a minimal role in the actual functionality of the VPN. At the other end of the spectrum, the CPE could be deeply involved in all of the protocols and functionality of the VPN. In this case, the actual *provisioning* of the VPN could be centered on the CPE without the least involvement from the service provider.

VPNs—A Business Discussion

At a high level, VPNs are the natural result of two strong evolutionary trends in Information Technology:

♦ The maturity and ubiquity of the Internet
♦ The maturity of the business process of delegating certain activities to third party specialists, known as *outsourcing*

Let's take a quick look at each of these phenomena.

Business Use of the Internet

Earlier we gave you a brief history of the roots of the Internet. In the next chapter we will give you an inside peek at the infrastructure and operations of Internet Service Providers. The Internet has clearly come a long way, but the more important fact is that the pace of growth, innovation, and maturity, is accelerating.

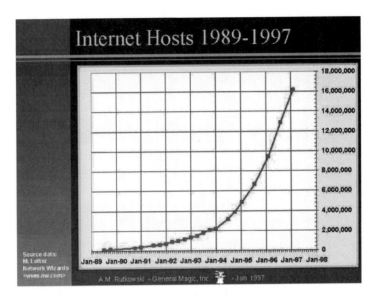

Figure 1.7 Exponential Growth of the Internet

Many people have an intuitive feel for the growth of the Internet. Those that don't may be more persuaded by the graph in Figure 1.7

Whether you prefer the psychic approach or cold facts, you cannot escape the truth. The Internet has become a de facto presence in the business and corporate landscape. Its impact rivals that of facsimile and even the telephone and may ultimately subsume both. Figure 1.8 below shows the growth of the Internet in terms of the growth in the number of three-letter Internet *domain names* (.com, .org, .edu, etc.) currently in use by organizations.

We stated that network-enabled applications have been critical business enablers for some time now. However, the applications in question generally ran only over a company's private network. The ubiquity and performance of the Internet, along with the newer security and VPN technology, have enabled a whole new class of company-to-company applications. These *extranets*, as they have been dubbed, support applications such as inventory management, customer support, joint development, and online ordering. In some cases, extranets are threatening to either supplant or subsume older and more closed Electronic Data Exchange (EDI) networks.

There are two key issues that businesses consider when evaluating the use of the Internet for any application, and VPNs in particular:

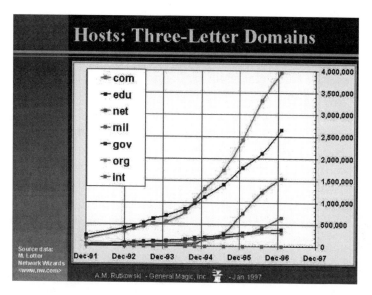

Figure 1.8 Exponential Growth of the Business Sector of the Internet

- ♦ Is the Internet secure enough for my operations?
- ♦ Is the quality (reliability, performance, etc) good enough for my application?

Is the Internet Secure?

There have been a number of high-profile Internet break-ins and hacker attacks publicized in the news. Universities, government agencies, and companies such as the venerable New York Times have had their Web sites compromised. There is a perception that these well-publicized incidents represent only the tip of the iceberg. It is felt that high profile companies shun the negative publicity associated with these attacks and suppress information relating to most incidents.

The Computer Emergency Response Team Coordination Center (CERT/CC) is located at the Software Engineering Institute (SEI), a federally funded research and development center at Carnegie Mellon University in Pittsburgh, Pennsylvania. Following the Internet Worm incident, which brought 10 percent of Internet systems to a halt in November 1988, the Defense Advanced Research Projects Agency (DARPA) charged the SEI with setting up a center to coordinate communication among experts during security emergencies and to help prevent future incidents. Since then, the CERT/CC has helped to establish other response teams while maintaining leadership in analyzing vulnerabilities and threats.

Since its inception, the CERT/CC has been tracking various security incidents, and vulnerabilities. Figure 1.9 shows the number of problems occurring since then. This chart, in conjunction with that showing the phenomenal growth of the Internet, paints a less disturbing picture.

In conjunction with this increased understanding of security vulnerabilities, technology has advanced to provide new foundations for Internet security. In particular, the maturity and increasing deployment of IP security (a.k.a. IPSec) has shown the way forward for equipment manufacturers, Service Providers, and their customers. IPSec, both in general and as a VPN tunneling "protocol," will be covered more extensively in Chapter 4.

To conclude, the reality is that today the Internet can be a surprisingly secure place. Notice we're not saying it *is* a secure place, because not enough security is actually implemented over the Internet, but it *can* be. We feel that the notion that the Internet is insecure is a notion born largely out of history and perception.

There are some interesting, albeit slightly off-kilter, laws to support this. The first is that fear is the strongest deterrent. The number of sensational articles that have surfaced in recent years regarding "hackers," credit card theft, and so on has led directly to a certain level of paranoia regarding the *in*security of the Internet. This, in turn, has spawned two phenomena. First, it has led many to be doubly sure (out of fear) about using security products and/or security features in existing products when they use the Internet for tasks requiring confidentiality or privacy. Second, organizations have developed a variety of products and standards that are designed to ensure the security of these frightened users.

This leads us to the second law. We're not sure it has a name, so we'll describe it with an example. When you hear a traffic report warning not to drive to a particularly crowded event because of potential traffic jams, it is almost guaranteed that there will be no traffic on the roads leading to the event. Being from the Boston area, Fourth of July festivities on the

```
Security (CERT) Incidents:

                1988 1989 1990 1991 1992 1993 1994 1995 1996 1997
               + ---- ---- ---- ---- ---- ---- ---- ---- ---- ----
  Incidents    |   6  132  252  406  773 1334 2340 2412 2573 2134
  Advisories   |   1    7   12   23   21   19   15   18   27   28
  Vulnerabilities                                     171  345  311
```

Figure 1.9 Security Incidents on the Internet

Charles River Esplanade come to mind as an example of this. You may be asking – how is that relevant?

Well, in terms of Internet security, it simply means that the perception...

"Traffic will be heavy" / "Internet is insecure"

. . . is not exactly in line with the reality.

"Traffic is actually light" / Internet is actually secure" (or at least can be, with the right security mechanisms applied)

In this case, the reality is a direct result of the perception. Get it?

There is also a perception that other public networks, like the packet switched networks described earlier or the public telephone network, are secure. The fact is that neither of these networks is truly secure, *in part because of the very perception that they are.*

Does Quality of Service (QoS) Exist on the Internet?

You breathe a sigh of relief as you approach the first-class check-in counter at a crowded airport. The economy class check-in line snakes around past the yogurt stand. You, however, with your company-paid first class ticket, have but a short wait before you verify that your frequent flier number has been recorded and you are off to the lounge for a refreshing beverage before your flight. The airline has a Quality of Service policy. After you land at Logan International Airport, however, and are late for your daughter's soccer game, the highway doesn't know how important or rich you are. You find yourself waiting along with everyone else because the road leading from the airport doesn't have a Quality of Service policy. All traffic is equal as you slowly snake your way past the tollbooth and into that blasted Sumner Tunnel!

In the above discussion on Internet security, we mentioned that the IPSec standards have largely coalesced and are now well on their way to widespread adoption for a number of security applications. The same cannot be said about technical standards relating to the management of bandwidth and performance on the Internet.

A lot of technical work is still going on with respect to Quality of Service (QoS) to ensure that applications such as VPNs and Voice over IP get the performance from the Internet that they need. We will study many of these in Chapters 6 and 8. In the absence of technical mechanisms to implement QoS, however, there are still alternatives.

If the traveler above lived in Utopia, all the roads would be engineered to easily support their peak demand. A permanent staff of "traffic engineers" would be available to quickly address any temporary or unusual situation that might occur. Roads could be widened or even added virtually overnight.

As a function of the increased use and utility of the Internet for business needs, these Internet Utopias are actually being built. A whole new class of Internet Service Provider (ISP) is appearing with very well-engineered backbones, which are aggressively managed for good performance. Of course, the rest of the Internet is reachable from these networks, and the technology, protocols, and addressing, are the same as those used by any ISP. Nevertheless, the goal of this new breed is specifically to offer services that are simply not possible on the crowded airport roadway known as today's Internet.

To answer the question posed above, then, no, Quality of Service does not yet exist on the Internet. Still, there is hope, as we shall see.

A Short Introduction to Network Capacity

In Chapter 2 we will take a more in-depth look at the basic telecommunications services that serve to connect networks, both public and private. In the past all telecommunications services were sold by AT&T, the telecommunications monopoly. These services ran over a wide range of transmission systems, from copper wire, microwave, satellite, and finally, fiber optics. Since then, two major forces have shaped the way data is transmitted in networking: the deregulation of the telecommunications industry allowing the spawning of a number of public and private telecommunications carriers, and the increasing use of fiber optics as the transmission media.

Fiber optics has a number of wonderful characteristics that make it ideal for transmitting data. The ultimate capacity of a single strand of fiber optics is still under debate, and rising at a rate that approaches Moore's Law (doubling every two years). A new technology in fiber optics has recently burst on the scene opening up truly vast reservoirs of bandwidth, called Dense Wave Division Multiplexing, or D-WDM. D-WDM allows the transmission of multiple streams of data, or "colors" over a single fiber. At the same time, deregulated carriers are in the process of using railway rights of way, power lines, and gas lines to lay down more and more bandwidth. Figure 1.10 gives an idea of this capacity explosion.

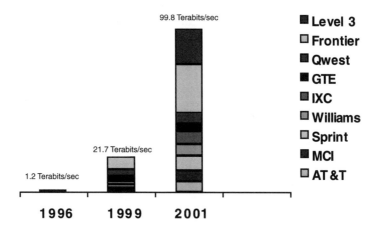

Figure 1.10 Rising Network Capacity in the United States. *Source:* Rafael King, "Too Much Long Distance," *Fortune Magazine,* March 15, 1999.

The result is that more network capacity is available to service providers for more applications. Although new bandwidth hungry applications such as multimedia are starting to appear, the increasing amounts of capacity in the network looks like it will more than keep up. Service Providers are eager to put this capacity to work. VPNs represent a business application available today that is truly enabled by this bandwidth.

A Short Introduction to Network Outsourcing

When an organization uses a "business class" Internet Service Provider, they are essentially paying a group of very specialized and focused people to manage a particular business need, good Internet performance. This concept of delegating activities that are not part of the "core competency" of the business is not new. Dubbed *outsourcing,* this business practice gained prominence in the early 1990s, in both Information Technology (IT) and non-IT contexts. Businesses talked of outsourcing all kinds of functions. Easy targets were Human Resources, Payroll, and Shipping and Receiving. New business models even appeared with completely outsourced manufacturing. In the IT area, certain computing tasks deemed not "core competency" were also sent out to companies like EDS and IBM. Some examples of these include not only programs such as General Ledger, but MIS functions, such as end-user help desks. The idea of an outside company specializing and focusing in these systems was quite compelling to beleaguered corporate IT staff, who were tasked with implementing the "next big thing" while still owning responsibility for the existing network and the systems that ran over it.

In the meantime, many small ISPs found that the entrance of deep-pocketed national providers and telephone companies was quickly eroding profit margins on end-user Internet access. The $19.95 a month "all you can eat" Internet account had become a commodity. The money (and profits) was clearly in the business customer. These resourceful and ambitious Service Providers began to look for value-added services that they could package with ordinary Internet access to attract the business accounts. Fortunately, for these ISPs this corresponded with the need of the corporation to establish their Internet "presence." The ISPs began to offer packages of Web site design, hosting, and E-commerce to the business community. The incredible growth of the World Wide Web is a testament to business appetite for these services.

If the ISP could actually become part of the business user's network, however, that would be the pinnacle of value-add. Being the manager and designer of the customer's network infrastructure could allow the service provider to drag along the whole portfolio of value-added services (Figure 1.11).

For the most part, these value-added services are natural extensions to the service provider's core business. Often, very little incremental investment is needed. The value-added services run over the same infrastructure and leverage inherent competencies such as customer help desks, network configuration, and troubleshooting.

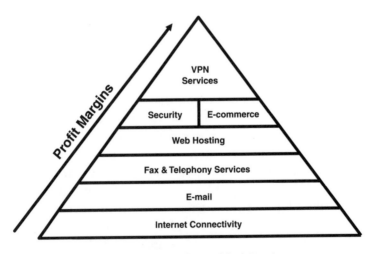

Figure 1.11 Service Provider Value Added Services

Another big problem for many retail Internet Service providers is customer "churn." A subscriber has a few problems logging on one day, maybe some perceived performance issues the next, and it is a simple matter to change providers. When a business engages a service provider for some of the value-added services shown in Figure 1.11, the relationship between provider and customer becomes much more strategic in nature. There is more consideration given when entering the relationship in the first place, and when problems occur, there is more of a tendency to work through the issues.

By this time, you should be thinking that offering VPN services is a "no-brainer" for most Internet Service Providers. We agree! For the customer, VPNs represent the next step in a progression of network refinements as shown in Figure 1.12.

When corporations were building their private networks from leased line facilities, the user had to take care of designing and configuring the network topology from multiple individual point-to-point circuits. A key reason for the popularity of newer Frame Relay services was that the service provider now handled many of the topology, capacity planning, and routing issues for the customer. The enterprise could be connected to the network via a single physical circuit, and the service provider could then pro-

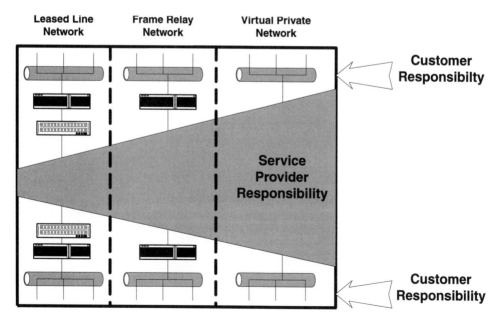

Figure 1.12 Evolution of User/Service Provider Division of Responsibilities

vision virtual circuits to all of the other facilities. We will discuss Frame Relay technology further in the next chapter, but it suffices to say that Internet-based VPNs continue this trend of giving the service provider more responsibility for the network. Management, capacity planning, and performance monitoring all may be included under the service providers purview in a VPN arrangement.

Thus, we see VPN technology being considered by the enterprise, along with Frame Relay and leased line, as a building block to an overall Wide Area Network (WAN) strategy. The chart below shows both VPN and Frame Relay access continuing to grow, while the share of more expensive and less flexible leased line networks diminishes. Still, not a lot of organizations are doing wholesale replacement of their leased line networks. After all, once entrenched, a particular network technology is hard to dislodge since it becomes tightly coupled with the applications and operational management. It is more that the *new* applications and network enhancements (such as the extranets mentioned above) are being implemented on the VPN and Frame Relay technology (Figure 1.13).

VPNs are a relatively new phenomenon. Like many new technologies, they follow a predictable pattern of customer acceptance documented by Geoffrey Moore in his book *Crossing the Chasm*. Initially, when a new technology appears, it is bought and used by a group of leading edge, technically literate buyers. As these trendsetters evaluate and analyze a new technology there is a lull before the mainstream consumer accepts the product. We believe that VPN have now crossed the chasm, and poised for wide spread acceptance by the general industry. Figure 1.14 shows the sharp uptake in the availability of Service Provider offerings for VPN services starting in 1999.

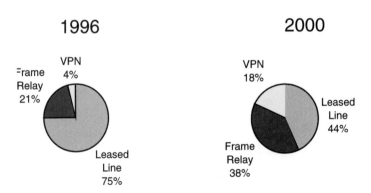

Figure 1.13 Network Implementations by Technology. *Source:* Telechoice.

VPNs Are Here

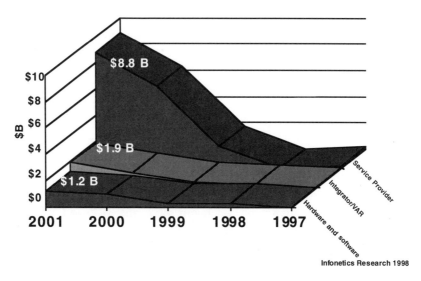

Figure 1.14 The Market for VPN Products and Services

Goals of This Book

We hope that the previous discussions have you thinking a little more about the possibilities, and yes, even the challenges associated with implementing a VPN or VPN service. Perhaps a better understanding of your own company's network, such as how it has grown and how it is now organized, has you thinking about possible changes. Maybe a reflection on the way your organization uses the Internet, or *could* use the Internet has you intrigued. If you are still with us, good! Here is a brief road map of what is ahead in the upcoming chapters.

In Chapter 2, we are going to take a closer look at the enterprise telecommunication facilities shown way back in Figure 1.1. VPNs have evolved and become popular just as each of these technologies and their facilities evolved and became popular. At each stage of the evolution, the newer technology introduced advantages over its predecessors. Still, each step in the evolution exposed issues that could only be solved with the next generation technology. And so it goes. We will provide a more in-depth overview of the technologies used in each of these applications (remote access, branch networks, backbone networks etc.), along with suggestions of where the current IP-based VPN technology provides an advantage. The chapter also gives a behind the scenes look at Service Provider operations designed to show potential VPN customers the kinds of equipment involved in providing VPN services. This may also serve to guide you down the sometimes-arduous path of evaluating Service Provider–offered VPN services.

In Chapter 3, we present a number of cost/benefit models that can be used to rationalize the choice of implementing an IP-based VPN as opposed to a more "traditional" networking technology. For the Service Provider we will look at the kinds of costs that are involved in entering the VPN business. We will also discuss some of the options in pricing VPN service packages. Like many things, costs and benefits are not always measured monetarily. This chapter also explores some of the non-monetary costs and benefits to VPNs.

In Chapter 4, we begin exploring IP-based VPN technology. We give an in-depth, pros and cons–oriented view of a number of VPN provisioning models and discuss the technical aspects of most of the contemporary tunneling protocols available today. These discussions are embellished with short case studies drawn from our experiences.

Chapter 5 covers most of the VPN product and solution types available in the market. This, too, gets into some of the pros and cons.

VPNs are not constructed from tunneling and encryption protocols alone. In Chapter 6, we look at many of the associated technologies, including management, policy, and directory services that are associated with VPNs. In Chapter 6, these are examined from the customer's perspective. In Chapter 7 we will look at the Service Provider environment.

Chapter 8 offers some forward-looking, and we hope interesting, insight on such emerging VPN applications as new access technology, Multicast, bandwidth management, and others.

We'd like to now tell you about three goals that we hoped to achieve when we began writing this book far too many months ago.

Our first goal in this, our maiden publication, was to provide an angle that we haven't seen very often in other data networking books. To that end, we will spend more than a little time looking at VPNs from the perspective of the Service Provider. After all, without Service Providers, there would be no Internet, and without the Internet, we probably wouldn't have been able to write this book! As well, Service Providers have a huge stake in the future of Virtual Private Networking as a service, since as we explained earlier, enterprises are, more and more, seeking to outsource large chunks of their network infrastructure. Service Providers, like their customers, need to understand their options, the issues they face with respect to deploying VPN services, and most importantly, what their customers and prospective customers will deem most important.

Our second goal was to focus a little more on the *practical* aspects of VPNs as opposed to just the technology. Don't get us wrong, we are huge fans of the engineers who develop the standards and actually build the products that are in turn used to build data networks. We're a little different in that we come at this more from the hands-on perspective, and, while we explain the technology to a level of detail that we think is quite adequate, we really seek to help you, the reader, through the various decision points as you embark on your VPN journey. After all, why else would you have purchased this book?

Our third and last goal was to write a *technology* book that was actually fun to read. We've been influenced by some of the best technical authors around and the ones we think are best are the ones that inject the occasional quip along with a healthy dose of humanity (and humility) into their words. If you've gotten this far, you've no doubt already seen our attempts (futile though they may be) to emulate these noted scribes.

All we can say at this point is that we hope you enjoy reading it as much as we enjoyed writing it! So have fun and learn something while you're at it!

CHAPTER

2

The Networking Evolution to VPNs

VPNs didn't happen by accident. They exist today largely because innovative types (yourself, for instance) are always seeking out new ways to solve old problems. The *term* VPN has actually been around for quite some time. The idea of using "public" network facilities to facilitate private communications was actually begun by the phone company (when there was only one phone company) to allow companies to extend their private telephone networks to include remote office locations. As you will soon discover, there were problems with the way intracompany, long distance telephony was originally deployed that led to the solution—the Voice VPN.

In this chapter, we examine the evolution of technologies that led to today's VPNs. The way we will approach the subject is on an application-by-application basis, examining each of the networking technologies found in the typical enterprise telecommunications environment discussed in Chapter 1. We will examine the typical costs and benefits of the "traditional" technologies that enabled (and in some cases, still do enable) these applications. Then we will examine the benefits and risks of using VPN technology for the same applications. From our perch high up on the soapbox, we will offer compelling reasons why the technologies evolved to where they are today. The vision of VPNs shown in Figure 2.1 may not be realized for many years, but it is useful to keep the ultimate promise of this technology in mind while reading the rest of this book.

This chapter starts out with a very brief discussion of the original VPN, the Voice VPN. We then quickly turn to examining three critical networking applications found in almost every enterprise: backbone, branch, and remote access networks.

Next, we shift our attention away from *intra*company applications so that we can tackle *inter*company applications. We explained in Chapter 1

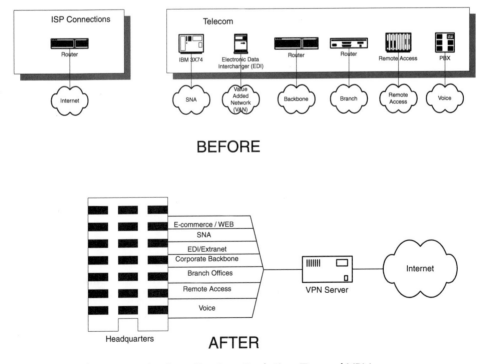

Figure 2.1 Telecommunications Services Evolution Toward VPNs

that much of this book would focus on the topic of using the Internet as a substitute for the networks that have traditionally been used to enable networked applications. Chapter 1 also introduced the concept of extranets, which use the Internet and IP-based applications to enable business transactions between different enterprises. Extranets are here in part to solve some of the problems inherent in the more established Electronic Data Interchange (EDI) applications and the Value Added Networks (VANs) over which they run. The one extranet that we will pay particular attention to is the Automotive Network eXchange or ANX, which stands as the current industry driver for business practices and standards in this area.

This will bring us finally back to the Internet. We will focus on how ISPs are typically structured in a networking sense. Then, since VPNs often require partnership with one or more Service Providers, we want to examine what makes a good ISP, including some of the important questions to ask ISPs about their service offerings.

Voice VPNs

The term *Virtual Private Network* was originally used to describe Private Branch Exchange (PBX) interconnection for private voice networks. To some extent, this is still the case. A recent meeting we had with a large telco to discuss VPN service requirements digressed into a long discussion on what was meant by the term "VPN." The representatives from the telco refused to apply the term VPN to a data-oriented service, insisting on calling the data-oriented service a VPDN (Virtual Private Data Network). Since we understood where they were coming from, we conceded the point if only to allow the presentation to continue!

Terminology aside, one of the main goals here will be to ensure that there is no confusion around VPNs when discussed in the voice context versus the data context. We've already explained that we are using the term VPN in the context of IP-based data services. One interesting twist to this is that we believe (as do many others in the industry) that IP-based VPNs will eventually be used to carry *packetized* voice (i.e., Voice over IP) between locations via the Internet.

Before the advent of Voice VPNs, organizations were forced to dial the full telephone number of the party being called in order to speak with their colleagues. Not only was this inconvenient, it was expensive.

Enter Voice VPNs. In the 1980s, as competing long distance carriers such as Sprint and MCI emerged as threats to AT&T, the competition for high-stakes commercial voice business really heated up. As a way to stave off these upstart phone companies, AT&T devised a way to reconfigure the software that controlled their voice switches to accommodate "internal" numbers defined between an organization's *publicly* numbered locations. At the same time, they cleverly linked the software definitions to their billing systems so that the new services could be billed at a lower rate than standard long distance. For the telco, the lower per-minute rates were easy to justify given the increased call volumes. Higher call volumes meant better economies of scale, elimination of complicated intercarrier bill reconciliation, plus better overall account control for the phone company offering the Voice VPN service.

From the standpoint of the enterprise, the Voice VPN meant lower billing rates combined with the convenience of having to dial simple 3- or 4-digit extensions as opposed to a full 10-digit number. In addition, the Voice VPN enabled the centralization of services such as voice mail, accessible from any corporate location, again by dialing a simple extension.

For all of these reasons, Voice VPNs quickly caught on with corporate America and they remain popular today. The popularity of Voice VPNs led directly to the availability of VPN services that applied some of the basic technical concepts (private addressing over public switched infrastructure, convenience, economies of scale, etc.) from the voice world to data transport.

Voice VPN Meets Pulp Fiction

After years of working in software development, Mary knew that her idea for developing a new Application Generator was a winner. The risks of starting her own company were high, but she felt that the time to do it was now or never. Before she left the security of her current job, Mary called the local telephone company to order new lines for her home office. She wanted to keep her private line private, so she ordered two new voice circuits, a line for her new fax machine, and a full time Internet connection. Had she shopped around, Mary could have saved

$11.87 on her monthly line charges (while earning 8000 frequent flier miles!), but she had bigger fish to fry. She needed to raise at least $3 million in venture capital—time to work the phones.

As expected, Mary's idea resonated, and she quickly had her funding. After staffing the organization (no problem given her extensive contacts), she opened her offices in a pleasant suburban technology park. But what to do about telecommunications? Her building services included the installation of a small Private Branch Exchange (PBX). This allowed all employees to have an extension on their desk. The PBX provided an easy-to-use voice mail capability, and a simplified internal numbering plan for abbreviated dialing of internal extensions. The PBX was connected to the outside world via a full T1 trunk with 23 lines. Mary wisely rejected the "Muzak on Hold" feature and configured the PBX to block all outbound access to 1-900 services.

So strong was Mary's vision and passion for her project that the product was ready in record time, and the sales and marketing team already had a sheaf of large corporate customers ready to implement her Application Generator. One morning in late spring, Mary met an old friend and mentor at a local bistro for lunch to celebrate her new and hard-earned success.

"If you're not in the Valley, Mary, you're nowhere," her friend told her with the wise look of experience. "If you want this product to really fly, you need to open an office on the West Coast—San Jose, Santa Clara, anywhere. That's how to get the *buzz*." Mary discretely removed the olive pit from her Salade Nicoise and, placing it into her napkin, resolved to call her real-estate agent that afternoon.

The week after her West Coast sales and support office was opened Mary reviewed her telephone bill. "Ouch," she thought. "Most of our calls seem to be between the two offices, and here I am paying retail long distance rates! There has to be a better way." She called the telecommunications consultant from the business card her friend had slipped her at lunch.

When Joe arrived, Mary was skeptical. He had a bad haircut and wore far too much jewelry. "Can this guy really know his stuff?" Mary asked herself. Her concern proved to be unfounded. Joe explained how Mary's company could lease circuits from the telephone company and implement a Voice

VPN. This would allow her to integrate the company's voice and data networks while keeping the existing internal numbering plan and voice-mail system intact. Mary was reassured. "Leave it to me," he said, "I'll order everything you need, but the circuits may take up to a month to be provisioned."

The payback period is about nine months, Mary thought, including the consultant fees. She called Joe. "Do it," she said.

Once the new network went in, things went well—for a while. Late one evening, Mary was reviewing her call logs. "If I had better call routing, my East Coast calls to West Coast customers could go through my private network. I also don't want my people getting busy signals—anything that can't be routed through the private network should fall back to the public network." She opened her contact manager and left voice mail for Joe.

Wide Area Branch Office and Backbone Networks

The networking model from Chapter 1 shows two basic types of site-to-site data networking connections:

♦ Those that connect major network centers to one another (called WAN *backbone* connections)

♦ Those that connect the major network centers to branch locations (called *branch* connections)

The differences between branch office networks and WAN backbone networks are somewhat arbitrary, so we will arbitrarily differentiate them as follows for the purposes of our discussion (Table 2.1).

Within LAN backbones that encompass buildings and campuses, multiple protocols happily coexist. Bandwidth is inexpensive and plentiful. Latencies (the time data takes to get from one end of the network to the other) are low. Once the data has to pass across the WAN, however, things become less rosy:

♦ *Performance becomes an issue*. In order to reach remote destinations, data may have to pass through many network routers, each of which add some delay, and if congested, may lose the data entirely!

Table 2.1 Attributes of Backbone Networks and Branch Networks

Attributes	Backbone Network	Branch Network
Number of sites	Few	Up to 1000s
Traffic	Unstructured	Often structured
Bandwidth	High	Low
Topology	Mesh	Star
Transmission	T1/T3/ATM	Fractional T1/Frame relay

♦ *Certain applications have special requirements.* Some of the LAN and PC protocols are not even routable and need to be handled specially for transport over the WAN.

♦ *Bandwidth is expensive.* Since the company is not free just to run its own wires over the public domain, it must lease bandwidth from public carrier networks. At this writing, long haul bandwidth is still somewhat scarce, and thus the bandwidth can be expensive. This is especially so if data has to travel overseas or into other countries.

♦ *WAN service deployment has become increasingly complex.* International networking used to, and to an extent still does, involve comparatively complicated regulatory, billing, and other business issues. Still, the U.S. telecommunications landscape since deregulation (a.k.a. the Telecommunications Reform Act of 1996) now often trumps those of other countries. Deregulation has spawned an alphabet-soup of players that are all involved with the transmission of data between cities. The entity providing the actual circuit to the site is generally called a *Local Exchange Carrier* or *LEC*. These used to be primarily run by the Regional Bell Operating Companies (or *RBOCs*), like Bell Atlantic or Southwest Bell. Lately a new group of independent or competitive local exchange carriers (called *ILECs* and *CLECs*, for short) have emerged. Greater competition has led to lower prices for these services but with a bewildering array of pricing plans and services offered. Getting data beyond a given metropolitan area generally requires the services of an Inter-Exchange Carrier or *IXC*. The complexity of bringing all of these parties together (1) for a reasonable price, (2) in a manner that doesn't lock the customer into repressive long term contracts, and (3) while ensuring reliable services that perform to specification, can rival the original consent decree on deregulation!

Do VPNs solve all of these issues? To some extent yes, and to some extent no. As we will see, however, the deployment of a VPN for connecting multiple sites can shield organizations from the complexities of leasing private telecommunications services while reducing costs significantly.

Point-to-Point Leased Line Networking

When organizations first went about solving the problem of connecting geographically dispersed sites to support computer applications, they did so using leased lines. Those days, the preeminent protocol carried over these circuits was SNA, which could run either over point-to-point or multidrop (imagine a long distance, bus-style Ethernet and you get the general feel for multidrop) connections back to a central hub.

In the 1980s, when LANs became *de rigueur*, organizations began to use leased lines to connect their geographically dispersed LANs. Thus was born the acronym *WAN*, short for Wide Area Network. WANs were initially constructed using devices known as *bridges*. As more protocols were introduced to the corporate network, multiprotocol routers, better able to handle multiple LAN types as well as multiple LAN protocols, replaced these bridges. Today, routers remain an essential component of the corporate WAN. Leased line, routed networks solved two important problems:

1. Leased WAN circuits afforded organizations the basic functionality of connecting multiple sites to one another. This was both an obvious and critical problem to solve if companies were to have any reasonable chance of consolidating their data infrastructure.

2. The same circuits could transport multiple protocols when multiprotocol routers were used. Without this capability, organizations had to run a separate circuit between locations for each protocol in use—a practice that was both extremely cumbersome and extremely expensive. With this capability, organizations could at last realize some economies in terms of the money being spent building the network infrastructure.

When organizations use point-to-point services to connect multiple sites, there are essentially two types of terminations—clear channel and channelized T1/E1—possible at the customer premise. Each will be described in the following sections. Regardless of whether the circuit uses clear channel or channelized T1 services, for our purposes, there are two essential characteristics of point-to-point leased line networks.

The first is that they form truly private networks (*Physical* Private Networks, as opposed to *Virtual* Private Networks, if you will). Circuits are provisioned between two private facilities. Hosts on these networks are not addressable (and therefore not reachable) from the Internet or any other public network. Referring to the leased circuit "hierarchy" described below, traffic from various subscribers is combined for long haul transmission (but only on the most basic electrical level) so each company's transmissions are generally considered private.

♦ The level of privacy offered by leased line, point-to-point networks is the "gold standard" to which VPN services can, and should be, benchmarked.

The second is that they deliver consistent levels of performance. The bandwidth leased from the carrier's "hierarchical" bandwidth is yours to do with as you please. If you only use a few kilobits per second every so often, the rest of the bandwidth on the circuit is wasted. For the most part, leased line services use a simplistic time division multiplexing hierarchy, so the sequential frames arrive at a constant bit rate and the end-to-end latency varies very little. Much of the equipment used for these applications are the same switches and multiplexers used for the telephone system. These mature systems are engineered for robustness; while outages do occur, they tend to be rare.

♦ The performance and reliability characteristics of private leased line services are the "gold standard" to which VPN services can, and should be, be benchmarked.

Clear Channel Leased Line Infrastructure

Clear channel circuits are named for the fact that the circuits are not *channelized*, that is, split into multiple "lanes" of equivalent bandwidth. A clear channel T1, for instance, consumes a full 1.544 Megabits per second (Mbps) of bandwidth regardless of how much data is actually being transmitted or received, and the circuit is terminated at a single destination.

The Bandwidth Hierarchy

Telecommunications carriers generally operate what are known as "multiplexing hierarchies" (Figure 2.2). They take circuits from all the customers in a given geographic area and combine them together into faster circuits. These circuits are themselves combined into faster circuits for efficient long haul transmission over fiber optic cables, satellite and microwave links, and older copper-based systems. What you are doing when you create a private data network is *leasing* a piece of the transmission hierarchy for your exclusive use.

Nowadays, the smallest "chunk" of bandwidth available is 64 kilobits per second. This corresponds to a standard voice channel, generally called a DS0 (technically, you may only be able to use 56 Kbps of this channel, for reasons that, for practicality, are beyond the scope of this discussion). 24 DS0s combine to form a DS1, which is rated at 1.536 Megabits per second, 8 kilobits per second is added for framing and overhead to make 1.544 Mbps. 28 DS1s is called a DS3, rated at 45 Mbps. Multiple DS3s can then be combined into *Optical Carrier* (OCx) Networks, which use fiber optic cabling and run at speeds up to 10 Gigabits per second, or 10 Gbps.

In Europe and many parts of Asia, an alternative multiplexing hierarchy defined by the CCITT is used. In this case, 32 DS0s are combined to provide the E1 rate. E3 is rated at 34.368 Mbps.

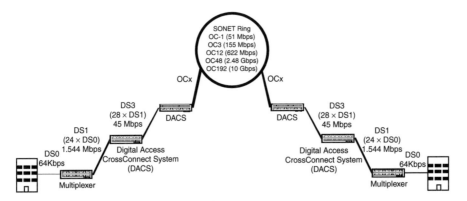

Figure 2.2 **Lease Circuit Facilities Organized into a "Multiplexing Hierarchy"**

A typical clear channel leased line environment is shown in Figure 2.3. It shows a three-node backbone data network deployed by a fictional company, Boffo Records, that we will use periodically throughout the book to illustrate points or specific topics. Boffo's factory, warehouse, and company headquarters are all connected to one another in a full mesh configuration, providing maximum availability and extra bandwidth. The factory and the warehouse are very close to each other and serviced by the same Local Exchange Carrier (LEC). An actual 4-pair copper wire is run from the LEC's Point of Presence (PoP) to the telecommunications "head" in each of the company's buildings.

The company's network is based on 64 Kbps DS0 service. The line from the service provider's PoP is a full T1, however only one of the 24 available channels is actually provisioned and usable. At the PoP, this channel will be separated and multiplexed (combined) with other channels according to the bandwidth hierarchy described in Figure 2.2.

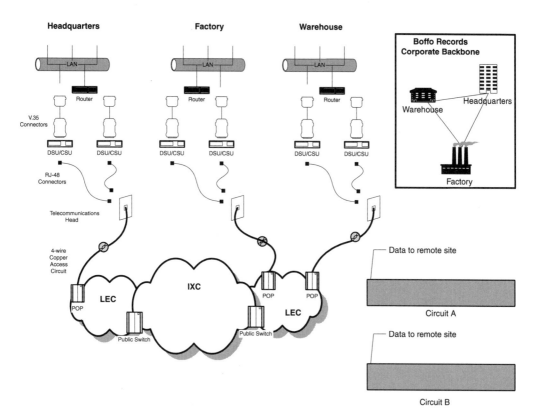

Figure 2.3 Leased Line Communications

Once the circuit is in place and functional, it is connected to an available router port. The router port is connected by cable to a device known as a CSU/DSU (Customer Service Unit/Data Service Unit). The job of the CSU is to provide timing, synchronization, and framing for the T1 line. The DSU converts the data coming in on the DS0 into a digital signal capable of connecting to computer or data communications equipment like network routers. There are several popular standards for performing the conversion (V.35 is perhaps the most common); the one used typically depends on the speed of the communications. In some service areas, the CSU/DSU is a commodity and can be bought from a third party, often with enhanced management features. In other areas, they are part of the leased line package, and are supplied by the carrier.

The router provides interfaces to both the WAN and the LAN and ensures that packets destined from the factory to the warehouse or headquarters take the right circuit to their destination. Each circuit is provisioned to terminate at one and only one far-end destination. The router also implements data link protocols suitable for point to point connections, typically Point-to-Point Protocol (PPP) or one of the proprietary point-to-point protocols implemented by makers of router equipment.

Channelized T1/E1 Leased Line Infrastructure

With clear channel leased line circuits, we need two physical circuits, two CSU/DSUs, and two ports on each of our network routers to implement the simple network for our friends at Boffo Records. A channelized leased line circuit, on the other hand, requires only one physical circuit and one router port per site, with the CSU/DSU typically built into the hardware supporting the channelized T1 port on the router.

Channelized T1 service allows each of the 24 channels on an incoming T1 circuit to be provisioned as if it were a *separate physical circuit*. Physically, the incoming circuit is still a T1; however, instead of a single channel being provisioned from the PoP, all 24 channels are provisioned and all 24 are usable *on a single circuit*. It becomes the router's job, then, to designate how to allocate and route each of the DS0 channels based on the Service Provider provisioning. For example, in Figure 2.4 the router at Boffo's headquarters will be configured that Channel 1 will contain data for the warehouse and should be demultiplexed and routed to that destination by the carrier. Channel 2 will contain data for the factory. When it is demultiplexed, the carrier should send it toward the circuit going to the factory, and so on.

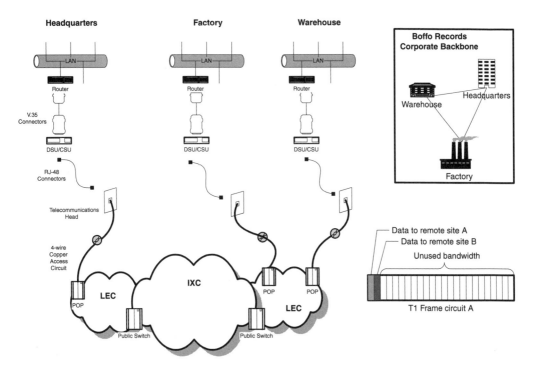

Figure 2.4 Channelized T1 Networks

Most of the equipment and cabling remains the same from Figure 2.2—there is just less of it. Most routers implement logic that enables them and the CSU/DSU to communicate which data should go onto which channel. In fact, many of them have built in CSU/DSUs. From the data networking point of view, however, each DS0 constitutes a separate point-to-point circuit. Each circuit has its own network address and the router runs the PPP protocol over each channel/circuit in order to establish and maintain a connection.

Channelized T1 can be very useful in constructing branch networks. To exemplify, suppose Boffo Records has nine warehouses and wants to construct a point-to-point network to connect its headquarters to each warehouse. Boffo might choose to allocate a DS0 to each warehouse, giving the service provider responsibility for demultiplexing each DS0 and transmitting separate streams of data to each warehouse (Figure 2.5).

The channelized T1 keeps all of the desirable properties of the leased line network mentioned above. It is private, secure, and has constant capacity, latency, and delay. In a large-scale branch network, the cost sav-

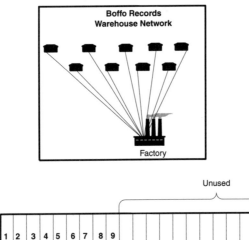

Figure 2.5 Channelized T1 Branch Network

ings (on router platforms, associated ports, circuits, management, etc.) can really add up by using channelized T1. Still, while it is certainly more efficient than clear channel, there is much room for improvement, as you will see.

Summarizing Point-to-Point Leased Line Networking

Point-to-point leased line networks solved some crucial problems. As with most technological solutions, however, a series of additional problems arose from point-to-point networking, which, of course, led to a "next generation" solution. As organizations began to roll out point-to-point leased line networks, they were quickly faced with the following challenges:

- ♦ *High circuit costs*. For short-haul circuits, leased point-to-point circuits are reasonably priced. Outside of the local exchange, however, the prices rise dramatically, with tariffs on point-to-point circuits based on both the speed of the circuit and on the distance between the two provisioned endpoints.

- ♦ *Need for more equipment and circuits*. The formula for determining the number of circuits in a multisite, fully meshed WAN backbone is:

$$X = \frac{N(N-1)}{2}$$

Remember, though, that there are ports, CSU/DSUs, and network addresses on both sides of the circuit.

For a five-site backbone, then, 20 of each item must be ordered, installed, configured, and maintained. For a 3- or 5-location WAN backbone that might not seem like such a hardship; however, for backbone networks that incorporate many sites, the cost and complexity can really add up. Although large networks are rarely full meshes, even partial mesh networks grow exponentially in cost and complexity.

Point-to-point networks, as we've established, are "physical," as opposed to "virtual," private networks. Still, point-to-point networking represented the first step in an evolution to site-to-site VPNs. The next, and even more significant step, was packet switched networks.

Packet Switched (X.25 and Frame Relay) Networking

Network managers seeking solutions to the problems exposed by point-to-point leased line networks were no doubt pleased to discover packet switched networks, first in the form of X.25, then later (and more successfully), Frame Relay.

X.25

Since its inception in 1976, X.25 has been a popular technology, particularly for branch networking. X.25 is essentially a protocol that defines the interface between data terminal equipment (DTE) and data communications equipment (DCE). In most X.25 data networks, the DTE interface is located on a router, while the DCE interface is located on an X.25 access switch owned by the service provider. Inside the "cloud," a third type of device defined by the X.25 standard, the DSE (data switching equipment), routes X.25 packets through the network.

As with point-to-point connections using channelized or clear channel T1, branches or stores using X.25 have a low-speed connection into the "cloud." Within that physical circuit, however, the branch networking equipment can create individual point-to-point network connections called *Virtual Circuits (VCs)*. The X.25 protocol defines the mechanism for the establishment and definition of VCs between DTE pairs. VCs can be switched, that is to say, dialed on demand like a telephone call or perma-

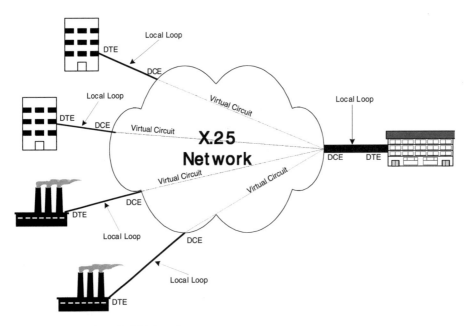

Figure 2.6 Typical X.25 Topology

nently established. The switched kind is called, predictably, a *Switched Virtual Circuit*, or *SVC*. The permanent kind is referred to as a *Permanent Virtual Circuit*, or *PVC*. At the headquarters or central site, the networking equipment typically has a faster circuit (i.e., a fatter "pipe"), where data from all of these virtual circuits arrives and aggregates on different logical channels for processing. Figure 2.6 depicts a typical X.25 topology.

Relative to the evolution to VPNs, Virtual Circuits were (and are) an important concept on a number of levels:

♦ In Virtual Circuit—based packet switched networks, the carrier, not the enterprise, was responsible for routing the data through the "cloud" at the packet level, not just at the transmission level. This required a new level of intelligence from the network, which from an equipment perspective brought the service provider network one step closer to the type of network on which the Internet was modeled.

♦ The "virtualization" of point-to-point circuits as replacement for physical circuits, including support for multiple LAN protocols over common VCs.

♦ These networks eliminated the economic challenges associated with long haul data transmission. Because the local loop provided the physical circuit termination between the DTE and DCE, organizations only had to pay the tariffs associated with the short haul circuit. This provided significant cost savings to the enterprise.

X.25 offered several advantages over point-to-point networks; however, other problems arose, particularly as the overall quality of carrier networks improved. X.25 was developed in the days when transmission systems were much slower and unreliable. In order to compensate for that, the X.25 protocol stack included a number of mechanisms to deal with issues of flow control, retransmissions, and error checking. This high amount of packet "overhead" became a burden as the overall quality and performance of the public transmission facilities improved. For example, X.25 does not support speeds greater than 2 Mbps, and even that is unusual. 64 Kbps access speeds are the norm for X.25 networks. This is clearly not sufficient for today's networks, which provide trunk speeds much higher than T1. Packet sizes, too, tend to be much smaller in X.25 networks than the 1500 byte packet size supported by most LANs.

As a way to provide a similar type of service to X.25 while improving efficiency and taking advantage of the improved transmission networks, Frame Relay was invented.

Frame Relay

Just as X.25 represented an advance over point-to-point networking, Frame Relay represented an advance over X.25. Frame Relay has many of the characteristics of X.25 but is much more efficient for today's high-speed, low "noise" transmission path. It provides lower overhead, error and congestion detection, but not correction. It is also better suited to today's client/server IP workloads with its larger packet sizes as it supports a larger frame size and no restriction on window size. The following list represents some of the important characteristics of Frame Relay relative to VPNs.

◆ *As with X.25, Frame Relay circuits are "virtual."* Using Frame Relay at Boffo's corporate headquarters, we could have a single high-speed circuit to our service provider. Over this connection, we could provision one or more *Permanent Virtual Circuits* (a specification for Frame Relay Switched Virtual Circuits is also available but not widely implemented).

- ♦ *Frame Relay PVCs can be provisioned to provide a guaranteed level of performance over the PVC.* This is handled using a feature of Frame Relay called *Committed Information Rate* or CIR. In addition, PVCs can "burst" up to the full bandwidth of the access circuit for short amounts of time. If these bursts last longer, packets are not immediately dropped, but marked as *Discard Eligible* or *DE*. If the Frame Relay network is not busy, such as at an off peak time, the packets get a free ride. For example, on a 64 Kbps access circuit, a customer requests a CIR of 16 Kbps. At 2:00 AM, the Frame Relay subscriber downloads a new price list. Since the Frame Relay network is not busy at that hour of the day, the site can use the entire 64 Kbps channel for the file transfer.

Figure 2.7 shows Boffo's network as implemented with a Frame Relay service. From the hardware point of view everything looks the same as our channelized T1 example. However, instead of being channelized, our T1 access circuit is a clear channel access circuit. The connection to each location is a virtual circuit multiplexed onto this single physical circuit. The access router uses a special packet format to label each packet with the Virtual Circuit number it will use. This number is known as a *Data Link Connection Identifier*, or *DLCI*.

Each Virtual Circuit has a Committed Information Rate that is less than the total bandwidth of the access circuit, but data is always transmitted and received at speeds up to the clocked speed of the circuit. When the data reaches the entry point of the Frame Relay service, at least the committed information rate is transmitted. If the switches and trunks that make up the Frame Relay itself are not busy transmitting data for other subscribers, data in excess of the committed information rate can be transmitted. The Frame Relay network is able to signal back to the premise router when congestion is occurring, and many routers are smart enough to throttle back their transmissions to the CIR. This is known as *traffic shaping*.

The previous telecommunication services (i.e., the point-to-point services) we discussed were part of a physical transmission hierarchy and were deterministic. If you subscribed to a 64 Kbps service, you got 64 Kbps, whether you needed it or not. Data was packaged in a fixed time-slot, so the end-to-end transmission time (or latency of the packet) is fixed, that is, it doesn't vary. Frame Relay is a packet-based service, much like an Internet in and of itself. Depending on conditions within the network, packets may arrive faster or slower (latency may vary) and the net-

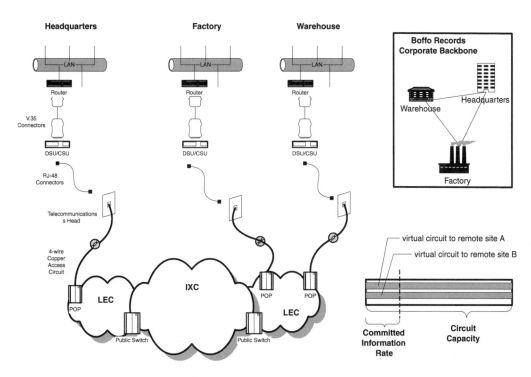

Figure 2.7 Frame Relay Networking

work may process more or fewer packets (although you would hope to always get at least your CIR's worth!). Frame Relay customers generally negotiate a service level agreement with their provider and often need to monitor whether they are in fact receiving the level of service they have paid for.

You might be thinking this sounds like a VPN. In many respects, Frame Relay services *are* VPNs, or at least share some of the traits of VPNs:

◆ A number of VPN services have Frame Relay networks at their cores.

◆ Although the switches and trunks inside the cloud are shared among all the subscribers using the Frame Relay service, each subscriber sees a private networking facility.

◆ From an "IP point of view," one Frame Relay subscriber cannot "see" packets belonging to another Frame Relay subscriber. (Although this is a fun debate in the security community!)

♦ Subscribers can use "overlapping" IP addresses (addresses that are identical to another subscriber's) or unregistered IP addresses, even though firewall and/or encryption software is not a (generally) necessary component when connecting to a Frame Relay service.

♦ It is viewed as private facility although its infrastructure is shared among many parties.

Frame Relay's popularity is proof alone of its many benefits. Still, Frame Relay was not and is not the be-all-end-all either. First, Frame Relay is not available everywhere. In some countries, it is all an organization can do just to get a single voice-grade circuit dropped into their site, let alone a high-speed digital circuit capable of supporting Frame Relay. Second, Frame Relay is optimized for LAN-to-LAN data applications but does not offer much in the way of support for other classes of service such as voice and video, in spite of recent standards of work in those areas. Enter ATM.

Cell Based Networking with ATM

Traditional IP networking is based on the transmission of synchronous data frames. For some applications, especially the long haul transmission of mixed media (voice, video, and data), it is more efficient to chop up the payload into small fixed length "cells." Because these cells are small (53 octets, in fact), they can be switched from one location to another very efficiently in hardware, allowing for extremely high-speed data transfer rates. This system is called *Asynchronous Transfer Mode*, or *ATM*.

ATM can be implemented over traditional T1 or T3 carriers, or on a special fiber optic carrier system known as the *Synchronous Optical Network* or *SONET*. Internationally, this is also referred to as the *Synchronous Digital Hierarchy* or *SDH*. SONET speeds start at 51 megabits per second (known as OC-1); OC-3 is 155 MBPS; OC-12 is 622 Mbps; OC-48 is 2.48 Gigabits per second (Gbps); and OC-192 is 10 Gbps. Most, if not all, of the highest tier (the OC-48 and OC-192) infrastructure is owned by carriers and used exclusively for high-speed trunking. Some large organizations, however, have implemented OC-3 WAN circuits running ATM. Some large enterprises even use OC-12, especially when they are privately networking voice, data, and video.

Like X.25 and Frame Relay, ATM divides the available bandwidth into separately routed Virtual Circuits (PVC or SVC). With ATM, however, there is a lot more flexibility concerning the characteristics of Virtual Circuits. ATM VCs, in fact, can be made to appear very much like Frame Relay VCs. An ATM VC can be assigned a *Sustained Cell Rate (SCR)* that corresponds closely to the Frame Relay CIR, and a *Cell Loss Priority (CLP)* that corresponds to the Discard Eligible bit in Frame Relay. The significance of this was not lost on engineers who were involved in both technologies. They found that Frame Relay services map so well onto ATM services that an *interworking* model and specification (defined in the document FRF.8, an *implementation agreement* produced and ratified by the Frame Relay Forum in 1997) is now widely deployed. Using services that implement FRF.8, an organization can have less expensive lower-speed Frame Relay connections at the branches that map onto ATM virtual circuits in a high-speed connection at the headquarters.

Unlike Frame Relay, ATM switches small, fixed-length "cells" instead of variable length frames. This allows ATM to reserve certain cells for a Constant Bit Rate service, giving ATM many of the features of a leased line, and ideal for voice. A key decision for many larger enterprises is whether they should provision ATM circuits to their Service Providers. In some large metropolitan areas CLECs are offering fiber optic 155 MB/s (OC-3) connections for little more than the price of a T3 (45Mb/s).

Comparing between ATM as a VPN protocol, versus IP as the basis for a VPN protocol, many in the industry feel that IP lacks the Quality of Service (QoS) capability enjoyed by ATM. Many in the IP community feel, however, that emerging Quality of Service mechanisms added to the IP protocol will eventually allow the Internet to provide differentiated services similar to those provided by ATM. In ATM, each of the small cells that make up the data stream requires a header to enable the routing of the cells. This overhead, or cell tax, as it is sometimes called, can be significant. In the IP alternative, frame-based IP packets will ride directly on high-speed optical carriers. Routers and switches in the network will be able to service delay sensitive or priority traffic without the need for the overhead required by the ATM protocol. We will look at some of these new IP QoS protocols in Chapter 6.

Remote Access

The technologies outlined in the previous section exist for the most part as a way to connect multiple sites to one another. In this section, we are chiefly interested in connecting individual remote users to the corporate IS infrastructure.

Of all the telecommunications services existing today on corporate networks, remote access is the service where VPNs have the biggest returns. Remote access is more critical than ever to enterprises and companies. Just about everyone is mobile these days. Corporate "road warriors" use remote access technology to send and receive E-mail, reference product catalogues and price lists, read technical reports, review presentations, and more. In an era where being cut off from the network feels like being cut off from the world, these users are demanding the ability to be able to connect to their network to get their work done.

In some industries, companies have integrated client server computing into their very business model, and remote access is a critical enabler. An insurance salesperson, for example, can visit potential clients, understand their needs, and onsite, configure and price a complicated set of options that would have taken several days turnaround in the past. These new services enable the salesperson with extended or complicated product lines to provide extremely detailed and customized proposals, often on the spot!

The growing societal trend of telecommuting is also driving remote access requirements. In some cases, state and local governments are strongly encouraging, even mandating, telecommuting to reduce air pollution, traffic congestion, and to enhance economic development. A 1997 Find/SVP survey entitled "1997 American Internet User Survey" reported 11 million people working as teleworkers and estimated that this could grow to 15 million people in 2000. Clear drivers for the trend to telecommuting were increasing penetration of home PCs and, you guessed it, the Internet.

An Introduction to Remote Access Technology

We don't want to date ourselves by starting this section on remote access technology with VT52™ asynchronous terminals and 300-baud acoustic coupler modems. We will also pass over the rise of client server computing and terminal servers with outboard modems and go straight to the 1990s-style environment pictured in Figure 2.8. Here we see the growing hordes of "road warriors" and telecommuters equipped for the most part with Microsoft Windows™ based PCs (laptops and desktops). There are also large and intrepid pockets of UNIX™, Novell IPX, and AppleTalk users requiring remote access. To serve these users, we will try to indicate

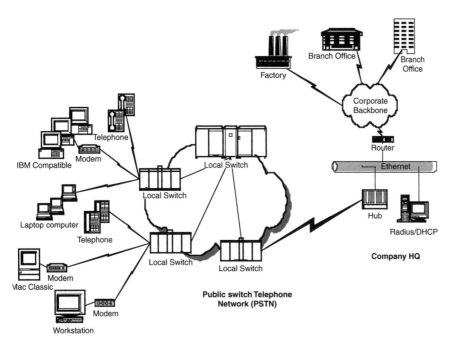

Figure 2.8 A Typical Dial-up Networking Environment

which, if any, of the following technologies relate to these "alternative" environments.

For the most part, users requiring remote access use the Public Switched Telephone Network (PSTN) to connect with their headquarters data center. Using the built-in Dial-up Networking (DUN) application, they connect using the Point-to-Point data link protocol-PPP. Once a PPP connection is established, they use IP networking to reach the destination host and use the desired application. In addition to switched connections over the PSTN, several other emerging physical access technologies are being used by remote users. We will look at some of these, including ISDN, Broadband CATV, and xDSL later in the chapter.

Figure 2.8 shows a user connecting to the local telephone exchange and being routed through the PSTN to the company data center. In the United States, we do not pay connect charges for calls in the local calling area. These areas have gotten smaller and smaller lately, as new numbering plans and deregulation leave their imprint. For mobile users, travelling either domestically or internationally, these dialup charges can be significant. Some companies have tried to control these charges by using a single 1-800 number that all users can dial to gain access remotely to the corporate network. For many enterprises these access charges can still add up to big money.

♦ VPN technology tries to replace long distance or 800 access numbers with local access numbers to a Service Provider.

Data calls tend to last significantly longer than voice calls (although readers with teenage children may disagree). A recent study suggested that data calls represent over 60% of the total traffic on the telephone network. While the access circuit connected to the dial-up users home is dedicated to that user, switching and transmission capacity at higher levels of the phone system have not been engineered for these calling patterns. Many service providers are facing costly upgrades of these network elements to accommodate these data calls.

♦ VPN technology enables service providers to remove data traffic from the voice network onto more efficient data networking circuits

Although the vast majority of the phone system is digital, most telephone sets are analog (like our voices). Modems transform digital computer data into analog signals for transmission over the voice network. Almost as soon as it gets there, it is transformed back to digital for efficient transport through the network. Just before arriving at the user's modem in the company headquarters destination, it is transformed back to analog (just in case it was really a voice call). Since the company will be receiving many data calls, it generally asks the telephone to bundle up the separate data lines into the company into high-speed channelized T1 circuits. A T1 circuit is 24 channels of 64 Kilobits per second (Kbps) digitized analog data, supporting 24 dial-in users. Even if the user only has a 28.8 Kbps modem, she will require an entire channel (64 Kbps) out of the T1 for her connection. For many users even before the first mouse-click, almost half the bandwidth they are paying for is wasted due to the analog to digital to analog conversions required. Once the user gets connected, maybe she only needs to do some Web browsing. She downloads a page, reads it, then downloads another, and so on. The effective bandwidth of this activity is even lower. Regardless, the user still consumes the entire 64 Kbps channel.

♦ VPN technologies use IP connections over unchannelized circuits. The same T1 circuit that supports only 24 simultaneous modem users can, as a 1.544 Megabits per second (Mbps) IP link, often support *hundreds* of users depending on their workload.

The example above assumed that the user's PC had a modem capable of 28.8 Kbps. This figure is typical of speeds achieved with a modem-signaling standard called V.34. New standards are constantly evolving to push modems toward their theoretical limit of transferring data at 64 Kbps. Most new laptops, for instance, now ship with new V.90 modems rated at 56 Kbps. With new compression standards, users can even think of achieving higher performance. Modem performance, however, is a two-way street. In order to benefit from new standards, not only does the *user's* modem have to support the new standard, but the modems deployed in the *access plant* at the home office need to as well. In contemporary MIS budgets and project priorities, modem upgrades tend to quickly fall to the bottom of the list.

   ♦ VPN technology pushes the burden of upgrading modem technology onto the Service Provider. Service Providers can use economies of scale to deploy cost effective high-density modem banks.

Modem technology, more so than many other aspects of data communications technology, needs to be backward compatible with an incredible range of multivendor, multistandard equipment. Many modems and remote access concentrators can be incredibly difficult to install and manage. Setting up a modem can involve a number of arcane feature initialization strings, dial codes, and other magical incantations. And it is often the least sophisticated and computer-literate user who is faced with this task. These issues have often required that the company MIS department staff a user help desk for these issues. Some mobile users require 24-hour, 7-day-per-week availability.

   ♦ VPN technology can enable the outsourcing of remote access help-desk services. Like modem banks, economies of scale and business focus enable Service Providers to provide a more professional and available service to all VPN customers.

Lastly, a whole new range of broadband access technology has burst onto the scene offering speeds that are an order of magnitude higher than what is achievable with analog modems (these are discussed further in Chapter 8). A new technology in modems called *cable modems* uses broadband signaling over the cable TV network to eventually connect to the Internet. xDSL (the "x" is a sort of wild card character, given the variety of DSL "flavors" available) is an emerging technology for running high-speed data over ordinary twisted-pair telephone wires. These are examples of two new services available in many areas. Once users have experienced the speed and simplicity of these services, they are truly loath to return to traditional modems. Cable TV operators and telephone companies generally deploy this technology for Internet access services. Secure access to corporate computing resources via these new technologies is simply unavailable outside of a VPN context.

♦ VPN technologies enable high-speed access to enterprise computing via new broadband services such as cable TV and xDSL.

After reading the last few pages on remote access, you are probably ready to turn off your corporate modems right now. Chapter 3 will consolidate these technological considerations into economic models and quantify the cost savings alluded to above. Chapter 4, which covers VPN tunneling protocols, will give you some basic design templates for possible VPN implementations for remote access.

Electronic Commerce

Even before the widespread acceptance of the public Internet, many companies recognized the usefulness of intercompany electronic transfer of data. The automotive, aerospace, and financial industries, along with organizations such as the federal government and military, share a huge volume of paperwork with their vast network of trading partners. Today, these organizations require their partners to be able to do business electronically. Since the World Wide Web burst on the scene, the business and commerce possibilities of this new medium sparked a great deal of imagination (as well as a few personal fortunes!). Let's look at two issues that are most relevant in terms of the evolution to VPNs: Electronic Data Interchange via Value Added Networks and the broader concept of intercompany extranets. For some companies, Web-based electronic commerce solutions can be an alternative to VPN technology. We will take a brief look at this technology to see how it positions relative to VPNs.

Electronic Data Interchange and Value Added Networks

Electronic Data Interchange or *EDI* is a standard format developed to exchange routine business information contained in documents such as purchase orders, invoices, or bills. The American National Standards Institute ANSI X.12 standard is the most popular format for such documents transmitted in the United States. Various industries and countries have also promulgated encoding standards suitable to their particular environment such as ODETTE and EDIFACT. Implementing EDI is not always a simple matter. The underlying processing of procurement, inventory management, accounting, and shipping/receiving procedures may need to be automated, if they are not already. Ideally, these applications should be integrated such that interconnection with EDI gateways is not overly complex. Happily, most of these systems fall under the processing "hygiene" we spoke of in Chapter 1 and are increasingly standardized and integrated out of the box.

Value Added Networks or *VANs* facilitate the interconnection of EDI-capable enterprises with their trading partners. Many VANs resemble a large electronic post office. An organization wishing to send an electronic purchase order, for example, can dial in to the VAN via their EDI software and transmit an X.12 formatted request to their supplier's EDI mailbox on the VAN. The VAN provides "value added" services on the message, such as error checking, protocol conversion, and transport to a mailbox close to the supplier destination. This way, access to the VAN is local for both the supplier and partner. Connection to a VAN is not always via dial-up. Many VANs offer leased line and X.25 connection in addition to dial-up. Interestingly, many of the major VANs are offering interconnection by—you guessed it—the Internet. Some of the major players in Value Added Networks run their own Internet service as well as other managed network services operations. Value Added Networks in support of EDI become just one item on a large menu of business communication services.

Extranets

An extranet is an intercompany network that uses Internet protocols to accomplish many of the same goals as Electronic Data Interchange. However, the scope tends to be much broader. EDI is only one application. Extranets can support joint product development, training and support, and diffuse any news or information that might be of interest to one company from another. This is in contrast to information diffused to the general public over a Web site, for example. EDI is a highly structured and tightly specified protocol environment. With extranets, many different protocols can be used. There is no "Registry of Official Extranet Protocols." The defining characteristic of extranets relative to other forms of Web-based electronic commerce is that the user community in an extranet is generally closed to a group of identified "members" specified in advance. VPN technology, especially IP-based tunneling (discussed in Chapter 4), is an ideal enabler of extranets.

Companies can and will run ANSI X.12 EDI exchanges over the public Internet using VPN technology. This can and will enable the retirement of older and more expensive VAN connections over X.25, dedicated low-speed leased lines, or dial-up networks. It is unlikely that the EDI framework and rigorous message definition protocol will give way to more unstructured and ad hoc transactions.

As in the original EDI rollout, the automotive industry is providing leadership in Internet-based EDI. The Automotive Industry Action Group (AIAG) Automotive Network eXchange (ANX) framework promotes the use of IPSec tunneling through a standard IP-based service provider network. The AIAG has selected the International Computer Security Association (ICSA) to certify the interoperability (and thus suitability) of vendor IPSec implementations for use in EDI applications for the "big three" automakers (Daimler-Chrysler, Ford, and General Motors). The buying power and pervasiveness of these companies is a major force driving the standardization and deployment of VPN and specifically IPSec technology. We will give an in-depth discussion of IPSec tunneling technology later in chapter 4.

♦ Look for ICSA certification of vendors' IPSEC-based VPN products and ANX Certification of ISPs as an indication of quality and interoperability.

Web-based Electronic Commerce

The number of things that both individuals and companies can do on the World Wide Web grows more wondrous every day. To support the desire of retailers, merchants, and brokers of various kinds for secure and authenticated commerce, a new series of standards have come to augment the relatively simple HTTP/HTML protocols that spawned the Web. Most Web browsers now support the Secure Socket Layer (SSL) protocol developed by Netscape. This protocol creates an encrypted connection between browser client and the attached server for secure transfer of data. The browsers also have the ability to store, present, and validate X.509 certificates (discussed further in Chapter 6) for authentication.

One significant difference between Web-based commerce and the Electronic Data Interchange that we discussed relates to the target populations for the two technologies. Web-based commerce is often targeted to the general public. It needs to be openly accessible to almost everyone. In general, you cannot know, *a priori,* who might want to purchase a good or service, or request information, through your Web site.

The Web interface does provide an increasingly functional interface for many business-to-business transactions as well. Web servers now contain sophisticated back-end interfaces to integrate into many of the supply-chain applications that support these transactions. Clearly the Web has moved beyond just flashy presentation of information to a critical business tool. In fact, Web servers with advanced security features are often seen as a competing technology to VPNs.

It is important to note, however, that Internet-accessible Web applications need to be individually updated in order to connect into the intranet servers supporting their function. Many of the extranet applications discussed above are much more ad hoc in nature. The flexibility to bring a partner into the intranet in a controlled way with VPN technology is often an advantage in certain applications. New applications can be added without specific programming or modification to enterprise firewalls.

While there is certainly no stopping the speeding train that is Web-based E-commerce, VPNs are a complementary technology that is often better suited to applications whose target user population can be determined in advance.

SNA Networks

In today's client/server networks, we often take for granted the incredible technological achievement of supporting a network of thousands of transaction-processing terminals. These terminals supported the applications that were at the heart of many businesses and impacted all of us on a day to day basis. Systems such as the Airline Reservation System, credit card authorization systems, bank teller systems, health care, and even the Internal Revenue Service all used IBM System Network Architecture or SNA. It seems amazing that so many terminals could support so many transactions over what seems to us little better than tin cans and string: 300 baud multidrop lines.

Today, 80% of the 2000 largest global customers run 50% of their mission-critical applications on an IBM or compatible mainframe (Yankee Group). Although 60% of these mainframes run TCP/IP today,

SNA still drives over 3 trillion lines of code in legacy applications. While there are many ways of dealing with SNA traffic in today's complex internetworked world, we will focus on two technologies that are useful for dealing with SNA in the VPN context: Frame Relay encapsulation and Data Link Switching. These are not VPN technologies *per se,* but both technologies prepare SNA data such that they are amenable to the IP-based or Frame Relay–based solutions discussed in the rest of the book.

Figure 2.9 shows a traditional SNA network based on long-haul, low-speed (e.g., 9600 bps) leased lines. These circuits connect remote cluster controllers, servicing 3270 synchronous terminals, or devices such as point of sale or teller systems, to a mainframe computer by way of a Front End Processor (FEP). These circuits are increasingly expensive to maintain and can typically only support SNA's Synchronous Data Link Control (SDLC) protocol. They cannot be shared with other voice or data traffic from the branches. Figure 2.10 shows how these long-haul SDLC circuits can be replaced with local frame relay connections. The SDLC circuits at the branches are terminated into a special adapter called a Frame Relay Access Device or FRAD.

These devices encapsulate SNA traffic into a standard Frame Relay packet for transport to the mainframe. At the headquarters site, one of three methods maybe used to get the data to the mainframe. Case *a* in Figure 2.10 shows a FRAD at the mainframe site as well, decapsulating the SNA traffic back to discrete SDLC circuits into the FEP. In this case the Frame Relay network substitution is transparent to the SNA hardware. Optionally, many newer Front End Processors allow direct attachment of the Frame Relay circuit as shown in *b* in Figure 2.10. This however would require a reconfiguration of the IBM networking software. Newer IBM mainframes allow direct attachment of the Frame Relay circuit via the Open Systems Adapter or OSA, as shown in *c* in Figure 2.10. This option also requires reconfiguration of the networking software, but allows the enterprise to potentially get rid of an old or very costly front end processor. Often the FRAD can be combined in a multiprotocol router platform. This allows IBM traffic to run over on virtual circuit with its own committed information rate and IP traffic to run on a separate virtual circuit. In this way the SNA traffic is unaffected by any bursts of traffic from the IP domain.

Some VPN services for the SNA world work by offering the FRAD function in the "cloud." That is to say the customer can replace the long-haul SDLC link with a short one to the service provider point of pres-

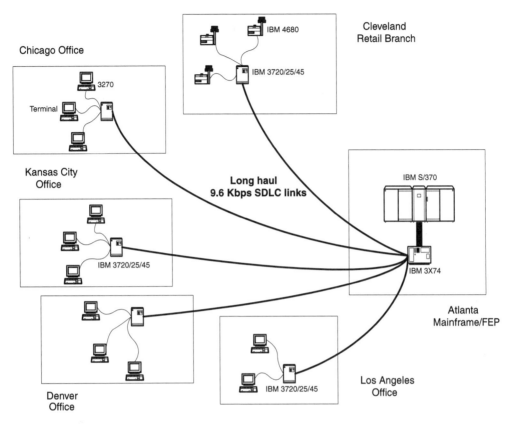

Figure 2.9 A Traditional SNA Network

ence where banks of FRADs encapsulate SNA traffic for many customers for transport over frame relay.

Despite these many compelling advantages, SNA Frame Relay Access Device usage is on the downswing. These special purpose devices are being replaced with a scheme to encapsulate SNA traffic within IP. Once this is done, separate telecommunications facilities for SNA and IP can be merged. The network can then be evolved using VPNs, Frame Relay, or ATM, as a whole; the SNA traffic just becomes another IP data stream. This technology, called Data Link Switching or DLSw, is well standardized and available in interoperable platforms from almost every routing vendor.

IP encapsulation is a technique used to adapt many legacy protocols for an IP centric environment. IP encapsulation protocols exist for Async terminal streams, X.25 and X.29 PADs, AppleTalk, and IPX, just to name a few.

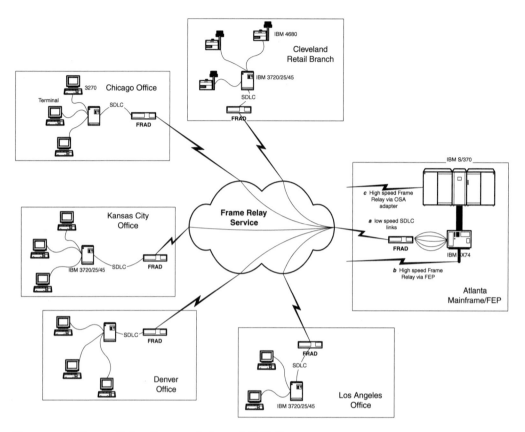

Figure 2.10 Frame Relay Encapsulation of SNA Data

The Internet and IP

One of the major themes of this book is that the public Internet can be used for many types of VPNs. Consequent to this is the fact that the Internet Service Providers (ISPs) are spearheading many of the VPN offers. In this section, we will take a closer look at the ISP as well as the main elements used in providing VPNs, and give a few pointers about what to look out for when selecting an ISP to provide VPN services.

The Internet Service Provider Point of Presence

Small Internet Service Providers (ISPs) generally have two types of customers: dial-in users and corporate leased line customers. Larger ISPs often have a third type of customer in that they often service smaller "downstream" ISPs. A Point of Presence (PoP) contains the remote access equipment, servers, and modems that support dial-in users and data network equipment that are used to provide leased line permanent Internet access to companies. Figure 2.11 shows some of the equipment that may be found in today's more aggressive ISPs.

Remote Access Facilities

An ISP uses the facilities of the local exchange carrier to provide transmission to its leased line customers, and T1 or ISDN primary access circuits to provide bulk telephone circuits for dial-up users. The dial trunks terminate onto one or more remote access servers or concentrators. These devices provide modem termination for dial-in users for basic Internet services or a subscribed VPN service.

♦ When evaluating ISPs for VPN partners, it is important to understand their dial-in modem capacity. If the ISP has too little, you may get busy signals when you try to connect at peak times.

♦ Verify that the modem capacity supports the modem types of your users. This is especially important for new standards such as V.90.

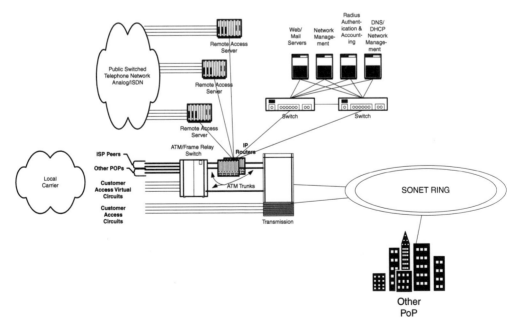

Figure 2.11 **A Service Provider Point of Presence**

You may want to discuss with your ISP the ability to guarantee access to a certain number of ports for your specific use. What might seem to be a reasonable customer access ratio during normal times might cause big problems, if say, there was a stock market crash, a snow day, or other event, and everyone wanted to log on. Some Service Providers are starting to implement a special protocol known as Signaling System 7 or SS7. This allows the provider to interact directly with the PSTN for these types of advanced applications, rather than passively receiving calls routed to it. These issues are discussed further in Chapter 7.

If you chose an ISP with a PoP in your area, you will be able to dial a local number to connect to the Internet. In the United States calls to a local number are generally free, irrespective of the time the user spends connected. Obviously, the phone companies are aware of this situation, and it may not continue into the future. As it is, the definition of "local call" is getting narrower and narrower.

♦ You will need to discuss the geographic requirements for remote access VPNs with potential service providers to insure that they can provide cost-effective coverage, both to mobile traveling users and/or work-at-home telecommuters.

The ISP may be able to augment its list of local dial-in numbers with 800 numbers, if required. As we will see in later chapters, ISP-enabled VPN architectures that require protocol support within the service provider may not be available across service provider boundaries. For instance, a nationwide service provider may not have a mechanism to provide VPN dial access overseas. If this is required, end-to-end models may be a better choice.

Port reservation and geographic distribution of users will be important factors in negotiating and pricing VPN service contracts. For service providers, these issues represent provisioning and billing requirements that will determine the success and profitability of the VPN service. Policy issues also come into play. The VPN subscriber may want to impose idle timeouts so napping road warriors don't tie up VPN resources. Another common VPN access service might be password management. These services and the mechanisms to enable them are discussed later.

Figure 2.11 also shows that the Service Provider is still beholden to public carriers for the "last mile" access to the customer access. This is a situation that many service providers are looking desperately to remedy. To them, this access represents a drain on margins, as well as a challenge to their position as total providers. Look for a number of new technologies on the horizon to chip away at this last barrier to the customer. Contenders include the previously mentioned data over cable TV and wireless transmission. DSL is excluded simply because the facilities used by xDSL are, for the most part, owned by the RBOC.

Leased Line Facilities

The ISP may also offer leased line Internet services out of the PoP over facilities ranging from low-speed DS0s to T1 links. For larger enterprises, Internet access via T3 links is not surprising, given recent reductions in tariffs for T3 access. Leased line Internet services may also be delivered as ATM or Frame Relay circuits. These circuits provide full time access to the Internet and allow an organization to send and receive data from the standard Internet application, typically E-mail and Web traffic. In the coming chapters we will show how VPN traffic can be delivered over these circuits as well.

Figure 2.11 shows leased line facilities from the enterprise terminating onto standard *bandwidth manager* systems provided by equipment makers such as a Nortel Networks or Ascend Communications. Bandwidth managers provide enhanced billing and provisioning to the service provider over and above what might be available on standard IP routers. Bandwidth managers also allow the service provider to provision Frame Relay or ATM Virtual Circuits through their private backbone. These Virtual Circuits are often used as a foundation for VPN services to enterprises.

Value-Added Services

Every ISP operates at least one major data center used to support the service provider's management and billing platforms. These data centers, and the people that implement and support them, are not always treated strictly as cost centers. To improve efficiencies, much of the equipment and manpower that are in place to run the data center are also used as a vehicle for delivering "value-added" services designed to contribute directly to the ISP's top line revenue stream. Traditional ISP services include hosting mailbox accounts for its subscribers and providing storage for personal web pages. The ISP provides caching of popular pages for the World Wide Web and Internet news. These important services allow much of the popular Web and news traffic to remain local to the ISP and not require bandwidth from Internet uplinks. The ISP may also host domain names for its customers and thus participate in Internet Domain Name Service (DNS).

ISPs are continually looking to provide new value-added services on their infrastructure. Profit margins on basic Internet access, including these basic services, have been driven down by the arrival of larger players with deeper pockets on the scene. An ISP may offer a complete package of E-commerce services, including the hosting of the site right in the ISP facilities. Outsourced service offerings such as these are somewhat beyond the scope of this book, except that a VPN or extranet connection into an organization's intranet may be packaged with these other services. Other popular service offerings include firewall and security management and implementation, Internet or IP-based fax and telephony services, and, of course, VPNs.

- Billing, provisioning, and management systems are critical components of successful VPN service implementation. Be sure to get a full understanding of the Service Provider capabilities in this area.

- Understand the fail-over, capacities, and load balancing strategies of key VPN systems such as tunnel management or accounting.

Internet Peering

The Internet today is highly distributed in nature. Smaller ISPs connect into one or more larger wholesale ISPs in an arrangement called *peering*. In order to provide higher availability and bandwidth, some ISPs peer with multiple upstream providers. The flow of traffic among these entities is controlled via a protocol called the *Border Gateway Protocol* or BGP. The BGP protocol may have importance to enterprises contemplating the use of Internet-based VPNs. Just as smaller ISPs can connect into more than one upstream provider, enterprises sometimes look to maintain several connections to the Internet via different ISPs so that they can control which traffic passes over which connection. Some larger national Internet backbone providers connect directly into the Network Access Points (NAPs) for peering, often in multiple places. Private peering arrangements between providers are also on the rise. Smaller or regional providers rely on larger ISPs to provide addressing and connectivity to the Internet.

- Know if your ISP is connected to an upstream service provider and at what speed. Your level of service will depend on how "far" you are from your VPN peers, be they branch offices, extranet partners, or dial-in users.

The Service Provider Network

Nationwide backbone carriers, who connect directly to switching centers located at the various NAPs, provide much of the actual transmission of today's Internet. From these switching centers, they branch out into a network of interconnected Points of Presence or PoPs, throughout the country. This network may be hierarchical with a number of distributed hub sites trunked together with high-speed, long-haul facilities such as T3 or OC-3. These hubs act as concentration points for smaller downstream PoPs and service providers, which may even connect with further levels of networking. These networks go beyond simple star-shaped hierarchies by implementing highly connected meshed networks for redundancy and load sharing.

In the past, service providers leased telecommunication facilities from the major IXCs. Increasingly, though, they are trying build or buy their own fiber optic transmission networks. A new technology called *Wave Division Multiplexing* (WDM) permits the purchase or lease of a private "color" on a fiber optic strand from fiber network operators such as Qwest. This recent development has provided a vast increase in terms of the bandwidth available for PoP networks.

The point we are making here is that with these private transmission facilities, service providers are more capable than ever to transform themselves into multiservice Competitive Local Exchange Carriers or CLECs.

Internet data from enterprise customers is routed through the Service Provider network topology to the most appropriate peering point by the BGP protocol. VPN data in the form of site-to-site Virtual Circuits or VPN tunnels for dial traffic will also route to their destination over this backbone. The service provider PoP network is no longer a monolithic IP network based on routers, but has interfaces at the transmission (OC3, DS0), and switching (Frame Relay and ATM PVCs) layers.

Conclusions

This chapter was designed to give the reader a more in-depth feeling for the character of telecommunications facilities that are used in contemporary enterprise networks. Some network seers foretell the day when all of these facilities are rationalized onto a single efficient and functional Internet. We do not know when and if this will happen. We have tried to give a feeling for the applications and requirements of these networks and some indications about possible evolution to Virtual Private Networks. Understanding the provisioning models and technical underpinnings of these network technologies, however, is a very useful foundation for understanding the business and economic models developed in the next chapter.

The Business Case
for VPNs

"Show me the money!" This famous quotation from the Cameron
Crowe/Tom Cruise movie "Jerry Maguire" has become the razor
by which most business propositions are judged. In this chapter
we will do just that. One of the chief reasons that VPNs are creating such excitement is the extremely compelling business case.
"For whom?" you may be asking. In most propositions there is a
winner and loser. In our mind, the business case for VPNs is
about as close as you can come to the proverbial win-win situation.

What follows is the proof. We will look at the business case for VPNs from the point of view of both the enterprise consumer and the service provider. For the enterprise customer we will look at the costs of implementing VPNs versus the costs of more traditional data networking. For the service provider we will examine some of the possible service offerings, look at typical pricing and revenue models, and discuss the costs associated with the delivery of the services. This should lead us to the bottom line.

We are going to present a series of analyses that will support our point of view, but there are some issues to be aware of. For the most part we will be using data collected at the end of 1998. Prices and cost information change. Furthermore, most of the examples come from implementations in the United States. Cost structures are different in other countries. The figures presented will give a reasonable overview of the big picture, enough to prove the win-win hypothesis of this chapter. The categories in the analyses are designed to be more useful. This chapter will help make sure your analysis is complete.

Last, we will take a look at some of the different business models available for offering VPNs. These will range from a single entity delivering a basic transport service, to a consortium of Service Providers providing comprehensive design, analysis, implementation, and support.

The Enterprise Customer

We will be concerned with two applications in this chapter: remote access and a branch network. Scale often is a major determinant of cost structure so we want to look at different-sized environments. Of course, this technology is of use to larger organizations; however, VPN deals for larger organizations are often custom quoted after long negotiations, and political and financial issues can be obscured.

LAN-to-LAN Networking

As we mentioned earlier, Frame Relay is the gold standard against which many LAN-to-LAN VPNs are judged. Many VPNs are in fact Frame Relay networks with the possible addition of Customer Premises Equipment (CPE) and perhaps management services. In order to understand the economics of IP-based VPNs, we will use the economics of Frame Relay as our yardstick.

Despite their maturity, Frame Relay offerings are far from commodities, and there isn't much standardization in service offerings. Conventional wisdom suggests that the only way to effectively compare Frame Relay offerings is via an RFP process. Even then, responses should be regarded as a starting point for negotiation, especially in regard to service level agreements and management reporting.

Table 3.1 gives an idea of the cost elements for a Frame Relay connection as well as a similarly configured Internet connection suitable for a LAN-to-LAN VPN.

This table shows us that many of the cost elements of both the Internet VPN and Frame Relay network are going to be the same! In both cases, each location will require a leased access circuit from the user location to the Service Provider PoP as well as pay a port charge to access the service. In the case of Frame Relay, the one-time installation fees are

Table 3.1 A Comparison of Cost Elements between Frame Relay and VPNs

Cost Element	Frame Relay	Internet Service
Monthly Access Charge: Leased line from customer premises to Service Provider Point of Presence	✔	✔
One-time Access Installation	✔	✔
Monthly Service Port Charges: Frame Relay or Internet	✔	✔
One-time Service Port Charges	✔	✔
Virtual Circuit Charges	Much variation	Not required
Provider Performance Reports	Optional	Not often available
CSU/DSU (often integrated)	✔	✔
Router	✔	✔
Management Cost	Can be outsourced	Can be outsourced
Service-level Agreements	✔	✔
VPN Device	Not required	✔
Internet Firewall	Not required	✔

often related to the length of time that the user is willing to commit to the service. A significant premium is usually charged for month-to-month access or a non-renewable contract.

In both cases, the network service requires the use of an IP router and CSU/DSU combination to connect the enterprise site to the network. More and more, both of these items are included in the basic access package, often in combination with some kind of shared management or provisioning service offered by the Service Provider.

When an enterprise is connected to the Internet, it is usually done in conjunction with a firewall. This is especially true if the Internet connection will support applications other than the VPN. The VPN capability can be then built in to the firewall, the Internet router, or deployed as a separate appliance. Some of these variations are discussed in Chapter 5, once we've had an in-depth look at some of the Internet VPN mechanisms.

Where frame relay differs from the Internet service is the provisioning of Permanent Virtual Circuits (PVCs). It is also here that there is the most amount of variation in pricing among different service providers. Variations include:

♦ Flat-priced PVCs based only on Committed Information Rate (CIR)

♦ Distance-sensitive PVCs

♦ Volume-based pricing

♦ Interprovider PVCs

♦ Simplex (single direction) versus bidirectional PVCs

♦ Tiered pricing based on number of PVCs

♦ Availability of low-cost "zero CIR" PVCs

In the United States, Frame Relay networks are ubiquitous. There are many different providers with hundreds and even thousands of points of presence. Due to competition, these services are very reasonably priced and typically offer good service. When analyzing the economics of Frame Relay and VPNs, it is important to be aware of not only the geographic situation, but also the application situation, to understand the relative economic benefits of one technology versus another. Blanket statements will simply not be satisfying. Below are a number of particular application scenarios that have clear economic advantages over the competing technology. Often individual cases are not so clear cut. It is hoped that these scenarios serve to clarify key indicators for one approach or the other.

Case 1: A new intranet star network configuration

(i.e., branch networks): In a limited geographical area or within the continental United States, Frame Relay, either in a Managed Network Service environment or self-managed, will tend to offer better price performance than a corresponding Internet VPN. Each location requires similar monthly access and port charges, one-time installation fees, and similar customer premises equipment (IP routers and CSU/DSUs). In the United States, this network would use a single flat-priced, bi-directional PVC per branch, which would cost little more than the corresponding Internet service.

Case 2: A new intranet mesh configuration

(i.e., interdependent business units): This type of network is often more cost effective as an Internet VPN. This is because of the large number of PVCs required to give the mesh connectivity. Even with bidirectional PVCs, a network of twenty branches would need 190 PVCs. Adding the twenty-first office then requires an additional twenty PVCs to attach it to each of the others. In this case, the geometrically increasing costs of the PVCs would become significant versus the other costs discussed above. An exception to this case might be if the mesh network was the core of a large corporate backbone. Here, concerns about emerging Internet VPN technology still favor a Frame Relay network, at this writing.

Case 3: Adding VPN application to existing Internet connections

The previous cases looked at cases where the networks were being built from scratch. Here the VPN application is being added to an already in-place Internet infrastructure supporting E-mail or E-commerce applications. This may be the case for the whole network or in just one or two branches. Here, much of the cost of the infrastructure will already have been sunk, and typically only a small equipment cost will be required to enable the VPN. This can be especially advantageous when traffic requirements are low.

Case 4: Connecting international sites

Building international private networks is still an expensive proposition. New telecommunications consortia, such as BT Concert or AT&T Worldnet, are changing this, but even these can offer a bewildering array of contract options, as well as still being pricy. In some countries, an international private circuit is simply not available. In contrast, the Internet is available almost everywhere on the planet. Even most third world or far-flung locations have some kind of Internet facility. These are often reasonably priced, and though they may suffer from slow performance or outages, the data does get through. Many VPN technologies are quite tolerant of these conditions due to their IP heritage.

Case 5: Connecting extranet partners

Connecting the facilities of two different cooperating companies is certainly technically possible, but it is fraught with many difficult questions concerning management and finances. Most companies have used third party networks such as VANs to accomplish the task in the past. An Internet VPN allows each company in a joint venture to safely use the Internet to collaborate. Each company separately funds and manages its Internet connections, and each can decide which set of facilities should be visible to the other partners. Almost all future extranets will use Internet VPN technology. This exciting new application is the momentum driving much of the development of VPN technology.

Case 6: Connecting multiple sites in a metropolitan area

Many urban centers are well wired with numerous fiber-optic transmission facilities run by competitive carriers. It is possible to lease private circuits from these carriers, but these are often priced relative to their traditional counterparts. Often more economical are high-speed Internet facilities accessed by easy LAN technology such as Ethernet or FDDI, or more recently cable modems and xDSL. This environment can offer a cost-effective, high-performance VPN environment.

Case 7: Connecting individual departments through a company backbone

With today's climate of mergers and acquisitions, it is often difficult to distinguish between "us and them." Decentralized operations such as human resources, engineering, and marketing often have the need to communicate sensitive information from one part of the company to another, where the network backbone very much resembles the public Internet in its collection of unvetted equipment. These departments will often use the VPN technology to securely communicate through the company backbone.

Remote Access VPNs

When we discussed remote access networking technology in the last chapter, we told you that this was where the really big savings appeared in using Virtual Private Networks. Let's take a closer look now at the business case and see why that is the case. The basic premise of remote access VPNs is that the company will replace its outdated hard-to-manage remote access servers with a new VPN server connected to the Internet as shown in Figures 3.1 and 3.2. The old remote access servers support channelized T1 circuits (or ISDN PRI circuits) each capable of supporting 24 simultaneous connections, regardless of the user workload. The new VPN appliance connects directly to the Internet via a clear channel, for example, which could support up to ten times the number of users (depending on the workload).

Note that in this case the remote users don't dial directly into the enterprise. They are given dial-in accounts with an Internet Service Provider. These no longer are limited to telephone circuits. Alternative technologies such as xDSL and cable modems can also be used.

Table 3.2 gives the output of one of the popular VPN savings calculators found on the Web. This calculator assumes that the organization is contemplating replacing its obsolete modems with a new remote access gear to support new modem standards. Remote users were dialing long distance at 60% of the time at $6 per hour. Now they all have Internet accounts at $20 per month. The figures given below may be obsolete by the time you are reading this, or vary for your part of the world. The $19.95 "all you can eat" Internet access accounts are popular for home users. Business

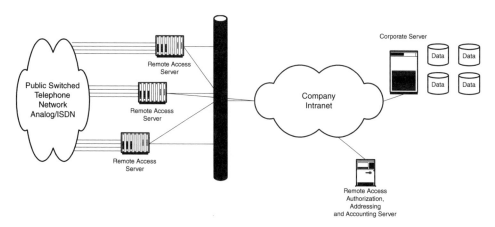

Figure 3.1 **Traditional Remote Access**

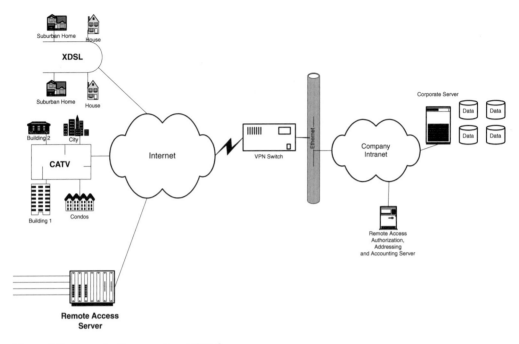

Figure 3.2 Remote Access via a VPN Server

class services may cost more, especially if value-added services such as port reservation, service level agreements, or help desk services are included. Nevertheless, the possibilities for significant savings should be evident.

Less obvious from Table 3.2 is new functionality, such as high-speed access and the ability to free up IT staff for more strategic or important projects. The company is freed from further obsolescence in modem and access technology and has a smoother growth (or shrinkage) path.

Other Benefits of VPNs

Examining monetary cost figures above only tells part of the story of the value of VPNs to enterprises. It is difficult to put cost figures on the capabilities described below. Nevertheless, these represent real value and need to be taken into account when evaluating whether or not to employ VPN technology.

VPN Technology is Easy to Understand

Upper management in many companies is perplexed by the complexity of networking technology. They see the capital and manpower expenditures in their financial statements and may even be able to

Table 3.2 A typical cost calculator for Remote Access VPN Savings

Cost	50 Users 20 Active 20 hrs per week		200 Users 50 Active 20 hrs per week		1000 Users 200 Active 20 hrs per week	
	Remote Access	VPN	Remote Access	VPN	Remote Access	VPN
Communications:						
T1 Lines	$500	$2,850	$1,500	$2,850	$4,500	$2,850
User Access	$3,600	$1,000	$14,400	$4,000	$72,000	$20,000
Equipment	$30,000	$20,000	$60,000	$20,000	$180,000	$20,000
Management:						
Equipment	$500	$200	$1,500	$200	$4,500	$200
Users	$1,250	$625	$5,000	$2,500	$25,000	$12,500
Total Monthly Cost	$5,850	$4,675	$22,400	$9,550	$106,000	$35,550
Monthly VPN Savings		$1,175		$12,850		$70,450
Yearly VPN Savings		$24,100		$194,200		$1,005,400

benchmark their IT budgets against comparable firms. However, it is more difficult to evaluate the merit and justification of individual projects and proposals. Is the new high-speed backbone circuit cost justified? How about the new network management systems? Do we require additional operations staff? VPN technologies often replace these questions with simpler alternatives: I'd like to open a new branch office in Texas, or I need to provide remote access to the staff of my new distributor.

VPN Technology Can Reduce the Risks of Obsolescence

The fast pace of technological innovation is often dizzying for enterprise management. New must-have technologies such as IP telephony, multicasting, content "push" applications, and the like seem to be arising almost every day. Will the platforms and process put in place today be able to support the new applications? Will new equipment be able to have a useful service life? What period should be used for Return on Investment calculations? With VPN technology, it is often the Service Provider that assumes the risk of obsolescence. The Service Provider keeps close relations with networking manufacturers and industry offerings and updates customer premises equipment as well as its own infrastructure to support technology advances.

VPN Technology Enables Scalability and Flexibility

Today's companies are constantly going through both internal and external restructuring. In addition to mergers and acquisitions, there are downsizing, spin-offs, and internal management reorganizations. These activities have wreaked havoc on network operations and finances. VPN technology is faster to adapt to these changes due to the underlying flexibility and ubiquity of the Internet.

VPN Technology Enables New Business Structures such as Extranets

As we have discussed in the previous chapter, a whole new segment of "networked" enterprises have emerged. In this business model, separately owned and managed entities cooperate to bring a product and service to market. One entity may do design, another manufacturing, a third distribution, a fourth service, and so on. A great deal of private communications is required to enable these activities. The design, implementation, management, and funding of traditional intranet technology would clearly be fraught with thorny problems of responsibility and finger pointing. VPN technology offers a convenient demarcation point between firms, as well as a simple and effective method for funding and managing the communications infrastructure.

Outsourcing

We have talked earlier about why a company might want to outsource its network operations to a Service Provider. This section takes a closer look at some of the economic and procedural elements to consider along with the decision to outsource.

Nowadays, there are two general forms of outsourcing: strategic and tactical. Tactical outsourcing can often be used where the task is well structured, the success criteria can be clearly articulated, and the cost/pricing structure is easily analyzed. Office cleaning services and the company cafeteria come to mind, and we suggest that remote access outsourcing using VPN technology will likely fall in this category. Simple LAN-to-LAN VPNs or extranets can also be tactical, but as service-level agreements, design services, and management are added, these can quickly become strategic.

Companies may also want to outsource less structured, less understood parts of their business. The operation of a company's wide-area network infrastructure certainly falls into this category. While the reasons for outsourcing are intuitive and compelling, the decisions of which Service Provider to choose and the associated contractual and financial aspects of the project need to be considered very carefully. The case literature is peppered with some spectacular debacles.

The outsourcing project may involve transfer of assets or personnel that can affect not only the financial performance of the company but its very existence. Contracts often have multiyear duration and may require a significant ramp-up period to achieve results. Throughout the book, we have been focusing mainly on tactical issues, but outsourcing arrangements are strategic business decisions and need to have the involvement of senior management to provide clarity on high-level goals and as part of the ongoing service monitoring and escalation process.

In-depth discussion of the outsourcing life cycle is beyond the scope of this book. Virtual Private Networks using tunneling technology or managed network services can quickly resemble outsourcing projects and due caution should be exercised. Retaining professional services with experience in the outsourcing during early phases of the project can often be well worth the effort.

From the Service Provider's Perspective

Pricing of VPN services remains a black art. As we will see in the next section, currently there is a large margin potential in VPN service offerings due to economies of scale in equipment purchases, bandwidth provisioning, staffing, and management. In addition to this relatively straightforward analysis, VPN services offer a platform for value-added services over and above the technology infrastructure. These include design and analysis services, proactive management, and end-user support services. Another area where the Service Provider has the ability to add value is by offering differentiated services. Differentiated services refer to the ability of the Service Provider to offer differing levels of service: response times, delay, network access, just to name a few, at varying price points. In this chapter, we will look at some of the pricing implications of differentiated services and will explore the technical details of their implementation later in Chapter 7.

Cost of Providing VPN Services

A naïve view of the VPN business might assume that there are no incremental costs to offering the VPN service on typical Internet Service Provider infrastructure. In some of the technical models for VPN services discussed in the next chapter, the service can merely be layered onto the existing infrastructure. The ISP uses existing dial and access concentrators, backbone switches, and routers to provision the service and is ready to go. While VPN services do strongly leverage the existing infrastructure, a number of elements need to be considered before the service is ready for the market. Some of these include:

Equipment

- ISP equipment upgrades to support increased traffic and new protocols
- Customer premises equipment that may be required for the VPN service
- Additional telecommunications capacity to support traffic requirements

Personnel

- Network design staff for customer analysis and proposals
- Installation teams for CPE and telecommunications installations
- Network operations staff to support the VPN application
- Customer support and help desk personnel
- Customer training
- Additional sales and marketing personnel for the service

Equipment Costs

When we were discussing the point of view of the VPN customer above, we said that a key advantage of VPNs was to remove the risk and cost of equipment obsolescence. The VPN customer expects the Service Provider to insure the network implements the latest standards and features. They want to make sure the equipment is appropriately sized to support the traffic load, and that in the event of equipment or telecommunications failures, the network will continue to run, perhaps with a stated degree of lost capability, and for a stated mean time to repair window. This is different from formal Service Level Agreements that we will discuss in Chapter 7. During pre-sales discussions for the VPN service, the customer will typically want to understand what approach the Service Provider takes engineering and maintaining its backbone. Further, Service Providers are receiving increasing scrutiny from the trade press and independent testing laboratories on the capabilities of their networks to support business class services. Their findings are reported in publications such as *Boardwatch*.

A new class of Service Provider is emerging to provide these business class services. They feature aggressively managed and generously provisioned network infrastructure. Their private nationwide backbones support a much smaller group of business users and connect into the public Internet at well-controlled peering points. These features are reiterated in the business case section to remind Service Providers that infrastructure investments may be required to enter the marketplace.

The next two chapters look at implementation details of VPNs. Some service models require special purpose VPN termination equipment at the customer premises. Others can use a standard network router on the customer premises, but the customer may want this sized and managed by the Service Provider. It is often in the Service Provider's interest to have the customer premises equipment as standardized as possible. Standard CPE provides a platform for integrated management and accounting capabilities and simplifies operations and troubleshooting. Economically it is also advantageous. The service provider can become a distribution channel for the equipment manufacturer. The channel relationship typically results in preferential pricing and discounts to the service provider. This results in higher margins on equipment sale or lease of the equipment to the enterprise customer. It also can give the service provider better access to technical information from the manufacturer as well a conduit for troubleshooting, the latest bug fixes, and input for enhancement and new feature requests.

People Resources

Human resources are the typically the most underestimated cost of providing the VPN service. The biggest miss in this area tends to be in the sales and marketing of the VPN service. An enterprise decision to outsource network operations to a service provider is a strategic decision. Contracts typically involve a significant monetary commitment, over long periods of time. As discussed above, it may involve transferring asset and personnel. As a result of these characteristics, sales cycles can be long and can involve months of negotiation and analysis before a long-term contract is signed.

The VPN market is relatively new. Service providers will typically need to engage in a number of demand generation activities such as seminars, conferences, and tradeshows. These require the production of brochures, white papers, reference accounts, and presentations. The cost of providing these resources has to be counted in any VPN business plan. None can succeed without these marketing activities.

Network performance analysis is an art. Many tools are available to help, but there is no substitute for experienced network designers. The enterprise VPN customer is essentially delegating this function to the Service Provider. Very few customers will have a precise understanding of their current or future capacity and performance requirements. A Service Provider consultant will often need to spend significant time interviewing various stakeholders in the customer organization and may want to use probes or monitors to sample the actual network activity before configuring the customer VPN environment. The design consultant will have to determine the impact of the new customer application on the service infrastructure as well as periodically review traffic and performance trends in order to adjust capacities both at the customer sites and internally. A key challenge for the Service Provider is making this value-add visible to the customer and charging for it. VPN packaging options and revenues are discussed below.

Staff may be required to deploy the VPN components. Customer premises equipment may need to be installed and configured in different customer locations. Software may need to be configured, including management or performance monitors and probes. Telecommunications facilities may need to be ordered, installed, and tested.

Once the network is configured, operations staff is required to insure the smooth operations as well as collect the operational data required for the design process. Administrative staff is required to process traffic, usage, and other billing data collected. This information needs to be fed back to the customer in the form of status reports and service level results. Of course, bills need to be sent and fees collected. The administrative staff needs to investigate discrepancies and respond to customer inquiries. VPN customers will typically have a better baseline feel for the network performance of their applications versus the general Internet user. As part of the VPN offer, the customer may require guaranteed service level agreements. Thus, in general, the VPN service offering is going to require closer management supervision as compared to many generic Internet service offerings.

End user support is also of significant value to VPN customers. We discussed some of the issues around dial-in support in the last chapter.

The customer may also require other end-user support activities. Opportunities exist for the Service Provider to provide application support for some of the standard office software products: E-mail, spreadsheets, and so on, as well as front line support for a broad range of intranet infrastructure issues. Where the VPN customer has no desire to hire and train support personnel, along with their respective backups during vacations and holiday, this can be an interesting proposition to the Service Provider. Typically, Service Providers are already providing this function to their retail Internet customers. The ability to spread the cost of personnel, their backups, and the technical infrastructure associated with the help desk function across many VPN and other customers can make this an interesting proposition for the Service Provider.

Last, VPN technology is new and can require a learning curve on the part of the user. This may involve new dial procedures, installation of client or other software, and perhaps new authorization procedures. A successful VPN deployment will include up-front training to the user population. Training can serve to preempt many satisfaction issues the end user may have with the VPN service and save calls to the help desk associated with deployment. The Service Provider needs to foresee the need for good instructors to work with the VPN clients on the deployment of the new technology.

Supplementary VPN Services

The above discussions on personnel highlighted various services that may be packaged with the technical protocol and transport services of a VPN:

- Design services
- Management services
- End user help desk
- Proactive monitoring service
- End user training
- Installation
- On-site problem resolution and troubleshooting
- Performance and usage reports

All of these services need not be provided to every customer. Customers will typically want to pick and choose which of these services they may want. The Service Provider needs to be able to provide flexible prices, contract boilerplates, and negotiate service level agreements around each of these. Here again, we can see that VPN services have the potential to be far more expensive that the corresponding do-it-yourself Frame Relay service. The difference is due to the outsourced services. Making this value-add explicit and visible to the customer is critical to avoid VPN sticker shock, especially in LAN-to-LAN offerings.

The Service Provider doesn't necessarily have to provide all of these services by itself. It can partner with other downstream Service Providers for fulfillment. This is especially common for front-line help desk and installation services. Much of the network design and training can be done in conjunction with system integrator partners that may be doing reengineering or other IT consulting for the VPN customer. The system integrator or consultant group may in fact serve as a sales channel for the VPN Service Provider under a formal business agreement. Thus, an ISP can concentrate on its core competencies in protocols and managed transport, while presenting a complete network solution to the end user.

As alluded to above in our personnel discussion, significant margin opportunity exists in these services. Profit derives from the fact that these network services are core competencies for the Service Provider, in the same way that manufacturing, retailing, banking, or insurance may be core competencies for the VPN customer. The Service Provider profits from economies of scale by spreading the personnel and technical infrastructure costs over a large customer base of both VPN and retail customers.

Service-level Agreements

Many ISPs offer guarantees concerning the performance on their networks in the form of service-level agreements or SLAs. These contractual arrangements specify specific levels of performance backed up by financial penalties or service credits paid to the customer for nonperformance. Service level agreements can be written against both technical and business characteristics of the network. These include technical metrics such as:

♦ Availability of network resources such as dial-up ports, and transmission capability on site-to-site virtual links

♦ Latency—that is to say, the time a packet takes to transit the network, including propagation of the signal, as well as queuing and switching delay through the Service Provider's routers. A typical dedicated phone connection is has a latency of about 50 milliseconds. Frame relay circuit latency can range from 100 to 300 milliseconds depending how the network is provisioned. VPNs can approach these figures, but if it is important for the application, the user should specify not only the level, but also the amount of variation (which can vary significantly with VPNs).

♦ Packet loss—the number of packets that have to be dropped due to congestion in the Service Provider network, or errors induced in packets while in transit.

♦ Network utilization—policies within the Service Provider network covering utilization of network routers and connecting trunks.

Table 3.3 A Sampling of ISP Service-Level Agreements

Company	Network Availability	Maximum Latency	Maximum Packet Loss	Penalty
AT&T World-Net	99.7%	100 ms North America (dedicated) 150 ms North America (dial) 250 ms outside North America (dial)	Not offered	5% monthly service charge per 10 minutes of downtime per day up to 25%
Saavis Communications	100%	200 ms	<5%	1 day service credit for each downtime event of 5+ minutes and option to cancel contract if service is unavailable 8+ hours/month
Sprint	99% (dial) 99.5% (dedicated)	140 ms (US only)	Not offered	10% credit on monthly dedicated port fee
Uunet	99.9% (12+ sites) 99.8% (6–11 sites) 99.6% (3–5 sites)	100 ms (US) 200 ms (International)	Not offered	25% credit on monthly service charge

Source: "ISP guarantees: Warm, Fuzzy, and Paper-tin." *BCR Magazine,* December, 1998.

Service-level agreements can also cover business aspects of the service such as mean time to repair, billing accuracy, or time to complete new order installations. Table 3.3 gives examples of some of the IP VPN service guarantees available at this writing. These are changing at a fast rate and should have improved by the time you are reading this. This table is more to give an idea what types of contracts Service Providers are writing.

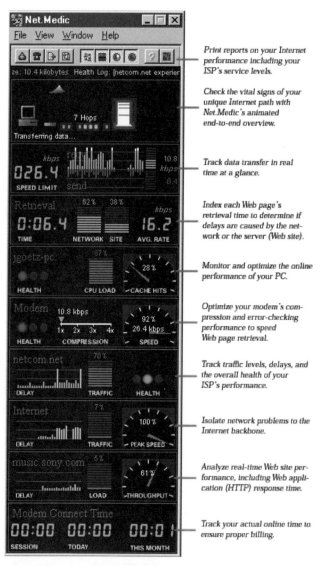

Figure 3.3 A Screen Shot of INSofts Net.Medic Application

Note that many of the technical guarantees are lost once more than one Service Provider is required, as for example, in an international environment. Another issue that comes up in service-level agreements concerns how conformance is measured. Many Service Providers insist that conformance to SLA contracts is based on their measurements. There is a more detailed discussion of the technical implementation of these service level and network management issues given in Chapter 7. There are also a growing number of tools available that allow the end user to measure the above mentioned technical metrics themselves. Figure 3.3 shows a screen capture of one of the more popular ISP monitoring tools: INSoft's (formally Vital Signs) Net.Medic.

Service-level agreements need to be clear about what specifically is being measured, what the measurement criteria are, how the service will be measured, what the escalation procedures are, and how any disputes will be resolved.

In Chapter 1 we introduced the concept of Quality of Service or QoS with short anecdotes relating to airport ticket lines and congested roads. Using technical methods discussed in Chapter 6 (as well as some not so technical methods such as service segmentation) Service Providers have increased their ability to offer differentiated VPN services. The Service Provider may be able to offer a "gold service" with no packet loss or a service offering a specific latency to all or some of the traffic. As above, the user should exercise caution when evaluating service guarantees to insure that they are clearly articulated as to what is being offered.

Tunneling

Now that we've set the stage, we will begin to delve specifically into the "essence" of Virtual Private Networks, beginning with the subject of tunneling. We've split this chapter into two distinct sections.

The first section introduces and examines three basic structural models for VPNs as determined by the locations of tunnel endpoints. For enterprises, you will be able to determine which of these, if any, suits the needs of your organization. For Service Providers, we will describe the basic infrastructure, deployment, and provisioning approach for each. After reading this chapter, you should understand and be able to describe the characteristics of each model, understanding the pros and cons enough to make an informed choice.

In the second section we will concentrate on the various tunneling protocols that have been developed specifically with VPNs in mind. As with VPN deployment models, each of these protocols have certain up sides and down sides. We will attempt to bring all, or at least some, of them to light. This is not designed to be an exhaustive discussion of details of the protocol headers or operation. There are other, more in-depth treatments of these protocols available and often the standards themselves are very readable. We are aiming for just enough detail for intelligent discussions with partners and vendors and for a strong platform for planning your own VPN implementations.

Fgiure 4.1 shows the two major VPN applications: remote access and LAN-to-LAN, along with the summary of the major protocols and VPN models used to implement them.

VPN Models

So many equipment vendors, Service Providers, software companies, and others have gotten into the VPN "game" that there is a practically infinite array of services and solutions from which to choose. The most important consideration, of course, is to deploy a service in a way that will best serve the business needs of the organization. With all of the choices out there, it's safe to say that every organization can find a solution that meets its own most important requirements to a "T." Of course, with all of this choice comes a certain level of confusion.

We are not even going to attempt to describe all of the possible ways VPNs can be built. Instead, this section will focus on what we consider the three most common models for VPN deployment. Why did we choose only three models? Well, we once heard a senior-level sales executive (he'll know who he is if he reads this book) say that salespeople can only remember three things about any given topic at a given time. Based on our interpretation of what he said, we'll paraphrase accordingly: If you can boil any subject down to three points, it tends to simplify the subject greatly. We are of the opinion that Virtual Private Networking is one subject that is screaming for simplification. Judging from articles we've read, we would say that we are not alone in this opinion! Therefore, we will boil it down to three models. If you start with these as a foundation, chances are you will quickly be able to determine the model that most closely suits your needs. Then you will have an easier time

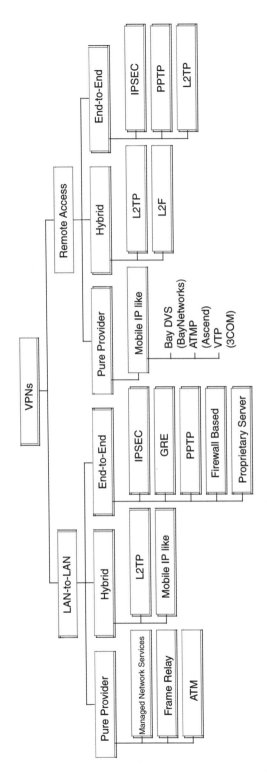

Figure 4.1 VPN Protocols, Models and Applications

choosing equipment, Service Providers, and the other components necessary to build your VPN.

These models are distinguished from one another by what we will refer to as *service endpoints*. More specifically, the *location* of the service endpoints distinguishes each model from the other. A service endpoint can also be referred to as a tunnel endpoint. Tunneling protocols will be discussed in the second section of this chapter.

Two of the models, the Pure Provider model and the Hybrid Provider model, involve direct Service Provider involvement in terms of VPN tunnel initiation (and in the case of Pure Provider, tunnel termination), Quality of Service, and management. Choosing either of these two is a direct indicator that the Service Provider will work closely with the customer to implement the VPN. The third model, which we'll call the End-to-End model, allows the VPN to be built in a fashion that, for the most part, disregards the Service Provider, using the public network somewhat transparently.

Since VPNs involve enterprise as well as Service Provider network infrastructure, a discussion about VPN deployment models must reflect the views of both enterprises and Service Providers. As much as possible, this section will attempt to convey pros and cons of each model from the appropriate perspective.

The Pure Provider Model

In the Pure Provider VPN model, all or most of the VPN value-add functionality is built into the Service Provider infrastructure and almost none of it is built into the customer network. Figure 4.2 shows this distinction. A Pure Provider VPN may or may not be built spanning multi-

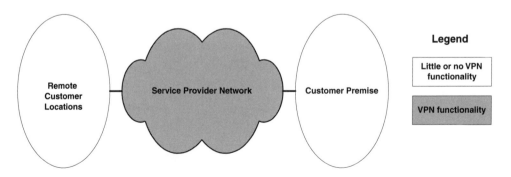

Figure 4.2 Pure Provider VPN Model

ple providers' networks. Today Pure Provider VPN services are most often deployed over one provider's network. Over time, the trend will be to build "inter-exchange" Pure Provider VPNs; however, much of the technology to make this happen is not available in 1998. We'll cover the subject of multiprovider networks later.

A Pure Provider VPN Scenario

Orion Enterprises chose Business Network's "Remote Access Link" service to implement its telecommuting initiative. Orion will be replacing its outdated remote access servers with a dedicated Frame Relay connection on an existing router to Business Networks, over which Orion will receive its dial traffic. Each telecommuter will receive a local access number to dial for remote access. Orion eventually plans to upgrade each telecommuter's 28.8Kbps analog modem to an ISDN link.

Another Pure Provider VPN Scenario

Small Country Telco has put together a custom remote access VPN service for the four major multinationals operating in the capital. Telco will host and manage traditional remote access servers in its facilities dedicated to each VPN customer. Although the network supporting the customers runs through the shared Telco transmission system, all IP routers and servers are dedicated to each customer. "Customers like to see equipment with their names on it in our racks," stated Telco's VPN marketing manager. "We don't have any religion around tunneling, we just want to get the job done."

Advantages of Pure Provider VPNs

With a few notable exceptions, VPNs deployed using the Pure Provider model have not been well publicized in trade journals or by network industry analysts. Nevertheless, this model is especially popular with Service Providers and carriers in particular, for a number of reasons.

Advantages to Service Providers   First, in the Pure Provider model, the service endpoints line up perfectly with "traditional" service demarcation

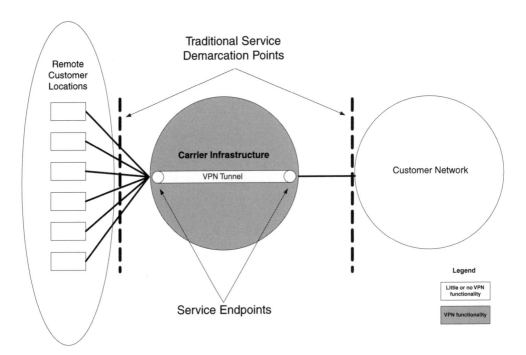

Figure 4.3 Pure Provider Service Endpoints versus Traditional Service Demarcations

points. That is, there is a very clear line of distinction between what constitutes the customer's network and what constitutes the provider's network. In this model, everything on the customer premise is owned and operated by the customer, while everything "inside the cloud," from the physical circuit on out, is owned and operated by the carrier. Although carriers have made great strides in recent years developing services that include management of customer premise equipment (CPE), they still, by and large, prefer the clear lines of distinction that characterize the Pure Provider model. The relationship between the VPN service endpoints and the traditional service demarcation points is illustrated in Figure 4.3.

Second, the carrier has much more control over the network in a Pure Provider VPN. This point touches many aspects of the network. Capacity planning, design, configuration, diagnostics, and troubleshooting are all made more difficult when the Service Provider and customer must share the responsibilities. Take the example of network configuration. More control on the part of the Service Provider typically translates to less chance of overall configuration error. Sharing of network configuration between Service Provider and customer increases the chance of configuration error. The Pure Provider model diminishes the risk of configuration mismanagement and these other potential "conflict" areas by focusing the responsibility for these elements on the Service Provider.

Third, the Pure Provider model places the burden of scaling squarely on the shoulders of the carrier. This works out well, since much of the equipment deployed in the carrier infrastructure is high-performance, high-availability, and high-capacity equipment that is shared among many customers. A carrier can make this a selling point, as well as a differentiator for its service.

Advantages to Customers   One key benefit of the Pure Provider model to the customer is the simple fact that the customer does not need any special equipment or software in order to get the full benefit of the VPN. There is no special software required for PC clients. There is no special equipment needed at the customer premise (only a router, usually). The existing customer equipment (again, typically a router) requires no upgrades in order to meet scaling requirements.

Another benefit to the customer of a Pure Provider VPN service is that the Service Provider assumes the majority of the responsibility for the management and administration of the VPN. With no client software to configure, and very little CPE to manage, a VPN service built on the Pure Provider model is much simpler to provision and deploy, but it also makes it much less complicated for the customer.

Finally, with a Pure Provider VPN, predictable throughput and high qualities of service in general are easier to obtain than with other VPN models. Because the provider assumes the overall responsibility for the service network infrastructure, the network can be designed specifically with the needs of the customer in mind. The network can also be scaled to meet the needs of multiple customers without compromising the performance delivered to any of them.

Disadvantages of the Pure Provider Model

We've spoken of the benefits of Pure Provider VPNs, now let's examine the down sides.

Disadvantages to Customers   The first and most obvious disadvantage of the Pure Provider VPN model is that the customer is completely dependent on a single provider. Since VPN tunnels are both initiated and terminated inside the Service Provider network, the customer has no recourse (other than what *may* be written into the service agreement) when the network fails. Even when the SLA includes financial rebates for nonperformance, the revenues and lost productivity from a network failure can be crippling to a business.

Dependence on a single provider also means that the availability of the service on a *global* basis may be compromised. Unless the Service Provider has struck agreements with other Service Providers, service availability is limited to locations where the Service Provider has points of access to the network. As was stated previously, interprovider VPNs are rare since the technology required to make them happen is not widely available in 1999. The number of Service Providers offering true global access in a manner that is convenient and transparent to the user is still quite limited as of this writing.

The second disadvantage is that Pure Provider VPNs tend to be premium services with premium price tags. In addition to the application provided, the Service Provider is also charging the customer for the peace of mind of delegating the network "problem" to the experts. They offer significant expertise, along with research, development, and management activities that a small enterprise may not be able to implement. Economies of scale often allow the Service Provider to earn very healthy profit margins.

The third disadvantage, though arguably less valid, is that with the Pure Provider model, the customer may lose some end-to-end functionality. Data encryption is one example of this. Customers requiring end-to-end data encryption in a Pure Provider VPN must implement it themselves since there is no way for the service itself to provide it. The same can be said for other typical end-to-end services such as payload compression.

Disadvantages to Service Providers   Pure Provider VPNs can be difficult to integrate from the perspective of the Service Provider. It is one thing to build a service infrastructure. It is another thing to offer the service in an end-to-end fashion taking into account the needs of the customer to preserve all of the functionality that is already in place. In order to preserve that functionality, the Service Provider is often placed in a position of having to develop customized functionality to meet those needs. Tasks that are typically considered routine in traditional remote access are easy to preserve in Hybrid Provider and End-to-End VPNs, but they are difficult to implement in a Pure Provider model.

Routing, address management, authentication, end-to-end encryption, and NAT are other examples of functionality that are (1) customer requirements, (2) not difficult to implement in Hybrid Provider and

End-to-End VPNs, and (3) challenging to implement with the Pure Provider model. We will discuss some of the technical details of these issues when we examine the protocols used to implement the various models later in the chapter.

The Hybrid Provider Model

In the Hybrid Provider model, both the Service Provider and customer networks play active roles in the VPN functionality as depicted in Figure 4.4. For instance, in a Hybrid Provider VPN, the VPN tunnel is usually initiated from a remote access concentrator inside the provider's cloud, but the tunnel is terminated at the customer premise.

With a Hybrid Provider VPN, the service demarcation points are a little fuzzier than with Pure Provider (Figure 4.2). As with Pure Provider, the Service Provider network plays an active role in initiating and delivering VPN functionality. Unlike Pure Provider, however, one of the service endpoints in Hybrid Provider is on the customer premise as opposed to both being inside the "cloud." The Hybrid Provider model lends itself nicely to the notion of outsourced remote access since the customer premise service endpoint in Hybrid Provider is in the same place as it is with traditional remote access (see Figure 4.5).

In a Hybrid Provider VPN, the Service Provider's chief responsibility is the initiation of VPN tunnels on behalf of remote users. This tunnel initiation function is typically handled during user authentication. If during authentication, it is determined that the user is a "tunneled" user, a VPN connection is initiated between the Service Provider and the customer. The user is then optionally authenticated for a second time in an authentication transaction initiated by the device serving as VPN service endpoint. Once

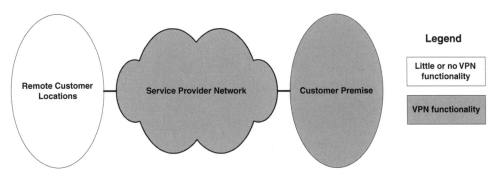

Figure 4.4 Hybrid Provider VPN Model

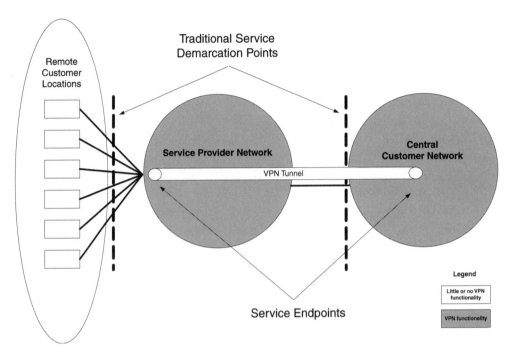

Figure 4.5 Hybrid Provider Service Endpoints versus Traditional Service Demarcs

authenticated, the user has access to the same network facilities he or she would have if connected directly to the corporate LAN via a traditional remote access solution.

A Hybrid Provider VPN Scenario

Yelp Records has been very happy with Telco Service Group's No Worries™ branch office managed network service. When Yelp wants to open a new warehouse, it simply calls up Telco Service Group and its Inventory Management Network is upgraded. The Service Provider handles provisioning the router, any circuits required, the address plan . . . everything. Yelp is now considering offering record store sales managers the ability to dial in to Yelp warehouses and order new inventory or look at upcoming promotions via a simple 800 number dial-up. Telco Service Group is proposing a Hybrid Provider VPN to run as an additional application on its warehouse router platform. Yelp would retain control of who would be authorized to access the system (via an authentication server), but Telco Service Group would continue to run and manage the network.

The Hybrid Provider Model has thus far been popular with Service Providers as evidenced by their desire to evaluate technology that employs this model. There *are*, in fact, VPN services offered today utilizing the Hybrid Provider model. It is still unclear, however, how popular this model will be with customers since the services that *are* based on this model didn't begin to roll out until late 1997. With the standardization of L2TP in 1998, the commercial viability of Hybrid Provider VPN services will become better known, since many Service Providers say they will support L2TP. L2TP is the IETF standard for Layer 2 VPN tunneling—one that the entire networking world has been waiting for. A recent study by Infonetics Research, Inc. showed Service Provider use of L2TP growing by a higher percentage than any other VPN protocol between 1997 and 1998 (Figure 4.6). L2TP is a technology that was, essentially, designed for use in a Hybrid Provider VPN service. It is important to note that L2TP is not the only tunneling technology that can be used in a Hybrid Provider VPN. It is just the one that has received the most fanfare.

Advantages of the Hybrid Provider Model

In spite of the dearth of Hybrid Provider VPN services currently available, it is easy to see why this model promises to be popular.

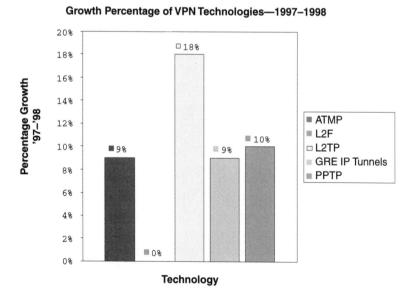

Figure 4.6 Growth of VPN Technologies by Percentage. *Source:* Infonetics Research.

Advantages to Service Providers   Many of the advantages to Service Providers accrue from the increasing standardization of protocols (like L2TP) that are implemented on the Hybrid Provider model. Service Providers want the competition and multivendor interoperability that strong standardization implies. Although other standards or models may be more robust or mature, Service Providers are often reluctant to commit to the single-vendor environments that they entail. Consolidation of standards also focuses industry efforts for more operational, economical, and secure products. If flaws are discovered or enhancements required, the vendor and standards community often respond quickly, as it is in the best interest of all parties.

Other Service Provider benefits are primarily economical. Service Providers are driven to offer VPN services for all of the reasons mentioned in Chapter 3. To the Service Provider, more customers mean more revenue, but lower costs mean higher profits. Of the two models (Pure Provider and Hybrid Provider) that feature high levels of value-add from the service infrastructure, the Hybrid Provider model adds less cost simply because half the service infrastructure exists on customer premises. While the Pure Provider model requires an investment in high capacity equipment designed to terminate VPN tunnels and perform proxy services for user authentication, IP address management, and so on, the Hybrid Provider model does not. If the service is set up in such a way that the customer assumes complete responsibility for the service endpoint located on the customer premise, then there are no costs to the Service Provider to manage the customer side endpoint. VPN tunneling in a Hybrid Provider-based service is simply a side order on the menu of services, not a complete service unto itself. Therefore, it is less costly to the provider. With the smaller initial investment required in capital and human assets, Service Providers view Hybrid Provider VPNs as a logical first step into the realm of value-added differentiated services.

Advantages to Customers   From the customer perspective, as mentioned in our discussion of the Pure Provider model, Hybrid Provider VPNs are easy to deploy without significant disruption to existing facilities such as user authentication and IP address management. Most solutions built for deployment in the Hybrid Provider model are designed with remote access outsourcing in mind. Most, therefore, have built these facilities in to their solutions.

The second advantage from the customer standpoint is that Hybrid Provider VPNs don't necessarily lock the customer into using a single

Service Provider. It is quite possible, as shown in Figure 4.7 to use more than one provider in a Hybrid Provider VPN with a common VPN endpoint on the customer premise.

The option of using multiple Service Providers translates to a number of benefits to the customer, including better leverage when negotiating billing rates, less chance of service downtime, and in all probability, better global reach.

Disadvantages of the Hybrid Provider Model

Although the Hybrid Provider model offers up many advantages, there are still some caveats to both Service Providers and customers.

The main disadvantage of the Hybrid Provider model to a Service Provider is the loss of complete control over the network. Since the Service Provider no longer controls the customer side endpoint, there is greater chance of configuration error. There is also no guarantee that the overall VPN will perform to the expectations set forth by the provider. Service Providers can overcome this obstacle by agreeing to manage the customer side of the VPN; however, management of CPE by the Service Provider is not always desirable to either party. The customer, for instance, may not feel comfortable having a Service Provider manage part of its network. The Service Provider may not want to assume the expense

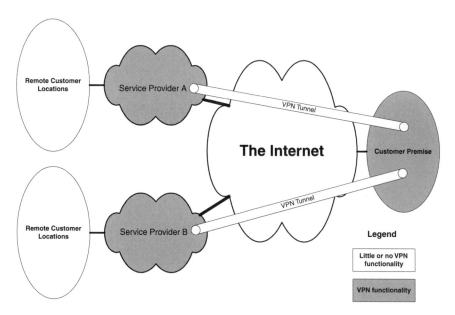

Figure 4.7 A Dual Provider Hybrid Provider VPN

of having to manage customer premise equipment. Unless there is a strong sense of partnership between Service Provider and customer, a Hybrid Provider VPN may not make the most sense.

The End-to-End Model

Of the three models described here, the End-to-End VPN model has thus far been the most widely deployed. End-to-End VPNs are flexible. They can be used to facilitate Internet-based remote access or to connect multiple sites securely over the Internet or another IP backbone. End-to-End VPNs appear to be firmly entrenched in terms of both mind share and installed nodes. There are many products already available for use in End-to-End VPNs.

In the End-to-End model, the Service Provider network plays little if any active role in the setup and tear down of the VPN (Figure 4.8), functioning primarily as a transparent transport for the VPN data. Internet access is performed as usual over any of the facilities normally used. In fact, access facility independence is one of the benefits of the End-to-End model.

> ### An End-to-End VPN Scenario
>
> All of the engineers working for Software Solutions live in communities served by the All Media Broadband Internet over CATV service. Software Solutions has purchased a high-end tunnel server that will allow their engineers to work at home up to three days a week. The engineers use special "crypto" software to make secure tunnels to Software Solutions over the Internet. "I'll never go back to modems," states one of the program's pilot members.

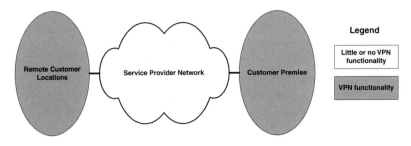

Figure 4.8 End-to-End VPN Model

It is important to note that end-to-end does not necessarily mean desktop to desktop. An end-to-end service endpoint, for example, can exist in a VPN device serving as a proxy for multiple desktops. The important factor is that the both service endpoints exist outside the Service Provider "cloud" as shown in Figure 4.9.

Because End-to-End VPNs are usually provider-independent, extranet VPNs are easiest to deploy using the end-to-end model, since it is unlikely that all companies participating in an extranet use the same provider. Of course, remote access and site-to-site VPNs are also deployable in an end-to-end scheme.

One might assume that End-to-End VPNs would have no appeal to Service Providers since the Service Provider network adds little to no value in an End-to-End VPN. This is not necessarily the case. There are many Service Providers today that perform integration and management of customer premise equipment and who are staffed to manage all aspects of an End-to-End VPN including software distribution, help desk services, and network planning. These providers simply resell VPN products from a selection of one or more manufacturers and then bundle VPN in-

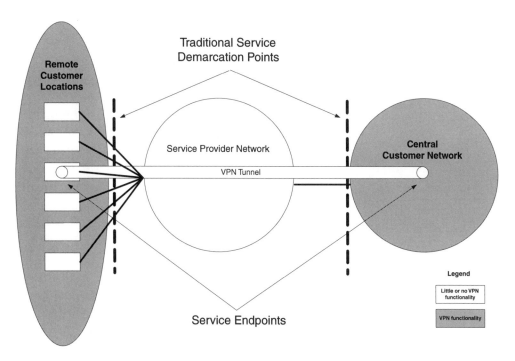

Figure 4.9 End-to-End VPN Service Endpoints versus Traditional Service Demarcs

tegration and management services with their standard Internet access contracts. The smart thing to do, should you decide that the end-to-end approach is best for your business, is to ask your Service Provider what types of VPN-related products and services are offered.

Advantages of the End-to-End Model

Advantages to the Customer   As mentioned earlier, complete Service Provider and access facility independence are two of the advantages the End-to-End model holds over the other two. Most Pure Provider and Hybrid Provider services are limited in terms of the number of different types of access facilities supported. Some providers, for example, support only analog access, while some additionally support ISDN. Others support data over cable broadband networks. Almost all offer some kind of leased line access. The End-to-End model is oblivious to all of this, allowing access over any of them. Service Provider independence carries with it a number of sub-benefits. These include better probability of global reach (Internet roaming services, which will be covered in a later chapter, can be quite useful when it comes to End-to-End VPNs), and less chance of lost productivity due to network outage.

Another chief advantage of the End-to-End model is end-to-end security. This is *not* to say that the other models are incapable of providing end-to-end security. All three can provide this dependent, of course, on the products, protocols, and other technologies that are used to implement the service. The End-to-End model, however, is the only one of the three that integrates a single, consistent security scheme all the way from the remote service endpoint to the other one located on the central network. This ultimately becomes easier to configure and otherwise manage.

Advantages to the Service Provider   From a business perspective, the End-to-End model does not seem to offer much in the way of revenue opportunities, particularly since the Service Provider network is not supplying the value-add functionality to the VPN. Still, there is a potential business benefit to the Service Provider with this model.

As more and more businesses use the Internet as an integral part of their overall network strategy, they will begin to demand higher qualities of service for all applications, including those that ride over VPNs. To meet this demand, a new class of Service Provider has emerged, providing what has been dubbed the "Business Class" Internet. These providers offer well-managed backbones solely devoted to the business community with controlled gateways to the Internet community at large. There are no large populations of students or home users on their networks. They are also often on the leading edge providing advanced IP services such as Quality of Service (QoS) implementations or multicast capabilities and are often willing to offer written Service Level Agreements (SLAs) to their customers. Business Class Internet backbones are the ideal platform for End-to-End VPN implementations. We expect to see many more of these Business Class providers emerge in the coming months and years.

If the Service Provider offers value-add services such as CPE integration and monitoring, help desk, 7x24 problem resolution, or others, these same services can be applied to assisting customers to implement and manage their own VPNs. Furthermore, this comes with little or no additional investment in their service infrastructure. The business upside comes from the pairing of revenues from value-added services with revenues generated from selling standard Internet access. With all of this, the Service Provider's network need not be upgraded to directly support any special VPN technology or protocols, therefore capital expenditures are kept to a minimum. As evidenced by the many Service Providers who are offering VPN "services" based on the End-to-End model, there is an advantage, after all, to using this model, even for a Service Provider.

Disadvantages of the End-to-End Model

Disadvantages to the Customer   The disadvantages of the End-to-End model from the customer's perspective lie not so much in the technology itself, but in business-related aspects of the VPN.

First, Remote Access VPNs that use the End-to-End model often rely on client software that resides in the user's desktop (or laptop) computer. The client software implements the critical VPN functionality (tunneling, encryption, etc.) for the remote user. The distribution and support of this software to a potentially large user population can be problematic for an enterprise IT organization. To complicate this issue, the users are not located in any one facility for easy access and troubleshooting, but tend to be geographically spread out.

If the customer is not staffed or otherwise properly resourced to manage an End-to-End VPN, the chances for failure are high. Any complete network deployment, be it a voice network, Wide Area or Local Area Network, or a VPN, carries with it a high price tag. Capital expenditures for equipment, initial investment in human resources for planning, design, installation, configuration, user training, and further investment in ongoing support must all be factored into the overall cost of the VPN. This does not even include the expenditures for Internet access! There are also high costs (in the form of lost productivity and/or revenues) associated with any disruption to the existing network that may be incurred by the deployment of the new VPN.

The second disadvantage is primarily technical: There is currently no way to ensure any kind of consistent performance in an End-to-End VPN when it uses the Internet as its transport. In the End-to-End model, network performance is completely dependent on the general performance of the Internet. For this reason, many Service Providers offering VPN services based on the End-to-End model do not allow the VPN traffic to "cross over" from their own networks to the Internet. Customers using the End-to-End model must, therefore, be careful about setting unreachable performance goals unless they decide to use a service such as the one described above.

Disadvantages to the Service Provider   The most obvious disadvantage of the End-to-End model to the Service Provider is loss of control over the network. This makes sense when you consider that End-to-End is more or less the opposite of Pure Provider, and Pure Provider offers the greatest degree of control by the Service Provider. This lack of control correlates directly with the likelihood that a customer will choose a different Service Provider based on that provider's ability to offer more than just "commodity" services. Unless the Service Provider offers the type of value-add services described earlier in conjunction with the End-to-End VPN, there really is no benefit to the Service Provider of this model.

Summary

Part of choosing a VPN is deciding first which model best suits the needs of your business. If your organization is somewhat short-staffed and/or you don't mind outsourcing much of the VPN functionality to a Service Provider, then chances are you will be more inclined toward either the Pure Provider or the Hybrid Provider models. If you have the resources necessary to build your own VPN, you may opt for the End-to-End model since it offers high levels of end-to-end security and a certain degree of independence relative to providers and access methods.

Whichever way makes sense, you are likely to succeed as long as you consider and understand the tradeoffs involved with each model and are able to choose the model that makes the most sense for you. As a way to simplify a bit further, figure Table 4.1 below summarizes the various tradeoffs involved with each VPN model.

Table 4.1 Summary of Pros and Cons of VPN Deployment Models

Model	Perspective	Pros and Cons	
End-to-End	Customer	Pros	➤Access facility independence ➤Service provider independence ➤"Guaranteed" end-to-end security
		Cons	➤Expensive to implement/manage ➤Inconsistent performance is a risk
	Service Provider	Pros	➤Possibly other related services ➤No additional infrastructure
		Cons	➤Lack of control ➤Competitive threats
Pure Provider	Customer	Pros	➤No special software, hardware ➤Predictable throughput/QoS ➤Little management/administrative burden ➤Premium service
		Cons	➤Dependent on single provider ➤Global coverage? ➤May lose end-to-end functionality ➤Premium priced
	Service Provider	Pros	➤Clear service demarcation points ➤Control over network ➤Infrastructure economies of scale
		Cons	➤End-to-end functionality difficult ➤Customized infrastructure ➤High implementation costs
Hybrid Provider	Customer	Pros	➤Integration with existing network ➤No single provider dependence
		Cons	➤Requires VPN capable CPE ➤Customer owns burden of scaling
	Service Provider	Pros	➤Strong protocol standards ➤Lower implementation costs
		Cons	➤Loss of complete network control ➤May require management of CPE

VPN Tunneling Protocols

Tunneling is the encapsulation of packets or frames inside of other packets or frames—like putting an envelope inside another envelope. Tunneling as a technique plays a number of significant roles in the deployment and use of VPNs; however, it is important to remember that tunnels are not VPNs and VPNs are not tunnels. Some of these roles include:

♦ **Hiding Private Addresses** Tunneling hides private packets and their addresses inside publicly addressed packets so that the private packets can cross the public network. For example, an organization that uses unregistered IP addresses in its private network can use tunneling to facilitate communications over the public network without having to change its IP addressing design. Network Address Translation (NAT) or other protocol gateways can also be used to accomplish this task, but there are number of issues to consider with those methods.

It is much more difficult to secure the traffic when NAT and/or gateways are used exclusively, because those techniques do not provide any inherent security for the payload. NAT and gateways do a good job of protecting private networks from outsiders, but they do not protect data, vis-à-vis encryption, from "eavesdropping" as it traverses the public network. NAT and gateways simply restructure the packet headers in order to assign those packets identities that are palatable to the network (usually the public Internet) over which they are being sent.

Some application protocols, like the TCP/IP file transfer protocol FTP, actually use IP addressing in the application layer headers. Ensuring that all of these application protocols continue to work can be a big job. The use of tunneling instead of NAT, in this case, is a far more simple way to solve the problem.

♦ **Transporting Non-IP Payload** Tunnels are somewhat akin to virtual circuits. The primary difference between the two is that virtual circuits are built at the link layer (Layer 2) of the OSI stack and tunnels are usually built at the network layer (Layer 3). The virtual circuit header usually contains a field, or in some cases, an entire subheader, that identifies the network layer packet to follow. The best known example of this is the Frame Relay frame with an RFC 1490 header appended to the Layer 2 header. RFC 1490 (Multiprotocol

Encapsulation in Frame Relay) is the IETF standard that describes how different protocol packet types are encapsulated in a Frame Relay Frame. Though it is a rough depiction (many apologies to our friends Caralyn Brown and Terry Bradley, two of the authors of RFC 1490), Figure 4.10 shows how this is implemented.

VPN tunneling also allows for the transport of non-IP payload, such as IPX or AppleTalk packets, by building an IP header, followed by a tunneling protocol header, around the payload. Depending on the tunneling protocol itself, the payload is either a Layer 3 packet or Layer 2 frame. This is exemplified (again, in a rough sort of fashion) in Figure 4.11.

Thus, the non-IP packet becomes payload that can then be transported over an IP network such as the Internet. Any network layer protocol can be encapsulated inside of an IP packet using the variety of standard and nonstandard tunneling protocols available. Again, we're not going to get into much detail here, since many of these protocols are described later in this section.

♦ **Facilitating "Data Shunting"** Tunneling provides an easy way to forward, or "shunt," entire packets or frames directly to a specific location. There, they can then be subjected to security, Quality of Service, or other network policy administered by the organization that owns the destination network.

♦ **Providing Built-in Security** Some tunneling protocols, most notably IPSec, add additional security layers (encryption, authentication, etc.) as built-in components of the protocol. Others, such as L2TP, make strong recommendations on how to implement security. PPTP also offers encryption as an option within the protocol.

VPN tunneling protocols are the topic of much "religious" discussion among networking types. We're not completely sure why, but we suspect that like anything else, the choice of tunneling protocol for a VPN will ultimately come down to what is most comfortable and feels the most safe. Like VPN deployment models, there are quite a few tunneling protocols out there from which to choose. We'll spend the most time on the

Figure 4.10 Frame Relay with RFC 1490 Header

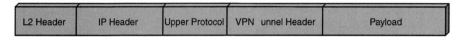

Figure 4.11 A "Generic" VPN Tunneling Packet

three that we feel offer the best overall chance for success in terms of maturity, long-term viability, features, and flexibility. Those three are IPSec, PPTP, and L2TP. Afterwards, we'll take a look at some of the other more popular ones.

IPSec

In many of the papers and articles we've read on VPNs, IPSec is referred to repeatedly as a "protocol." Interestingly, though, IPSec is not actually a single protocol. IPSec (short for IP Security) is actually a *collection* of protocols. These protocols are defined in a number of Internet Request for Comments (RFCs) and Draft Specifications that are collectively overseen by the IETF's IPSec Working Group. As of this writing, the IPSec "protocol" consists of over *forty* RFCs and drafts.

Now that we've cleared up that little technicality, we will confess that we too are going to refer to IPSec as a tunneling protocol, for simplicity, nothing more and nothing less.

IPSec is supported both for IP Version 4 (IPV4) and for IP Version 6 (IPV6). With IPV6, IPSec is a standard component of the protocol.

IPSec was first formally defined in 1995 with the introduction of RFC 1825, "Security Architecture for the Internet Protocol." This document was important in that it set up a baseline definition for securing IP packets that networking vendors could actually implement in their solutions. IPSec provides integrity and confidentiality for IP packets. As a means for providing these services, IPSec is comprised of three basic elements, all of which make it useful as a VPN protocol: authentication (packet-level, as opposed to user-level), encryption, and key management.

- ♦ **Authentication** is the act of verifying that the senders of data are who they claim they are and that the data sent is the same as the data received.

- ♦ **Encryption** is the act of "scrambling" data so that it is incomprehensible to anyone not in possession of the proper key.

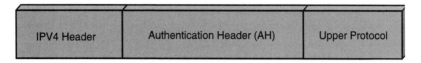

Figure 4.12 IPSec AH in an IPV4 Packet

♦ **Key Management** refers to the act of reconciling or negotiating the value of a security "key" between the sender and receiver.

Packet-level authentication in IPSec is provided by the IPSec Authentication Header as defined in RFC 1826. This is commonly referred to as IPSec *AH*. Figure 4.12 illustrates an IPV4 packet with the AH header added, while Figure 4.13 demonstrates the integration of the AH header in an IPV6 packet.

IPSec supports payload encryption via the Encapsulating Security Protocol as defined in RFC 1827. This is commonly referred to as IPSec ESP. ESP and AH can be and frequently are used together.

ESP has two modes of operation—Tunnel Mode and Transport Mode. The difference between the two modes can be summed up as follows:

♦ **Tunnel Mode** encapsulates the original IP packet inside of an "outer" IP packet (creating a completely new packet with the original packet as its payload).

♦ **Transport Mode** simply adds the ESP header to the original packet header before it is forwarded.

Figure 4.14 illustrates the use of IPSec ESP in an IPV4 packet. Tunnel mode is especially useful when the user is using an "unregistered" IP address or for some reason wants to hide the addresses of network elements within the network.

It is important to note that VPNs use both modes of ESP. Tunnel Mode is frequently used as a "stand-alone" VPN tunneling protocol.

Figure 4.13 IPSec AH in an IPV6 Packet

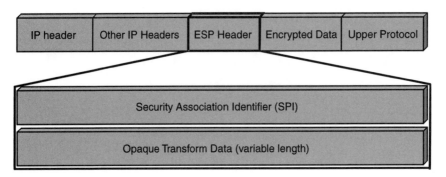

Figure 4.14 Use of IPSec in an IPV4 Packet

An IPSec Tunnel Mode Scenario

Jerry wants to connect to his corporate LAN securely via the Internet. However, since Jerry's company uses unregistered IP addresses, Jerry must "tunnel" his data inside a packet that uses Internet-registered source and destination addresses. IPSec software running on Jerry's laptop provides not only the tunneling function (IPSec Tunnel Mode), but encryption and authentication services as well. A VPN device on the corporate LAN is able to authenticate Jerry's packets using IPSec AH. The same device also decrypts Jerry's encrypted packet using IPSec ESP and strips the "outer" IP header, leaving the original packet with its unregistered destination address intact. The packet is then forwarded to its destination host.

Transport Mode is used in two related, though not identical, VPN scenarios. The first is the case where the payload from the original packet is secured prior to being sent on the network. In this scenario, then, the payload has already been encrypted and is decrypted after the packet has arrived at its destination. The second scenario involves a Pure Provider or Hybrid Provider VPN in which the tunneling protocol used by the Service Provider requires protection from denial of service or theft of service attacks.

An IPSec Transport Mode Scenario

WireSpeed, a national ISP, offers a VPN service based on the Hybrid Provider model. The tunneling protocol it uses in this service runs over IP with UDP encapsulation. WireSpeed is concerned that network interlopers or even unscrupulous competitors may attempt to disrupt its service by attempting to "spoof" tunnel disconnect messages purportedly initiated by WireSpeed's equipment. In reality, though, the disruptive messages would be generated by the intruder. To combat these attacks, WireSpeed secures all of its tunnel command and control messages using IPSec Transport Mode as shown below:

The user sends an IP packet (using PPP over a dial connection) to the RAS: **[PPP][IP Packet]**

WireSpeed's RAS creates a tunnel for the users packet: **[IP][UDP][Tunnel Header]**[PPP][IP Packet]

WireSpeed secures the tunnel using IPSec: [IP]**[IPSec ESP]**[UDP][Tunnel Header][PPP][IP Packet]

In doing so, it is practically impossible for an intruder to spoof the tunnel command and control messages. WireSpeed can now legitimately advertise its service to customers as being "secure."

How Does IPSec Work?

IPSec always involves two parties. We'll call them the sender and the receiver. In IPSec-ese, the relationship between sender and receiver is called a *security association*. (Occasionally, people refer to IPSec associations as "connections" or "sessions." Technically, this is inaccurate; however, it is understandable, since from the user's perspective, a connection does exist between the user and the remote application. When IPSec is used this way, it is sometimes referred to as a "secure" session, so it's perfectly understandable that the terms are sometimes misused. We probably do the same more often than we'd like to admit!)

In spite of the fact that executing the IPSec protocols can be fairly resource intensive to devices that implement it (we'll cover this a bit more in Chapter 5), the actual operation of IPSec is reasonably straightforward. First, both sender and receiver must obtain a shared key using one of the methods supported by IPSec. The key may be obtained either manually, through static configuration, or dynamically using any of a number of "standard" methods. Once this key is negotiated (or simply assigned), and the sender and receiver maintain identical keys, the security association exists.

Next, the sender "hashes" its data using the keyed value, producing a digital signature that can only be read by the receiver with the right key. When ESP encryption is used, the sender also encrypts the data according to the algorithm being used. The scrambled text is called *ciphertext*. ESP does not mandate an encryption algorithm. Still, the most popular encryption algorithms used in IPSec include DES (Data Encryption Standard), 3DES (a.k.a. "Triple" DES), and RC4. The sender then transmits the secured packet over the network towards its destination.

56-bit, 64-bit, 128-bit, Hike!

We've recently encountered a bit of confusion regarding the size/length of the keys used by DES and 3DES. Let's see if we can clear it up . . .

A DES key has a 64-bit value. However, eight of those bits are used to check parity, and are effectively thrown away by the algorithm. This is why DES is typically classified as a 56-bit algorithm, though the keys themselves take up 64 bits.

One might assume that 3DES uses a key that is three times the length of a single DES key. Using this logic, a "full" 3DES key, comprised of three separate single DES keys, would actually take 3 * 64 = 192 bits to store. 3DES, however, uses a key that consumes 128-bits (two 64-bit blocks as keys for the three encryptions/decryptions). The actual length of the key, however, is only 112 bits (2 x 56 bit keys) with the remaining 16 bits (2 x 8 bits) used for parity checking.

Triple encryption is an entirely different story. Triple encryption uses three different keys with the same single DES algorithm. This method, however, turns out to be only as strong as two times the length of the key. In actuality, the statement that 3DES is twice as strong as DES implies an effective key length of 112 bits.

Regarding 3DES, by the way, there are at least two different variants, one of which uses two independent DES keys and one of which uses three. For IPSec, the three-key variant is the one used.

Get it? We didn't think so. For a full explanation of all this, see Bruce Schneier's excellent book *Applied Cryptography*, Second edition, Chapter 15.

At the other end, the receiver gets the packet and, using its key, runs the same algorithm in reverse in order to return the data to its original clear text form and again forwards the packet toward its destination.

If the receiver is a VPN appliance or other device responsible for handling multiple IPSec associations, a library of keys and algorithms must be kept—one for each association. This is where scaling and performance are likely to be a concern. It is difficult enough for a device to manage its own keys, encryption, and the like. Imagine the processor burden of managing this for hundreds or thousands of associations simultaneously! It is therefore important, when evaluating products, to find out how many security associations can be supported simultaneously by the device and what kind of performance to expect under *real* network conditions.

Practical Use of IPSec

IPSec can be and is implemented on a variety of platforms and in a variety of models as shown in Figures 4.15 and 4.16.

Another IPSec Tunnel Mode Scenario

National Insurance wants to use VPN technology to enable its agents to price and configure insurance policies through the Internet, right in the customer's home. Because they are especially concerned about privacy, they want the security of 3DES encryption. Agents will be given an ISP account in their local

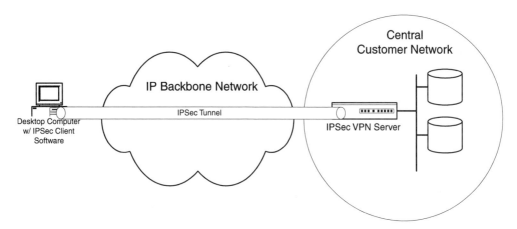

Figure 4.15 IPSec Client-to-Dedicated Server VPN

---

area, along with IPSec client software. National has updated its Internet connection to a full T1 to support 400 agents and has bought a well-respected dedicated IPSec tunnel server. National now specially permits IPSec connections to pass through their firewall, but only to the dedicated tunnel server.

Hosts (such as PCs) typically run IPSec client software provided by a variety of hardware and software vendors. Eventually, IPSec will be included in standard operating system software either as a standard component of the IP Version 6 stack or as a configurable option in IP Version 4, the stack that is included in most operating systems.

General purpose servers (such as firewalls or others) can also be enabled with IPSec server functionality. For firewall products, IPSec functionality is a natural extension to the embedded security functionality. Integration of VPN and firewall functions seems like a great idea; however, price, performance, and scaling needs should be considered before this integrated approach is chosen.

IPSec "appliances" (usually dedicated to VPN applications) have begun to take a stronger hold in the market over the past twelve months or so.

An IPSec-based VPN Service

Retail Solutions Inc., a small systems integrator, wants to set up a temporary extranet with its two subcontracted programming firms and the end customer. Only a small number of systems within each organization will participate in the VPN and all of them have public address on the Internet. The firms contract VPN Associates to implement an IPSec-based VPN. VPN Associates uses commercial IPSec servers in transport mode to dynamically encrypt packets from any partner firm going to one of the other partners. Packets destined to systems other than those that are members of the VPN user group are dropped. VPN Associates provisions and manages the VPN servers and sends each partner a usage report each month.

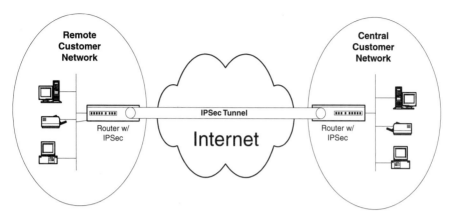

Figure 4.16 IPSec Router-to-Router VPN

Advantages of IPSec as a VPN Tunneling Protocol

IPSec, when it is used as a tunneling protocol, is by far the most popular Layer 3 tunneling approach used in VPNs (PPTP is the most popular Layer 2 approach). There are several reasons for this. First, IPSec supports built-in encryption but is, in fact, quite flexible in terms of how encryption is implemented. IPSec doesn't dictate an encryption algorithm—only the format of the encryption header itself. This makes it easy to implement IPSec in software while using hardware—usually in the form of ASICs (Application Specific Integrated Circuits)—to handle processor-intensive activities such as key management and packet encryption. Developers of VPN solutions have leveraged this flexibility by utilizing IPSec as their "cornerstone" technology. It is available both in software running on desktop clients and in hardware "appliances" that function as Internet-attached security proxies for users, groups, or even entire organizations. This product mix offers a "best of both worlds" scenario. Other reasons for the popularity and long-term viability of IPSec are:

♦ The wealth of standards work that has been and is being done around IPSec.

♦ Widely publicized adoption by several large organizations and key industry groups such as the ANX (Automotive Network Exchange) and Kinko's Business Centers, among others.

♦ IPSec leverages the popularity of IP—most applications are now written specifically to run over IP networks.

♦ IPSec headers are built in to the IPV6 packet format. This assures long-term viability, which, for many organizations, provides a high level of comfort with the decision to implement the technology.

IPSec Limitations

One shortcoming of IPSec is that is does not address network protocols other than IP. For non-IP traffic to be protected by IPSec, it first has to be tunneled inside of IP. This adds a layer of unnecessary overhead to data packets, so IPSec is not considered optimal when transporting protocols such as IPX/SPX, AppleTalk, or others.

Another limitation, albeit one that is sure to be solved over time, is interoperability. Most currently available versions of IPSec are not interoperable between vendors. This reflects not only the status of the many standards involved, but the options available for encryption, key management, and so on.

Summary

To summarize, you will want to seriously consider IPSec as your VPN tunneling technology of choice when:

♦ There is no need to encapsulate multiple protocols—IPSec only addresses IP.

♦ Built-in security is of the utmost concern—IPSec contains built in encryption and authentication.

♦ You want to use a single device to enable security on behalf of a number of users. There are many IPSec "appliances" on the market that support LAN-to-LAN VPN functionality.

♦ You are looking for a "standard" approach that will eventually guarantee interoperability with solutions from other manufacturers.

PPTP

PPTP (*Point-to-Point Tunneling Protocol*) was first defined in a now-retired Internet draft specification. It is now considered a "work in progress"; however, as of July 1998 there was a new version of the Internet draft.

PPTP was designed to facilitate secured data transfer from a remote client to a private enterprise server using the Internet access infrastructure as a common transport. PPTP creates a VPN by tunneling PPP frames over TCP/IP-based data networks such as the Internet. Although

Microsoft's implementation was the first available and is still the best known, there are now several implementations available.

PPTP was initially developed by a team of engineers from Microsoft, ECI/Telematics, Ascend Communications, and US Robotics (now part of 3Com Communications), and it has found wide use in VPNs thus far. There are several reasons for this:

- ◆ **Marketing**   Because of its huge installed base, Microsoft's involvement with and sponsorship of any given technology always sends a powerful message to the industry. As one of the inventors of PPTP, Microsoft has used its omnipotent marketing muscle to promote PPTP heavily.

- ◆ **Timing**   The developers of PPTP were among the earliest to recognize the potential of outsourcing the remote access component of the corporate network to the Internet and its omnipresent dial access infrastructure. Then they acted on this vision and introduced PPTP-based solutions before competing solutions could come to market. In short, PPTP had quite a head start.

- ◆ **Flexibility**   As is the case with IPSec, there is more than one way to implement PPTP (more on this to come). Because it encapsulates the entire PPP frame, PPTP can support multiple network protocols (theoretically, any protocol that runs over PPP). We say *theoretically* because the PPTP server must have a forwarder for the appropriate protocol built into its system, as the following case illustrates.

PPTP and AppleTalk

Suppose you have a PPTP client that runs on your Macintosh and can set up the PPTP tunnel around an AppleTalk packet. Roughly speaking, the packet looks like this as it exits your system:

[IP][PPTP][PPP][AppleTalk Packet]

When the PPTP packet hits the server, it is processed normally as a PPTP packet. Once the IP, PPTP, and PPP headers are stripped, however, the server has no idea what to do with the AppleTalk packet, so it simply throws it away. This is not good.

PPTP is flexible in other ways as well. It can run over dial-up lines, local area networks (LANs), or wide area networks (WANs). It can run over the Internet or any other TCP/IP-based network, private or public. Later, we'll touch on a couple of more aspects of PPTP flexibility.

How Does PPTP Work?

PPTP uses two basic packet types—data packets and control packets. Data packets contain actual user data. These are encapsulated using the GRE (Generic Routing Encapsulation) protocol. Control packets are used for signaling and status inquiry. Control packets flow over a TCP session that is set up between the two devices serving as tunnel endpoints. There is actually a third type of packet, the management packet, defined in the PPTP specification; however, the contents of these packets are not currently defined.

To initiate a PPTP tunnel, the PPTP client must first establish a TCP session with the server. Once this session is established, PPTP control messages can be sent between the client and the server. These control messages are used for all aspects of the operation of the tunnel. Once the tunnel has been successfully initiated, GRE-encapsulated data packets can flow in either direction over the same tunnel between the client and server.

When the user is finished working, the PPTP client sends a control packet to the server that disconnects the session and tears down the tunnel.

PPTP Implementation Models

As we mentioned earlier, PPTP employs a client-to-server architecture; however, the identity of client and server are left largely to the whims of the implementation. Consistent with our "three is the most likely to be understood before mass confusion sets in" theory, we'll now discuss the three most common PPTP implementation models we know of. They are: client-server, RAS-server, and server-server.

Client-Server   The most prevalent model involves a remote client, usually a PC with PPTP client software installed, connecting to the Internet and then tunneling over the IP backbone to a PPTP server installed on the user's "home" network. The PPTP client software can also reside on a dial-up router. The Client-Server PPTP model is consistent with the End-to-End VPN model described in the previous section.

Assuming you choose PPTP as your tunneling protocol, we'll leave the specifics of the installation to you. In short, though, the first step in running PPTP is to install the PPTP server in the enterprise network, usually in what's known as the network DMZ (De-militarized Zone). The DMZ is the area of a network residing between an external firewall and an internal firewall as shown in Figure 4.17. As a point of reference, most companies' external Web servers are installed in the DMZ, while private Intranet servers are installed behind the internal firewall. The external firewall implements security policy that is designed to keep all unwanted external traffic from entering the corporate network. It also may apply security policy to outbound traffic. The internal firewall plays a more complex and active role in deciphering which traffic can go where within the network.

In Figure 4.17, for example, the intranet server would probably be installed in the "Trusted" network, while an extranet server accessible by business partners from the outside would be installed in the "Semi-trusted" network. The internal firewall would ensure that traffic from the "Semi-trusted" network couldn't penetrate the "Trusted" network. The "Untrusted" internal network would be used by visitors to the campus with the internal firewall only allowing traffic from the "Untrusted" network to stay on that network or get out to the Internet.

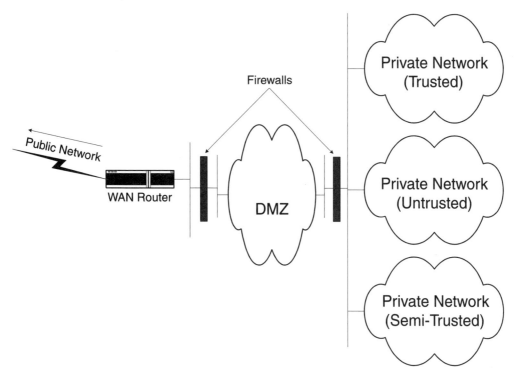

Figure 4.17 **The DMZ**

The second step is to install and configure the PPTP client software. Once the client and server are installed and properly configured, PPTP can be used.

To use PPTP, the client must first connect to the Internet (or other IP backbone) using his or her standard account. In doing so, the client obtains a registered IP address that serves as the "outer" IP address in the PPTP packet. As well, the PPTP server located in the DMZ has a registered IP address. The external firewall would then allow PPTP packets (TCP port 1723) with the destination IP address of the PPTP server through to the DMZ so that the PPTP session can be established and later torn down.

A Simple Client-Server PPTP Scenario

Design Interiors is a small ten-person interior decoration firm. The decorators occasionally need to upload price lists over the Internet. The contract MIS manager enabled the PPTP service on Design Interiors' existing NT server and set up Microsoft Dial-up Networking VPN client on each Windows 95 PC.

The benefits of the Client-Server PPTP model are:

♦ **ISP Independence** The Service Provider network does not require any special tunneling capability or other policy associated with the VPN.

♦ **End-to-End Compression and Encryption** The most secure network is one that implements end-to-end security including the "First mile" connection to the Internet.

♦ **Integration at the Desktop** The PPTP client is already included with Windows NT version 4.0 as well as Windows 98. Windows 95 supports a number of PPTP clients, including one available as a free update from Microsoft. In general, though, no special software must be purchased to implement a PPTP-based VPN.

RAS-Server The popularity of PPTP has motivated several remote access equipment manufacturers to develop and implement PPTP on their products, giving rise to the RAS-Server model. In this model, the RAS in the Service Provider PoP takes on the role of PPTP client and initiates the PPTP tunnel to the server on behalf of its remote client or clients. The PPTP client functioning this way is called a PPTP Access Concentrator, or PAC. Because a PAC can multiplex several PPP sessions over a single tunnel, each individual remote user does not have to set up a separate tunnel. All users from within a single login domain share the single PPTP control channel that exists between the PAC and the PPTP server, otherwise known as the PNS (PPTP network server). If you hadn't guessed already, this model conforms to the Hybrid Provider VPN model. The benefits of the PPTP RAS-Server model are:

♦ **It supports clients not capable of tunneling.** This model provides an easy approach for organizations that support Windows 3.1 clients, early versions of the Macintosh, and even Unix or Linux workstations that support PPP but have no integrated tunneling capability.

♦ **It provides the benefit of "data shunting."** Having the Service Provider handle the task of tunnel initiation means that the user has less control over destinations, which may be attractive to certain employers. For more on this, refer to the introduction at the beginning of this section.

♦ **It is server-efficient.** Client-Server PPTP tunneling is somewhat inefficient because each remote user represents a single tunnel. One hundred users equal one hundred tunnels, and so on. With RAS-Server PPTP, the same one hundred users can be connected using a few tunnels at the most. This represents a decrease in server load relative to the number of TCP sessions that must be maintained in support of PPTP users.

♦ **It supports no-maintenance/Low-maintenance clients.** Having the PPTP client on the remote user's desktop means it has to be installed (to a certain extent), configured, and supported. This can be costly to an IS department in terms of time and effort. "Out-tasking" the tunneling function to the Service Provider is a way around having to bear the cost burden of supporting individual clients.

Server-Server Microsoft is the only known vendor that currently supports server-server PPTP. A Server-Server implementation would look something like the router-router IPSec example from Figure 4.16 substituting the two PPTP servers for the two IPSec routers.

A Simple Server-Server PPTP Scenario

After opening several successful branches in the northeast United States, Antique Reproductions wants to make an assault on the lucrative UK antique market. Even a slow private data circuit between the Boston head office and the Maidenhead site in the UK would be prohibitively expensive. Antique Productions decides to implement a Server-to-Server PPTP connection through the Internet to support its simple file-sharing–based applications.

The benefits of the Server-Server PPTP model are:

♦ **"Blanket" Coverage**   This model applies a PPTP tunnel to all traffic from all users between networks without each client having to run a PPTP client.

♦ **Inexpensive if You are Already an NT User**   If you already have NT servers and connections to the Internet for most of your sites, this model provides a "quick and dirty" Wide Area Network. There is no need to implement separate circuits and/or technology to handle site-to-site connectivity.

Other Features of PPTP

As we mentioned earlier, there are some other aspects of PPTP worth mentioning.

End-to-End Data Encryption   At the very end of the current PPTP draft, there is a short section on security considerations. It states plainly that security is not discussed in the specification. Rather, security is left up to the PPP protocol that is, of course, encapsulated within PPTP. PPP handles security at the link layer as part of the Link Control Protocol (LCP) options that are established during PPP session establishment. What this means is that encryption is negotiated between the remote client and the PNS when PPP comes up.

A Scenario Involving Encryption with PPTP

Phil is running Windows 98 on his desktop, which is configured to support 128-bit RC4 encryption as an option for PPP connections. Phil's company has installed and configured PPTP on a server back at the home office. The server is configured to support 128-bit RC4 encryption for some users' PPTP sessions, including Phil's. When Phil initiates a PPTP tunnel to the server, PPP negotiates the 128-bit RC4 encryption. The data is encrypted before it is tunneled inside of PPTP by Phil's dial-up client. The server, since it terminates the PPP session, decrypts Phil's data after the PPTP header is stripped from the packet. The result is strong end-to-end encryption over the PPTP session.

128-bit encryption keys can be used in the United States and Canada. Most international law requires the use of 56-bit keys. Regardless of the key and encryption algorithm, though, as long as the PPP client and the PPTP server support the same key and algorithm, the user's data can be secured end-to-end.

End-to-End Data Compression   Just as it supports end-to-end encryption, PPTP supports end-to-end compression, again based on the compression method supported by both ends of the virtual PPP link. Again using the Microsoft implementation as an example, MPPC (Microsoft Compression Control Protocol) using the well-known LZS compression algorithm can be negotiated during the PPP LCP bring-up. Compression is important because it preserves bandwidth by shortening the length of the payload. Since PPTP supports MTU sizes up to 1583 octets, not including the length of the extra packet headers that PPTP adds, this becomes even more important because most networks are configured for a *total* MTU of 1500 or so octets. Without compression, packets (especially larger ones) would almost certainly be fragmented impacting overall throughput and performance.

Outgoing Call Support   With enterprise-located remote access, one of the traditional applications has been PPP dial-out. Dial-out enables the RAS to be used as a modem pool for these outgoing sessions, saving network managers the cost, inefficiency, and management burden of installing and maintaining individual modems at user desktops. When this modem pool is moved out of the enterprise computer room (as in the case of remote access outsourcing and the use of a Remote Access VPN), the dial-out functionality is taken away unless an alternative can be found. The alternative, when PPTP is used, is the Outgoing Call Request.

Usually, PPTP is used to initiate a tunnel from a remote client to the enterprise-installed PPTP server. In the case of the Outgoing Call Request, the process is reversed. The PPTP Network Server (PNS) actually functions as the PPTP client, initiating a connection to the remote PPTP Access Concentrator (PAC). The PAC then actually performs the dial-out function.

Outgoing Call Support in PPTP

Mickey, a research analyst, has software on his PC that redirects modem calls from his PC COM port to a LAN-connected Remote Access Concentrator. Mickey's company has recently entered into a contract for a Remote Access VPN service with Edge Access, a regional ISP. In the past, when Mickey required a dial-out session to gain access to the Lexis-Nexis online information system, the Remote Access Concentrator would dial the Lexis-Nexis computer directly. With his company's new VPN service, Mickey's dial-out session is redirected to the corporate PPTP Network Server (PNS). When the call request arrives from Mickey's system, the PNS initiates a PPTP Outgoing Call Request message to the PPTP Access Concentrator (PAC) in the Service Provider's PoP. Upon receiving this control message, the PAC initiates a modem connection to Lexis-Nexis. The PPP session is then set up between the PPTP Network Server and the remote Lexis-Nexis host. Mickey can now perform his research on Lexis-Nexis as he always has.

PPTP Limitations

PPTP as a VPN tunneling protocol does quite a few things well; however, we feel it is important to also point out some of its shortcomings and general things to watch out for.

Performance Issues   PPTP may have performance issues over high-latency networks. There are a couple of reasons for this. First is the use of TCP for PPTP control packets. TCP is a session-oriented protocol, meaning a session exists between the PPTP client and PPTP server during the life of the tunnel. TCP implements flow control based on configurable send and receive window sizes. The window size is the number of input or output buffers available for sending data. The size of the window is similar to the length of time a traffic light stays green before changing to yellow and red. When the road ahead is congested anyway, it is all right if the light is green for only a short period of time (small window). When the road is wide open, the longer the light stays green the better (large window). Usually, larger window sizes lead to higher performance on faster networks. The problem is that performance over the Internet can fluctuate widely so it is difficult to predict an optimal window size.

Microsoft did issue an update to NT 4.0 and Dial-up Networking (DUN) version 1.3 that was designed to improve PPTP performance over high latency networks and networks prone to packet loss. The update increased the default receive window size. It also included the ability to run "packet-by-packet" (i.e., history-less) compression and encryption. Theoretically, these are good things; however, they are both items that should be configured after a network analysis to determine if the updated settings would really be useful.

Scaling Issues   The PPTP network server is called upon to terminate PPP sessions as well as PPTP tunnels. The requirements for terminating PPP, including all of its options, are significant. The "typical" Microsoft NT version 4.0 server should not be called upon to terminate more than a dozen or two PPP sessions. There are, however, devices on the market designed to terminate large numbers of PPTP connections simultaneously, including compression and/or encryption. An important consideration should always be the number of users that will require connectivity via PPTP simultaneously.

Security Issues   An enlightening report on PPTP security was issued in June 1998 by Counterpane Systems, a well-known security consultancy. The report exposed security holes in Microsoft's version of PPTP. Among them:

♦ Weak authentication using only the Challenge/Reply Authentication Protocol (CHAP) as the way to authenticate the PPTP client.

♦ Poor encryption using easy-to-crack keys based on easily obtainable users' passwords. There were also flaws in the encryption algorithm itself.

♦ Unauthenticated TCP control packets, which left the VPN open to denial-of-service attacks.

The report was not an indictment of PPTP per se. It simply pointed out issues with the Microsoft implementation. Microsoft has since fixed most or all of the flaws. Still, these issues should be properly evaluated before implementing a VPN based on PPTP.

Multiprotocol Issues   In spite of the fact that PPTP tunnels PPP, which itself supports many protocols, most implementations still do not support more than IP and IPX as payload. This was covered earlier in our AppleTalk scenario.

Summary

PPTP merits consideration as your VPN tunneling technology of choice when:

♦ Microsoft is a strategic vendor and/or your organization is most comfortable using widely deployed and/or mature technology.
♦ Transport of IP and/or IPX is a requirement.
♦ You are implementing a business-to-business extranet. Because PPTP clients are available "for free," your partners can implement the client software themselves.
♦ Performance, scaling, and security are less important to your network.

L2TP

Once upon a time, there were two protocols, each designed to encapsulate PPP frames and deliver them to the corporate network. They were both very popular and each was capable of initiating its tunnels from RAS equipment. They each set out to accomplish the same thing—facilitate Remote Access Virtual Private Networks via the Internet. They were each sponsored by a different industry powerhouse. Realizing how very important they were, they each traveled to the governing body of Internet standards, the IETF, in search of the IETF's blessing. The IETF was not convinced that either protocol was the one true solution. They were, however, impressed with certain aspects of each protocol. So they instructed the two protocols to get together and combine the best features of each to arrive at a single combined (and standard) protocol. The protocols announced their new, combined mission to the world. Then, after months and months of discussion, development, more discussion, and more development, the new protocol was finally sent to the IETF standards track. Bells rang, grown men wept in the streets, lovers embraced, and birds sang. Then one of the original protocols decided to continue forward along its own path anyway. The other just faded away.

Thus goes the story of L2TP. L2TP (Layer 2 Tunneling Protocol) came about as the result of a merging of the PPTP and L2F specifications. The protocol that doggedly continues forward is PPTP. The protocol that is, or will be, fading away is L2F (Layer 2 Forwarding).

Hype or Hope?

Sometimes technology is hyped up by trade magazines or by certain industry analysts. L2TP is one of those technologies that was hyped even within the standards bodies since it first came into existence, sort of the networking protocol equivalent of Tiger Woods. It is interesting to note that most Internet draft specifications feature one or two authors. Occasionally you'll find one with three listed. The L2TP spec, by comparison, features no less than ten authors representing six separate companies! The good news is that with all that support, chances are that the technology will succeed if for no other reason than so many developers and their companies have so much time and effort invested in the success of L2TP.

We've already discussed PPTP, but before we get too deep into L2TP, it makes sense to briefly mention L2F. L2F was developed by Cisco Systems as a mechanism for setting up UDP-encapsulated tunnels between remote access equipment and its routers. In reality, L2F has been "retired" as a standard specification; however, its installed base, particularly among makers of networking equipment such as Cisco, Shiva, Northern Telecom, and Compaq/Microcom, has made it somewhat of a *de facto* standard. We also know of a few Service Providers that have deployed VPN services that use L2F as the tunneling protocol. Still, we believe that L2TP will quickly supplant L2F because:

1. The two are very similar, but not interoperable.
2. L2TP is the *industry* standard—many, many vendors are implementing it.

3. Cisco, the chief proponent of L2F, has begun to ship L2TP and has effectively retired the L2F protocol.

Given the status of L2F, both technologically and standards-wise, we feel it does not make much sense to cover L2F to any level of detail in this book. Had we written this book a year or two ago, L2F would have been an integral part of the discussion. Today, however, it would be a waste of time and space, but we suppose that's just how it goes when you're dealing with "Internet time" where technology becomes obsolete in the proverbial blink of an eye. If you have a yen to learn more about L2F, we suggest either finding a copy of the now-expired IETF draft, or better yet, read the product documentation supplied by the companies that still support L2F as a product feature.

Unlike L2F, L2TP is experiencing widespread popularity throughout the industry and will most likely emerge as *the* standard for RAS-initiated tunneling.

How Does L2TP Work?

For the most part, L2TP is used in Hybrid Provider VPNs. Consistent with our earlier definitions then, L2TP tunnels are initiated inside the Service Provider network and terminated on the customer premise.

The central components of an L2TP network are the *LAC* (L2TP Access Concentrator) and the *LNS* (L2TP Network Server). Figure 4.18 depicts a typical L2TP network. Note that PPTP, in its latest version,

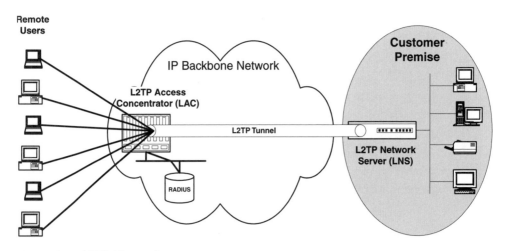

Figure 4.18 L2TP Network

uses terminology similar to L2TP. The LAC in L2TP is a *PAC* in PPTP. The LNS in L2TP is a *PNS* in PPTP.

In an L2TP network, the LAC performs the following functions:

- Termination of modem and ISDN calls
- First-level authentication and tunneling via RADIUS
- Some level of initial PPP setup, much of which is overridden at a later stage by the LNS
- Execution of the L2TP protocol in terms of command and control messages and encapsulation of the remote user's PPP traffic in L2TP packets

The LNS can be thought of as a Remote Access Concentrator that resides "virtually" as a software function inside of another piece of networking equipment on the customer premises. The LNS is responsible for executing key aspects of PPP, such as the Link Control Protocol (LCP) and Network Control Protocol (NCP) that were previously handled by the Remote Access Concentrator. Other traditional RAS functions such as RADIUS (Authentication, Authorization, and Accounting), filtering, Multilink PPP termination, and dial-out are handled by the LNS as options.

It is important when considering a Service Provider for your remote access VPN, to understand which remote access or RADIUS features you are currently using and which features you will continue to need. Then you can ensure that these are or can be implemented as part of the VPN. This is one reason why the choice of tunneling protocol is important and why you should ask the provider which protocol or protocols they support.

One Company's Reason to Use L2TP as Opposed to L2F

Moon-Net is a local ISP offering a variety of advanced services over and above the "standard" menu of Internet Access and content-related services. Townsend Industries recently signed a contract to use Moon-Net's remote access VPN service. Townsend uses its remote access concentrators for tasks that require dial-out as well as dial-in functionality. Moon-Net's service currently uses L2F tunneling, which does not support the dial-out capability through a tunnel. Townsend was dismayed to learn this only after the VPN contract was signed. It threatened to take its business elsewhere until Moon-Net told them that it would soon be transitioning to L2TP, which *does* support

> dial-out through the tunnel. They renegotiated the contract such that the monthly charges would be prorated according to the lost level of functionality. When the full range of capabilities is available, billing will revert to the full rate that was negotiated prior to the misunderstanding.

In most cases, the LAC initiates a tunnel to the LNS—the method illustrated in Figure 4.19 and described step-by-step in the following paragraphs. Keep in mind that this is a very high-level description of L2TP initiation.

1. The user (user@acme.com) calls the Remote Access Concentrator (RAC). After the call is answered, the RAC sends a RADIUS Access-Request packet to the RADIUS server that contains the user name, including the domain identifier.

2. It's assumed that the RADIUS server has implemented a dictionary of RADIUS attributes that are used for L2TP tunneling.

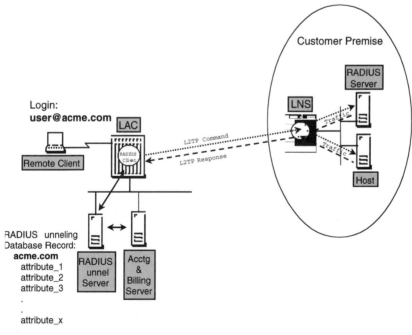

Figure 4.19 **L2TP Tunnel Initiation**

Logic in the RADIUS server initiates a database lookup based on the user's domain name, in this case acme.com. If there is no record for acme.com in the tunneling database, then the user is authenticated in the typical fashion. If there is a record for acme.com, then the values of the RADIUS attributes in the tunneling dictionary under acme.com are sent to the Remote Access Concentrator in a RADIUS Access-Accept packet. The information contained in the packet is sufficient to enable the RAC to initiate an L2TP tunnel to the LNS.

3. The LAC initiates a tunnel to the LNS using a series of L2TP command and control packets called *Attribute Value Pairs,* or *AVPs.* AVPs are responsible for setting all tunnel parameters as well as the initialization, maintenance, and teardown of the tunnel.

4. When the user wishes to disconnect, he or she simply logs off the network. The LAC then sends an AVP to the LNS to disconnect the session and sends an accounting message to the RADIUS server indicating that the tunneled session has stopped. The RADIUS server responds affirmatively to the LAC, thus officially ending the tunneled session.

Between 1997 and 1998, there has been a series of Internet Draft Specifications designed to instruct developers on implementing RADIUS in conjunction with VPN tunneling. Our descriptions are admittedly not very detailed since our intent is to give you a more general flavor for VPN operation while not becoming too bogged down in the gory details. We highly recommend reading these concise, well-written documents in the event you are searching for more detail.

As is the case with PPTP, L2TP features both command and control packets as well as data packets. While PPTP uses a TCP session to carry the command and control packets, L2TP does not distinguish between packet types. All L2TP packets are UDP encapsulated. Because of the connection-less aspect of L2TP, L2TP utilizes more command and control messages than PPTP, but will also perform better over high latency networks.

Performance, Scaling, and L2TP

PPP is a mature, well-understood, and widely adopted protocol. By definition, PPP runs over point-to-point links. These links can be transient (like analog or ISDN) or permanent. Because of its maturity, broad acceptance, and most importantly, its design, PPP as a protocol offers a plethora of options and capabilities. These capabilities, however, come at a price in terms of equipment resource requirements, since many PPP options and capabilities must first be negotiated then managed at the two PPP endpoints.

A Brief Retrospective on PPP Scaling

Why wasn't PPP scaling an issue prior to the advent of technology such as L2TP? Well, until recently, the scalability of PPP has not been problematic, since most networking equipment never had to handle hundreds or thousands of simultaneous PPP connections. The majority of Remote Access Servers and Concentrators, for instance, are designed to handle up to 48 or 96 PPP connections. Some of the current breed can terminate up to a T3's worth (672) of PPP calls; however, most of these devices feature multiple processors designed to balance the load across the box.

As corporate Wide Area Networks expanded, routers too were called upon to terminate increasingly high numbers of PPP connections in the form of short- and long-haul point-to-point leased T1 or E1 circuits. This drove the need for increasingly powerful processors and higher port densities on backbone routers. Then, Frame Relay emerged as an alternative, partly because it didn't require a physical connection to each remote location and partly because it didn't carry the overhead that PPP (or for that matter, X.25) did. Once Frame Relay became the preferred WAN protocol in the market, *larger* networks could actually be built using *smaller* routers, and the number of PPP connections a router could support became practically irrelevant.

In an L2TP network, the LNS terminates the PPP connection but it is a virtual connection, not a physical one, as is the case with traditional remote access or leased point-to-point. In traditional remote access, a single T1 carrying individual modem calls must only support up to 24 users, or PPP sessions, simultaneously. The same T1, on the other hand, carrying L2TP traffic may be called upon to support as many users as the available bandwidth will allow. It is entirely conceivable that with L2TP, several hundred active PPP sessions could be simultaneously connected over a single T1. Most equipment (routers, servers, etc.) that runs L2TP is not designed to handle this level of activity.

Sessions and Tunnels, Tunnels and Sessions

With Frame Relay, the question was always "How many PVCs can your Frame Relay router support?" The comparable L2TP question seems to be "How many tunnels can your LNS support?"

In order to answer this question, we must first draw a distinction between a "tunnel" and a "session." A tunnel is essentially defined by the IP addresses of the LAC and LNS. Tunnels also feature command and control messages sent back and forth between the LAC and the LNS. A session is essentially a single PPP connection. PPP sessions are encapsulated within L2TP tunnels.

L2TP can and does multiplex numerous PPP sessions within a single tunnel. Each of these sessions, constituting a remote user's individual PPP connection, is terminated at the LNS. Each PPP session must be negotiated individually (LCP, NCP, etc). Each session maintains its own encryption and/or compression library. Each maintains separate status regardless of the status of the "tunnel." All of those are somewhat resource intensive.

Since many more resources are consumed at the session level, the real issue with L2TP is not the number of tunnels as much as it is the number of sessions constituting "virtual" PPP endpoints.

An L2TP Scaling Scenario

Plant Manufacturing uses an L2TP-based VPN service offered by a national ISP. The ISP has hundreds of Points of Presence but currently only twenty are hosting remote access sessions for Plant. Plant currently has 200 remote users logged into the corporate network. The breakdown of users per PoP is as follows:

Point of Presence	Number of Users
Saratoga Springs, NY	3
Burlington, VT	3
Boise, ID	2
St. Louis, MO	10
Reston, VA	20
Paducah, KY	8
Framingham, MA	3

Norwalk, CT	5
Tarzana, CA	10
Oakland, CA	12
Denver, CO	15
Asbury Park, NJ	5
Knoxville, TN	9
Boston, MA	17
Port Washington, NY	12
Duluth, GA	10
Durham, NC	10
Salt Lake City, UT	7
Las Vegas, NV	25
Seattle, WA	14

L2TP tunnels are dynamically provisioned via RADIUS. Currently there is a tunnel between the L2TP LAC in each of the 20 PoPs and the L2TP LNS installed in Plant's DMZ. This means that the LNS is currently supporting 20 tunnels; however, it is actually terminating 200 PPP sessions, one for each remote user. Plant's routers, which are running the L2TP LNS function, use a single processor, so performance tends to degrade at this level of usage. Plant is considering an upgrade to a more powerful router with hardware-assisted encryption to accommodate the increased demand it anticipates over the coming months.

The way to alleviate concerns about L2TP scaling is to first look for a L2TP LNS that (1) features multiple processors, (2) offloads some of the more processor-intensive tasks, such as encryption, or (3) does both. Another thing to consider is a dedicated L2TP server that is optimized for high performance VPN applications. General-purpose routers do not often implement efficient VPN protocol engines because they perform so many different tasks. Finally, test the LNS in your own network to ensure that it lives up to its manufacturer's claims. Some manufacturers are already talking about scaling L2TP up to a couple of thousand sessions simultaneously. That would certainly constitute an improvement over what is currently available in 1998.

Security and L2TP

L2TP-enabled Remote Access Concentrators make IP connections to the destination LNS as shown in Figure 4.19. This means that all of the VPN customers as well as the Service Provider are on the same Internet. As of this writing, L2TP does not support encryption or any advanced security for that matter, although it *does* implement CHAP-like authentication during tunnel setup and a set of hidden commands, otherwise known as hidden AVPs. More advanced security is currently being developed for next generation L2TP implementations.

Both Service Providers and enterprises need to pay special attention when implementing Hybrid Provider VPNs based on L2TP. VPN customers of the Service Provider should not be able to use the shared network to gain access to resources either in customer networks or within the Service Provider network.

Often, VPNs based on L2TP are implemented as managed network services where the Service Provider provides the LNS (tunnel server or router) and is responsible for implementing IP addressing and filtering rules.

The L2TP Working Group recommends that L2TP command and control packets be secured by the use of IPSec Transport Mode. IPSec Transport Mode was discussed earlier in the chapter. Figure 4.20 illustrates an L2TP packet that has been secured using IPSec Transport Mode. The shaded area is the secured area. The unshaded area is "in the clear," as it must be in order to traverse the IP backbone.

L2TP Limitations

We've already discussed some of the issues and limitations of L2TP having to do with scaling and performance. The other main issue with L2TP as of this writing is simply immaturity. Several shipping versions of L2TP are available; however, none of them has implemented the full protocol in the initial release. This will make interoperability challenging until shipping versions have been available and revised once or twice to eliminate early bugs and implement missing functionality. The good news is that many of the vendors supporting L2TP have gathered periodically to test

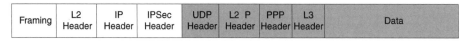

Figure 4.20 Protecting L2TP Packets Using IPSec Transport Mode

their versions for interoperability against versions from other vendors. "Bakeoffs" such as these will only help this protocol become more widely deployed and used as an integral component to VPN services.

The immaturity of the protocol also manifests itself through the lack of L2TP-based services available. Until Service Providers have had a better chance to test L2TP in their labs and test networks and begin to understand how they will use the technology as a component to their service offerings, L2TP will remain a mystery. When L2TP *does* begin to show up in VPN services, it is largely unknown how it will perform under real conditions over the actual public network. This is a large question mark.

The other issue as of late 1998 is security. None of the shipping versions has implemented the IPSec recommendation. Secure versions of L2TP will become widely available in 1999.

Summary

L2TP is a good protocol. It's not great and it's not poor. It's just good. It has certain limitations, to be sure; however, there is another important aspect that should be considered. L2TP is widely supported. By widely supported, we're not talking about "this manufacturer supports it or that manufacturer supports it." By support, we mean that there are already several supporting IETF draft specifications recommending proposed enhancements to L2TP. These include proposals for standard MIBs (Management Information Blocks), Quality of Service (QoS) proposals, recommendations for standard RADIUS compulsory tunneling attributes, security, and the list goes on.

The abovementioned issues surrounding its immaturity and lack of "real-world" exposure will go away over time. Eventually, L2TP should emerge as a widely supported, quite capable protocol.

If your organization is considering a VPN service based on a Hybrid Provider model and you are interested in standards-based service offerings, then chances are you will be very interested in evaluating L2TP as a tunneling protocol. If not now, then certainly later.

GRE (Generic Routing Encapsulation)

Generic Routing Encapsulation, established in 1994, was one of the pioneer tunneling protocols and is, in fact, used as the encapsulation technique for other tunneling protocols such as PPTP, Ascend's ATMP, and Bay Networks' BayDVS. GRE is defined in IETF RFCs 1701 and 1702.

GRE came about as a response to other early encapsulation proposals that the authors of GRE deemed too specific in terms of their ability to handle the number of payload types that existed in networks at that time. The resulting proposal mandated only that GRE packets include a "delivery" protocol header, the GRE header, and the original packet. The key to GRE, then, lay in its protocol type field, which defined twenty different packet types that could be encapsulated with GRE.

The other aspect of GRE that made it attractive as a VPN protocol is its built-in ability to identify and/or authenticate the source of a GRE packet. This is based on the inclusion of a four-octet "key" field in the GRE header. The presence of a security mechanism such as this makes the deployment over the public network a much more viable option.

Although the delivery header in GRE is left open, IP is by far the most common protocol used for the delivery and routing of GRE packets.

Common GRE Implementation Models

The most common model for GRE is point-to-point between two routers, where the GRE source and destination endpoints are manually configured. Where the VPN is deployed over the Internet, the GRE implementation is likely to be based on RFC 1702, since IP represents the delivery protocol. As is the case with most tunneling protocols, not every device in the VPN has to support GRE. A standard IP router, for example, has no knowledge that it is forwarding a GRE packet, since its only concern is the IP header.

GRE leaves the key management technique open to the GRE implementation. Therefore, depending on the authentication key used to identify the source of the packet, an external key server may be required. Some implementations of GRE use standard Message Digest 5 (MD5), which does not require an external server, but many do not support any security methods at all.

A GRE VPN Tunneling Scenario

When First and Second National Bank merged, the MIS directors thought they would never be able to consolidate their IP networks. Second National used a mix of registered and private address that made it hard to use shared wide area routers and replace redundant IP circuits to the same city. The MIS department decided to use GRE tunneling so that some of the Second National branches could use the First Bank network as a backbone cloud. Although the tunnels pass through many router hops, the First Bank network looks like a single circuit to Second Bank routers. The "outside" of the tunnel has "public addresses" on the First Bank network, but the "inside" keeps the original Second Bank's private addresses.

Another GRE VPN Tunneling Scenario

When All-Media Cable Company wired Morgantown, Wisconsin for cable TV service, it reserved three channels for the free use of the city. The city used these channels to implement a citywide Metropolitan Area Network (MAN) via cable modems. The fire stations, police stations, municipal offices, and the three school buildings each have its own private network through the MAN. Each building has GRE tunnels configured to their peers through a GRE capable router and cable modem. The police, fire, and municipal offices also implement MD5 encryption for privacy.

Other Models

There are a few other VPN tunneling protocols that may be of interest, particularly if you are the customer of one of the vendors that feature the protocol in question in its products. More specifically, the correlations are as follows:

Protocol	Vendor
ATMP	Ascend Communications
BayDVS	Bay Networks/Nortel
VTP	3Com Communications

Perhaps the most interesting aspect of these three protocols is how eerily similar they are. All three are based either directly or indirectly on Mobile IP, for better or worse, but have "extended" the Mobile IP protocol to suit the needs of their specific protocol. All of them use RADIUS-based compulsory tunneling and are typically deployed in Pure Provider VPN services. All three of them terminate PPP at the Remote Access Concentrator and use GRE to encapsulate IP or IPX payload. They are all more or less proprietary to their specific vendor.

ATMP

Ascend Tunnel Management Protocol (ATMP) is actually an informational RFC (2107); however, the only vendor that has implemented ATMP is Ascend Communications. ATMP is a Mobile IP-like protocol, although it borrows Mobile IP terminology more than it does the actual protocol. ATMP was specifically designed with Service Provider-offered VPN services in mind. ATMP can be deployed using either the Pure Provider (called "Gateway Mode") or Hybrid Provider model (called "Router Mode"). Figure 4.21 shows ATMP functioning in Gateway Mode in which the connection to the Home Network is via Frame Relay.

The primary components of an ATMP network are the Foreign Agent (FA) and Home Agent (HA). ATMP uses compulsory tunneling to build the tunnel between the FA and HA, then tunnels the Layer 3 packet inside of a GRE packet. ATMP is a little light on security, using only a CHAP-like challenge mechanism for the HA to authenticate the FA. It is possible to use other security mechanisms, like IPSec transport mode, to secure tunnels and their payload. GRE, which is the encapsulation used by ATMP, also offers the option of using keyed MD5 as a security mechanism. Neither of these is mentioned in the RFC; however,

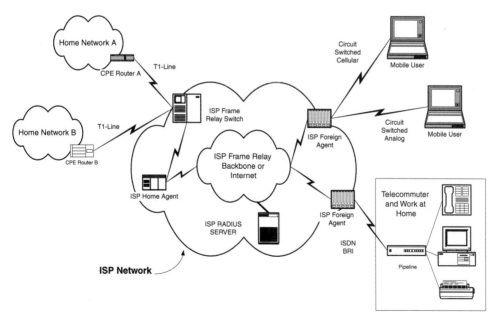

Figure 4.21 ATMP Elements (Gateway Mode)

they should work as long as their implementation does not interfere with actual ATMP operation.

As a tunneling protocol, ATMP is fairly lightweight but can be useful to Service Providers as the means for another flavor of VPN service. Since many Service Providers already have Ascend gear deployed as part of their service infrastructure, ATMP is usually an option in spite of its propriety nature.

BayDVS Tunneling

BayDVS (Bay Dial VPN Services) is quite similar to ATMP in terms of form and function; however, there are some noteworthy differences between the two. First, the terminology is slightly different (the word "RAS" is used in place of FA and the word "Gateway" is used in place of the term HA). Second, BayDVS is actually based on the IETF standard Mobile IP (RFC 2002). Mobile IP is a protocol that was devised to "extend the existing Internet Protocol to allow a portable computer to be moved from one network to another without changing its IP address and without losing existing connections."

BayDVS breaks the RFC with private extensions that enable functionality such as IPX support, mapping tunnel endpoints to Frame Relay virtual circuits, and obtaining IP addresses and WINS name server resolution via DHCP. Another deviation from Mobile IP is that it is not assumed that the mobile node will actually continue to use the same address. It is expected that the remote node will obtain a new address with each login.

Another difference between ATMP and BayDVS is the security architecture. BayDVS has implemented stronger security than ATMP. For instance, BayDVS tunnels are authenticated using digital signatures generated by an MD5 hash. ATMP uses a weaker CHAP-like method. Also,

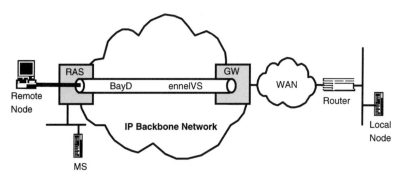

Figure 4.22 **BayDVS**

certain components of ATMP networks, such as the RADIUS server used for compulsory tunneling, are "in the clear," meaning they are publicly addressed and thus susceptible to attack. BayDVS has implemented its tunneling architecture in such a way that the Service Provider network is unreachable from the private, or customer, network. Conversely, the private network is unreachable from the public network. An overview of BayDVS is shown in Figure 4.22.

BayDVS is a proprietary technology that is attractive as long as you are a Bay Networks customer. Those Service Providers wishing to build their VPN services on non-Bay gear will have to search for a technology other than BayDVS.

VTP

VTP stands for the *Virtual Tunneling Protocol*. It is a Layer 3 tunneling method that was devised by US Robotics and Bay Networks engineers in July 1996, though only US Robotics ended up implementing it. As you might have guessed, Bay Networks branched off on its own and developed BayDVS. Like BayDVS tunneling, VTP is based on Mobile IP.

Over time, a few subtle differences have emerged between VTP and BayDVS—however, they are not really worth mentioning, much less researching! The important things to consider, if you are in a position to do so, are the actual capabilities of the service implementation in terms of capacities, protocols, and level of functionality supported. Just remember that the whole point of a Pure Provider VPN is to "hide" the tunneling protocol along with all of its quirks from the enterprise customer!

Summary

If you are a Service Provider and use Ascend, Bay Networks, or US Robotics (3Com) remote access equipment, you can deploy a Pure Provider VPN service today using the Layer 3 tunneling protocol or technology that's available from your vendor. All three protocols have been available for some time on their respective products.

If you are an enterprise organization and have decided that Pure Provider VPN services best suit the needs of your organization, you first must seek out a Service Provider that is offering Pure Provider VPN services. From there, it is a question of asking which tunneling protocol the Service Provider is using for the service. Chances are good that it is one of these three. Make sure that the service will accommodate all of your requirements and if not, inquire as to what it would take to have the service customized to fit your needs.

VPN Products and Solutions

Now that we've had a chance to examine the models and some of the core technology comprising VPNs, it's time to look at the kinds of products and solutions that are used to build VPNs.

This is the hard part—choosing products and/or solutions. As of this writing, there are literally hundreds of products available on the market from a variety of large and small vendors. Don't believe us? Try walking the floor at one of the large networking industry trade shows. Just about every vendor's booth these days showcases something having to do with VPNs. For simplicity's sake, we'll break them out into two categories—software-based solutions and hardware-based solutions—although one could rightly argue that the best overall solutions require some of both. As with the various models, the key is choosing the right solution, or combination of solutions, for your business. In general, we'd say that software offers a bit more in the way of flexibility, while hardware-based solutions usually feature better performance—though we'll delve a bit deeper on this topic later.

An important note regarding this chapter—we don't want it to serve as a space for product reviews/comparisons. You can get those from any of a number of usually reliable, relatively unbiased (did we really say that?) trade periodicals. Instead, we will focus on the high-level information surrounding each *type* of solution. That should be enough to help you narrow your search to some extent.

Software-based VPN Solutions

When the idea of mass marketing IP-based Virtual Private Networking products first popped as a light bulb over some product manager's head, software-based solutions represented the easiest and least expensive way to take the idea from concept to shipping product. After all, there were many platforms already available and capable of implementing protocol-level solutions. The operating systems, APIs (*Application Program Interfaces*), and to some extent, the protocols themselves, were well known to software engineers. The concept itself, which was to securely connect remote user desktops to the corporate network and its resources, also lent itself neatly to a software-based model, since both the requisite hardware and software were already deployed on the network.

It should come as no surprise, then, that software-base products and solutions such as Digital Equipment Corporation's AltaVista™ Tunnel and Microsoft's PPTP were early product/technology entrants to the VPN market. Alta Vista Tunnel has been around since 1996 while Microsoft introduced PPTP as a patch-level enhancement to Windows 95 Dialup Networking (DUN) in 1998. Firewall products, also software-based and for the most part designed to operate on "standard" Unix platforms, were also clear candidates to implement software-based VPN services. This was especially true given the security-oriented nature of both firewalls and VPNs.

Software-based VPN products exist largely within two categories—firewalls (which are usually software based) and "function-specific" software.

VPN Firewall Products

For almost as long as the Internet has been a publicly accessed network, there have been firewalls. Originally, firewalls were developed as way to fil-

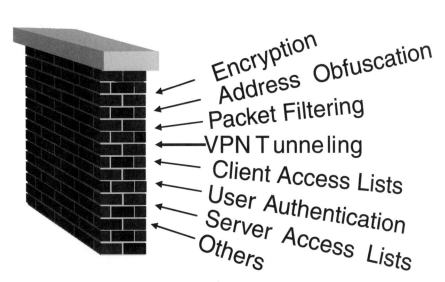

Figure 5.1 Firewalls—A Growing List of Capabilities

ter (the dropping or forwarding packets based on a criterion or set of criteria) packets in a more sophisticated way than standard routers. Filtering was, and is, used as a way to keep selected (read *undesirable*) traffic off private networks and allow other selected traffic in. Over the years, however, firewalls have evolved to encompass a variety of security-related functions beyond simple packet filtering. Today's firewalls authenticate users, sessions, and even applications as well as individual packets, provide proxy services,[1] translate addresses, encrypt data, and the list goes on (Figure 5.1). The latest capability related to firewalls is, of course, their ability to implement Virtual Private Networks. Most of the better firewall products have by now added VPN functionality to their growing list of features.

Firewalls with built-in VPN capabilities have been used frequently by Service Providers as components of VPN services; however, the "services" lean more toward managed CPE services than actual VPN services. When you think about it, this is a natural fit. Service Providers selling Internet access to organizations often bundle a router and firewall with the service (similar to a Chinese restaurant that includes white rice with your takeout). Taking this concept a step further, as long as the firewall supports tunneling, encryption, authentication, and most other required VPN technology components, why not just configure and turn on the

---

[1]Proxies are software functions that carry out instructions on behalf of one or more entities within the network—like sending a representative to a meeting instead of attending yourself.

features and call it a VPN service? Indeed, the customer enjoys the benefit and the Service Provider enjoys a new revenue stream without much in the way of additional capital investment.

Firewalls are also used by enterprises directly, both as part of the corporate Internet connection (from Figure 1.1 in Chapter 1) and internally as a way to design and create secure zones within the corporate network. In effect, the firewall, for many organizations, is the vehicle upon which their network security infrastructure is built. And since the security function is so integral to the VPN, it stands to reason that the VPN would somehow be woven into the services provided by the firewall. To paraphrase the saying from the 1980s (or was it the 1970s?)—if you got it, use it!

Firewall-based VPN solutions typically run in two modes. In the first, two firewalls establish a security association and tunnel data between them as shown in Figure 5.2. In this mode, the VPN is established between two sites. Which data is tunneled depends on its IP destination address. Data that is destined for the Internet is not tunneled. The rules governing the decision to tunnel or not to tunnel (THAT is the question!) are established during the configuration of firewall policies.

Note that this mode is typically useful only when the firewalls are from the same manufacturer. The current state of interoperability among firewall products for VPNs, while improving, is that interoperability does not really exist. We expect this to change over time as:

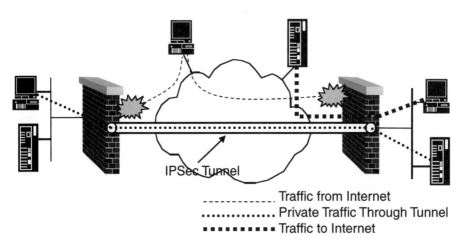

IPSec Tunnel

- - - - - - - - - - Traffic from Internet
· · · · · · · · · · · · Private Traffic Through Tunnel
■ ■ ■ ■ ■ ■ ■ ■ ■ Traffic to Internet

Figure 5.2 Firewalls Managing Public and Private Traffic

1. Industry standards tighten up around such problems as key exchange and the acquisition of digital certificates for authentication.

2. More products coalesce around the more popular tunneling standards such as L2TP and IPSec.

3. More vendors seek certification by the ICSA, ANX, and other groups focused on multivendor interoperability. Chapter 2 covered these organizations in more detail.

The second mode involves remote users individually tunneling to the corporate firewall. Special client software, sold by the maker of the firewall software, is installed on the remote client and configured to set up a security association (in "tunnel" mode) with the destination firewall. When the user connects to the Internet, she launches the client application. The client application initiates a VPN tunnel to the firewall on the home network. All traffic destined for the home network is subsequently encapsulated in the "tunnel." Traffic destined for the Internet is not encapsulated, allowing the user to freely communicate back and forth with hosts on the public network. The bifurcation of traffic to private (tunneled) and public (nontunneled) destinations simultaneously from the same client is sometimes called *split tunneling* (Figure 5. 3).

Not all products support split tunneling. With some products, tunneling is an all-or-nothing scenario, meaning if the remote client invokes a tunneled connection, all data is tunneled to the private network regard-

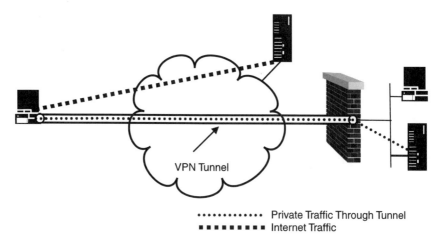

·············· Private Traffic Through Tunnel
■ ■ ■ ■ ■ ■ ■ ■ ■ Internet Traffic

Figure 5.3 Split Tunneling

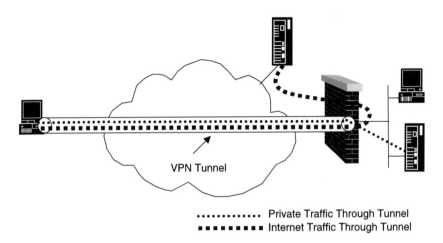

Figure 5.4 VPN "U-turn"

less of its ultimate destination. Even traffic that is destined for the Internet must be decapsulated prior to being sent back out through the firewall to the Internet in a kind of "U-turn" (Figure 5. 4). While this is fundamentally inefficient (especially if optimal Internet performance is desired), in some cases, the "VPN U-turn" is a way for companies to better control the activities of their employees.

Let's say, for example, that a company has "bulk" contracted Internet access for its employees with a national Internet provider as a way to further drive down the cost of its VPN. Let's also say that one of the employees is a miscreant, abusing the Internet "perk" to conduct illegal or immoral activities of one kind or another when not tunneled into the corporate LAN. In such cases, it may be in the company's best interest to force the VPN U-turn, since the company's firewall can then control Mr. Bad Apple's access to Internet sites that promote or facilitate activities inconsistent with company policies.

With the advent of more fully featured client software, split tunneling is a configurable option, which is a good thing. Organizations can set their own policies regarding employee use of the Internet and the corporate VPN. As you consider which direction to take for your own VPN, you may also want to consider the performance ramification of directing all client traffic through the firewall. The VPN U-turn scenario places more of a burden on firewall resources (CPU cycles, memory, etc.) than a scenario featuring split tunneling, since *all* traffic (not just tunneled traffic) must be handled by the VPN software running in the firewall.

As a summary, we'd like to point out some of the relative pros and cons of using existing firewall products for VPNs:

Firewall Advantages

♦ Firewalls that are already in place can be easily reconfigured or upgraded for VPN use.

♦ Additional hardware is usually not needed (unless scaling is a concern).

♦ Many service providers are equipped and trained to manage firewall products as a component of an outsourced VPN service.

Firewall Disadvantages

♦ Many firewall products have proprietary aspects to them, particularly with regard to VPN functionality and management, meaning the same firewall product must be used everywhere in the VPN.

♦ Encryption usually degrades performance in firewall products, limiting their applicability when the requirement is to support a large number of VPN users.

♦ Firewalls are not purpose-built for VPNs, meaning certain functions, such as network management, are or can be potentially cumbersome.

Function-Specific VPN Software Products

Despite the security tie-in between firewalls and VPNs, many organizations have chosen to keep their VPN separate from the firewall, in terms of deployment, for any number of reasons. It could be that the organization is concerned about taxing the firewall, a critical component of their network, above its scaling and performance capabilities. It could be a cost issue—maybe the firewall's VPN capabilities are a pricy option and more expensive than purchasing separate product. It could be that certain protocols used within the organization are not supported as part of the firewall's VPN implementation. It could be that the salesman selling the nonfirewall VPN product is a very good salesman!

Regardless of the reason, the good news is that there are a number of nonfirewall VPN solutions, which also run on "standard" server platforms such as Windows NT, Novell NetWare, or Solaris. The bad news is that these other platforms are oftentimes running other tasks and applications themselves, which means that using one of them as opposed to the firewall is akin to jumping from the proverbial frying pan into the fire.

Software-based VPN products typically involve two components—a client and a server. The client (usually) installs on a Windows desktop while the server runs as an application on the server. While it is possible (Microsoft's PPTP server comes to mind) to set up a VPN running between two servers, it is also less prevalent a model.

Early software-based VPN solutions were to an extent based on proprietary tunneling schemes—Digital's AltaVista (TM) is one product that comes to mind. Recently, though, most products are based on "standard" protocols or protocol sets such as IPSec or PPTP (assuming you consider PPTP a standard). Check to make sure, when evaluating a software-based solution (or *any* VPN solution for that matter), that the product implements standard protocols. This is particularly true if your goal is to develop an extranet, since you have no say as to which products your partner is using.

SOCKS Version 5

One notable technology that has been integrated into popular software-only solutions is a technology known as SOCKS. While we don't deign to understand the words behind the acronym (that is, if it *is* indeed an acronym), we can explain a little about SOCKS.

SOCKS is a protocol that operates at the session layer of the OSI stack (Figure 5.5). There are several versions, with SOCKS Version 5 being the most recent as of this writing. SOCKS functions as a proxy, meaning it controls the flow of data by establishing a kind of "virtual" circuit (or *session*) between a client and a host for use with one or more specific applications. By monitoring all data and providing strong authentication, SOCKS provides strong security to applications that *require* strong security. Applications not requiring strong security are simply not configured to utilize the SOCKS protocol.

From a product perspective, SOCKS is installed and used as a software "shim" on the user's PC. In many cases, it operates in conjunction with browser-based security protocols such as Secure Socket Layer (SSL), as well as the corporate firewall. Because it operates at Layer 5, SOCKS can also operate alongside other VPN protocols that run at either Layer 2 (PPTP, L2F, L2TP, etc.) or Layer 3 (IPSec, etc.). The combination of strong security and ease of use makes SOCKS a nice bit of technology for use in VPNs. The only notable disadvantage with SOCKS is that it can

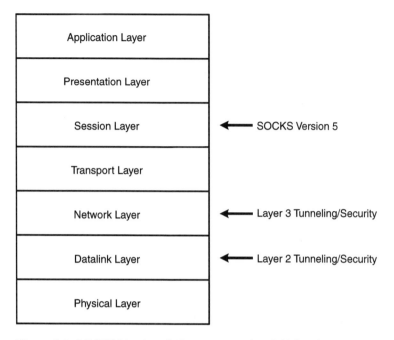

Figure 5.5 SOCKS Version 5 Operates at the OSI Session Layer

impact an application's performance; however, this problem plagues other software-only solutions as well.

A summary of the relative pros and cons of nonfirewall software-only VPN solutions:

Software Advantages

♦ Easily installed on standard desktops and network servers.

♦ Typically does not require additional hardware—reducing capital expenditure.

♦ Easily upgradable compared to hardware.

Software Disadvantages

♦ Lower overall performance, primarily due to security functionality running in software as well as in competition with other server processes.

♦ Servers usually can't scale to meet the demands of a large (more than a dozen or so simultaneous sessions) VPN.

♦ Client software must be distributed to each device, creating a fair amount of administrative burden to the organization.

Hardware-based VPN Solutions

When you really think about it, VPN hardware platforms are designed with the needs of multiple consumers in mind. They are used both by enterprises in the "roll your own" motif and by Service Providers that use them as the foundation for their VPN service offerings. Regardless of who's using them, for the most part they can be divided up into two categories:

1. Hardware solutions built on "general-purpose" platforms, such as routers
2. "Function-specific" hardware solutions designed from the ground up specifically for use in VPNs

Routers

Although routers are hardware platforms, much of the intelligence in routers is derived from software. Many of the leading router vendors (and many of the trailing ones as well!) have either implemented VPN features in their software or are going to. The most popular router features for VPNs have been the addition of VPN-enabling technologies such as IPSec (Tunnel Mode, as well as Transport Mode) and L2TP. Routers have also implemented ancillary protocols that are used to implement VPNs such as Network Address Translation (NAT), RADIUS, and Generic Routing Encapsulation (GRE). Additionally, some routers have begun to offer performance-enhancing options such as encryption coprocessors that are designed to make routers more usable in VPNs.

Routers are used for VPNs both by enterprise organizations and by Service Providers as tunnel initiators and terminators. Service Providers, for example, typically use routers for WAN edge access concentration in Pure Provider VPNs. We touch on the WAN edge aspect a bit later in this chapter. Still, routers that support VPN tunneling and encryption are primarily used by enterprises. According to a recent publication by industry analysts Infonetics Research, 40% of the respondents in a recent survey of current and future VPN users plan to use their routers to implement VPN-specific functionality.

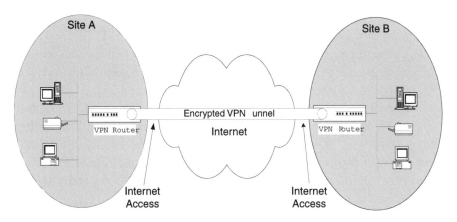

Figure 5.6 Routers in a Site-Site VPN

Routers today are used in both Site-Site VPNs and Remote Access VPNs. We'll cover both.

Routers in Site-to-Site VPNs

In a Site-Site VPN, VPN tunnels are built between two routers as shown in Figure 5.6.

These tunnels are sometimes implemented using Generic Routing Encapsulation (GRE); however, more and more routers are using IPSec (Tunnel Mode) for this application. The GRE or IPSec tunnels can be thought of as replacements for Layer 2 Virtual Circuits (a la Frame Relay). The primary difference is that IP-based VPN tunnels are fundamentally connectionless, while Layer 2 circuits are fundamentally connection-oriented.

Where this makes a difference is in the service's ability to deliver deterministic (i.e., predictable) performance, otherwise known as Quality of Service (QoS). At this point, we must digress into a brief discussion of QoS. A more in-depth treatment of QoS mechanisms is given in Chapter 6.

Quality of Service (QoS)   QoS is a topic that has the capability of spawning arguments that reach religious-like fervor. From our vantage, QoS can be boiled down to two fundamental aspects. The first aspect deals with the topic of separating different types of traffic into classes that, in turn, are processed differently by networking equipment (such as routers). CPU reservation, egress queuing, and packet buffering address this aspect of QoS, which we'll refer to as *internal QoS*.

The second aspect deals with the ability of the network as a whole to sustain the performance of each class according to the values of parameters (throughput, latency, "jitter" tolerance, etc.) assigned to each class. Frame Relay CIR (Committed Information Rate), ATM PCR (Peak Cell Rate), and ATM service classes (VBR, CBR, etc.) address this aspect, which we'll call *protocol-level QoS*. Most protocol level QoS today is found in Layer 2 networks.

Networks that use connectionless protocols (such as IP) can deliver internal QoS today consistent with the capabilities of routers and other networking gear. Connectionless networks (like the Internet) have not yet mastered protocol level QoS, however, even though the IETF (to its credit) is making great strides towards standardizing QoS protocols that can be used in connectionless networks.

While connection-oriented networks can already deliver protocol-level QoS, not all regions of the world have access to Layer 2 services such as Frame Relay, ATM, X.25, and so on. Organizations that have remote branch locations with access to the Internet, but not Frame Relay, X.25, or ATM services, can now use VPN-enabled routers to securely tunnel back to the home office or to other branches. As well, Layer 2 services are frequently more expensive than simple Internet connections, so connecting many sites via the Internet is usually cheaper than connecting them via a VC-based service. Chapter 3 covered this issue.

The business case notwithstanding, it is important to note that raw cost should not always govern the decision to use a router-based *IP* VPN versus a router-based *Layer 2* VPN. For one, not all traffic types can be transported through IP-based VPN tunnels. Sure, there are protocols such as Data Link Switching (DLSW) and AppleTalk Update Routing Protocol (AURP) to encapsulate SNA and AppleTalk respectively inside TCP/IP packets. But these protocols add a significant amount of packet overhead to the network compared to Layer 2 VPN technologies, which accommodate multiprotocol traffic using simple (and small) multiprotocol headers, such as Frame Relay's RFC 1490 header. The additional complexity of the "value-add" protocols such as DLSW and AURP also creates havoc with regard to performance in large networks. SNA, which is particularly intolerant of network-induced delay, is not a good candidate for use in a VPN running over a connectionless network; however, it runs great over a connection-oriented Frame Relay network! Got it? We hope so. We're not even sure *we've* got all the issues sorted out!

Regardless of your own religious stance on QoS, there is one point that is important to raise at this juncture—security, which is, of course, crucial in the deployment of *any* VPN, makes the QoS problem more difficult, not easier.

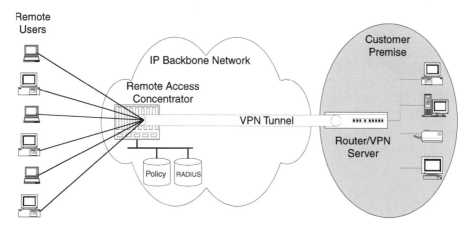

Figure 5.7 Remote Access Concentrator to Router VPN

Routers in Remote Access VPNs

In a remote access VPN, the router functions as a tunnel server, either for voluntary tunnels initiated by remote clients, or for compulsory tunnels initiated by remote access equipment located in the Service Provider network (more on this topic later). Using a router for this function is advisable particularly when there is excess bandwidth on the circuit connecting the router to the Internet, and/or the router itself is not already overtaxed with compute-intensive tasks. In Remote Access VPNs, the tunnel is usually built between a Remote Access Concentrator and a router as shown in Figure 5.7.

The primary advantage of using a router as a VPN device is the simple integration of functionality. If a router is already deployed and functional at a location, simply adding and configuring a new protocol feature to the existing equipment is a quick-and-dirty solution to building a multisite VPN without having to add more equipment. This is similar to the concept of adding VPN functionality to firewalls as discussed earlier. Furthermore, consolidation of the existing *Inter*net and *intra*net facilities from two connections to one (as shown in the before/after example of Figure 5.8) for each site provides a significant reduction in monthly line and service costs.

So what are the gotchas? Well, for one, routers are designed primarily for making packet-by-packet forwarding decisions based on the network layer address found in the packet header. Even with the recent improvements in router technology that have them forwarding packets at gigabits or even terabits per second, routers are *not* designed to perform

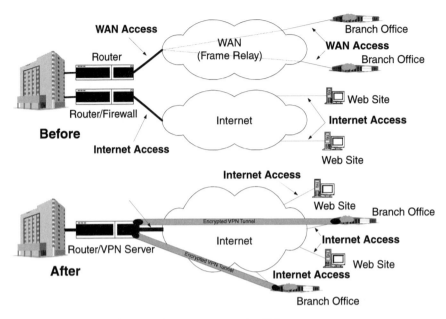

Figure 5.8 Consolidation of WAN Access Facilities

highly mathematical computations such as those involved with cryptography. So routers that support packet encryption in software are not of much use if high overall performance is expected. Routers that support encryption in hardware are better; however, their implementation, which could necessitate upgrades or even wholesale replacement, could prove costly. These important factors should be weighed carefully before building a VPN on existing routers.

The second problem associated with building a VPN on the existing router network involves the handling of multiprotocol traffic. A network that is already based 100% on IP and IP-based applications poses little challenge in this regard, since both VPN and non-VPN traffic are treated the same way by the router. Networks that incorporate SNA, AppleTalk, and/or the ever present IPX, however, pose challenges since they too must be considered if the VPN is to deliver the expected service and cost savings. SNA in particular is problematic since SNA is also sensitive to latency and other network performance variations that the Internet has not yet completely addressed (refer back to the previous QoS digression). The multiprotocol problem is not a problem limited to routers, by the way. Lack of support for non-IP protocols is a problem with VPNs in general. It's just worth mentioning here because routers were *designed* for use in multiprotocol environments. Therefore, it is more likely that network managers will be exposed to this issue when trying to build a VPN using existing routers.

To summarize, routers are most often used for site-to-site VPNs in which they serve to connect multiple sites together securely over the Internet. They can also be used in remote access VPNs as VPN tunnel termination points for stand-alone clients or service provider RAS gear.

Despite their flexibility, however, using existing routers as the basis for a VPN is a hit-or-miss proposition. Performance and scaling are likely issues, since routers are not particularly fast when called upon to encrypt and decrypt packets. This hurdle can be cleared if the router employs hardware-assisted cryptography. Another issue is the handling of multiprotocol traffic, since most routers today have not yet integrated multiprotocol routing with IP-based VPN capability. If performance and multiprotocol support are not crucial requirements for the VPN, routers may be a cost effective and simple solution for providing secure site-to-site or remote access connectivity over the Internet.

Dedicated VPN Equipment

The recent popularity of Virtual Private Networking has given birth to a new classification of internetworking device. Being somewhat new to the scene, they are called many different things—multiservice dedicated VPN devices, VPN "appliances," you can choose your moniker—but we'll keep it simple by calling them dedicated VPN equipment, or DVE. (We could have alternatively used the term dedicated VPN devices (DVD), but that would have confused the multimedia types who consider DVD an acronym for digital video disk, so we'll just stick with DVE.)

DVE is designed and built from the ground up for use in VPN applications. To illustrate what we mean by this, most DVE comes packaged with interfaces that are clearly marked "Public" and "Private" (how many routers can you say that for?). All support one or more Ethernet interfaces with the better ones supporting Fast (100 Mbps) or even Gigabit (1000 Mbps) Ethernet. Most support WAN connectivity as well; however, the preferred method of deploying DVE, particularly at central locations, is by placing it *behind* WAN access equipment. The focal technologies of DVE are VPN tunneling and encryption; however, most DVE also offers integrated filtering, some level of routing, and support for user level authentication and/or policy via RADIUS, tokens, LDAP, or others. Because they were designed with a single purpose in mind, their performance is optimized for critical services such as encryption and hosting a large number of sessions and/or security associations. Management of these devices is usually handled through user-friendly, Java-based tools that make it easy to set up, configure, and otherwise manage the device.

The chief advantage of DVE is in the high price/performance ratio relative to other hardware, software, or hardware/software combo solutions. As evidence, many DVE vendors are now claiming wire-speed T3 (45 Mbps) throughput for high priority sessions with *Triple DES* encryption! Sorry, but last we checked there weren't many routers claiming this. DVE also tends to scale much better than non-DVE since (1) all they do is VPNs and (2) their hardware and software design is optimized to host many remote sessions. High PPP scalability, for instance, is usually optimized in DVE—in fact, it is usually a specific requirement—while standard issue routers are typically required to scale PPP only as high as the number of physical interfaces on the router. Another advantage of using DVE for a VPN is the overall emphasis on security compared to other VPN devices. Manufacturers of DVE have built security features into their equipment that is not normally found in networking gear. How many routers, for instance, encrypt the configuration file? How many require even managers to establish secured connections, each requiring its own separate key negotiation, before even attempting to manage the device. Most don't. For most routers, if you can figure out the "manager" password (mere child's play for most network intruders), you can do irreparable damage to a network and by extension, a business. Simply stated, routers by today's standards do not protect themselves even adequately, making them suspect as potential VPN devices.

Looking at the disadvantages of DVE requires a little reading between the lines of the marketing materials. Many of these products advertise their ability to perform functions typically found in other kinds of devices, like routers and firewalls. In terms of technology such as integrated "firewalling" and routing, however, most DVE can't hold a torch to firewalls and routers that are dedicated to *their* respective applications. Most DVE that claim to support firewalling, for instance, really support policy-based traffic filtering but not other advanced firewalling features such as seven-layer stateful packet inspection. Some of these products support Network Address Translation (a standard feature in most firewalls) and some don't. Most DVE that support routing support routing for only one protocol (IP) and support very little in the way of dynamic routing protocols.

As opposed to routers, which are deployed either at the customer premise or within the Service Provider network, dedicated VPN equipment, with few exceptions, is almost always deployed at the customer premise.

In general, we recommend DVE as the way to go if you consider the VPN a critical component of your organization's overall networking strategy.

Service Provider–Located VPN Products

In Chapter 7, we will spend much more time exploring the Service Provider aspect of VPNs from a pure *services* perspective. Since this chapter is more centered around VPN products, however, we're going to peek under the hood and describe some of the VPN-enabled products that you would likely encounter on a tour of your Service Provider's network facilities.

As we pointed out earlier, many of today's VPN "services" are really managed CPE services that utilize the End-to-End tunneling model using the Service Provider's network for transport only. Increasingly, however, services are rolling out that incorporate new functionality that is being built into the provider infrastructure. Some of this functionality is being built into a new generation of edge access platforms and some is being built into dial access concentrators. We touched earlier on the use of routers running VPN functionality deployed at the service provider WAN edge. Let's now explore this further, as well as a couple of other types of platform used to provision VPN services in the "cloud."

"New Breed" Edge Devices

The Internet edge (i.e., the ingress, or entrance, points to the Internet) is a topic that we covered back in Chapter 2; however, to frame the topic at hand, we'll throw in a brief review.

The presence of edge access routers in the Internet is a trend that has come and gone but is now making a comeback. In the early days, Internet Service Providers placed an IP router at the network ingress to accommodate the increasing number of organizations that required or desired access to the Internet. As demand grew, particularly in the early 1990s, Service Providers began to realize that the typical router would not and could not scale to accommodate the increasing growth. Thus, a new idea was born featuring the concept of "front-ending" the IP access routers with high-capacity, high-density Layer 2 access switches. These switches, less software-burdened than routers, were able to handle as many as twice the number of T1 interfaces per slot (and consequently, twice the amount of service revenues per shelf). Additionally, a single, high-capacity interconnect (such as 100 Mbps FDDI) between the access switch and the router was sufficient to handle all of the aggregated traffic without requiring significant slot build-out on either device. In effect, the access switch functioned as a kind of "Internet Access Mux." Internet Service Providers bought and deployed them by the bushel (to the unbounded delight of Cascade Communications' stockholders!). The switch/backbone router tandem has been the prevailing Internet access architecture throughout most of the 1990s and is depicted in Figure 5.9.

Recently however, a new breed of high-capacity edge platform has emerged that threatens to break the prevailing model. Some of these platforms are simply high-end high capacity routers with some value-add service-level functionality built in. Others don't do much routing at all, preferring to focus on other services while leaving the routing function to the existing Internet infrastructure. Regardless of what they are called by their manufacturers, these devices feature the port density and throughput capacity of edge access switches and much, if not all, of the IP smarts inherent in "traditional" Internet routers. With embedded Quality of Service, better redundancy than their predecessors, and the ability to connect directly into multigigabit optical networks, these devices are well

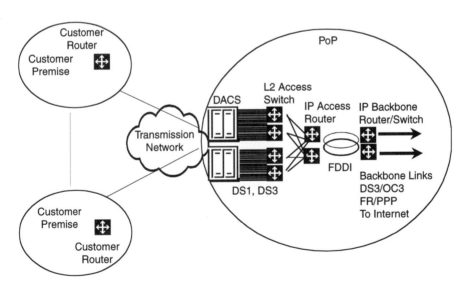

Figure 5.9 "Traditional" Internet Access using the "Tandem" of Layer 2 Access Switches and IP Routers

suited to meet the demands of what has come to be known as the "Business Class Internet." The design goals of these new edge platforms are largely driven by three fundamental truths in today's IP services market:

1. Services are provisioned at the edge of the carrier network.
2. To remain competitive, Service Providers must differentiate their service offerings from those of their competitors.
3. To remain competitive, Service Providers must simultaneously increase revenues per unit of rack space while decreasing cost.

VPN services are, of course, on the "A-list" of features that are being developed for these products. In many cases, the VPN capabilities that are being touted by the manufacturers of these products (many of which are networking startups, by the way) are based on MPLS (MPLS is examined in further detail in Chapter 8). More and more of these products, however, are building other "high-touch" IP services into their platforms. From many of these manufacturers' Web sites, we've read about service capabilities in these products such as:

♦ IPSec SA termination
♦ Layer 2 tunneling termination
♦ Other PPP termination (PPP over ATM, PPP over Ethernet, etc.)
♦ Virtual firewalling
♦ Virtual routing
♦ Per session QoS
♦ And others . . .

All of these services have traditionally (remember—in "Internet time" anything up until the last few months can be considered "traditional" at this point!) been deployed at the customer premise. All or many of them are found in VPN products today, again deployed primarily at the customer premise. What this new breed of product has done, through a combination of ASICs, coprocessors, software, and shear capacity, is move all of this functionality into multiple virtual *instances* of service terminations residing in a single edge platform.

For the most part, many of these products have not yet hit the market in terms of being generally available as of this writing. Still, all of them are being built with the promise of changing the fundamentals of how IP services such as VPNs are outsourced to carriers and other service providers.

Remote Access Concentrators (RACs)

Previous discussions about remote access VPNs have centered on the End-to-End model from Chapter 4 in which VPN tunnels are built between software-based "clients" found in remote PCs and VPN "servers" found on customer premises. This model assumes that the transport network (in many instances the Internet) features none of the VPN "smarts" required to actually build or tear down the VPN.

More frequently, however, Remote Access equipment is featuring high-end capabilities in the area of VPN service deployment. There are actually two emerging VPN applications for Remote Access Concentrators (RACs): Virtual Private Dial Network (VPDN) services and ISP wholesaling of VPDN services.

Remote Access Concentrators Used in VPDN Services

In VPDN services, the typical role of the Remote Access Concentrator is one of tunnel initiator. All of the major Remote Access vendors have by now developed and introduced VPN software capabilities in their platforms. These functions allow a service provider to deploy a provider-based VPN service in which the remote access infrastructure plays a role far beyond its traditional one as a modem shelf/PPP terminator for Internet access.

The type of tunneling used by remote access gear is called "compulsory" tunneling. Compulsory tunneling is called that because the user doesn't have a choice as to whether his or her session will be tunneled. Essentially, whether users are tunneled depends on who they are! Let's take a look.

Compulsory tunneling is usually based on the RADIUS protocol deployed with a twist: Rather than look up and authenticate a single user, the RADIUS server used for compulsory tunneling looks up an *organization*. Each organization record configured in the server database contains a number of attributes and values that are used to assist the RAC in building and tearing down VPN tunnels. When the user first logs in to the networks, the RAC first sends out a RADIUS request to look up the organization in the tunnel database. If the RADIUS server finds a match, it returns all of the necessary attributes to the RAC, which proceeds to establish a tunnel based on the attribute values returned from the RADIUS database entry for that specific organization. Figure 5.10 depicts this interaction based on an L2TP-based service.

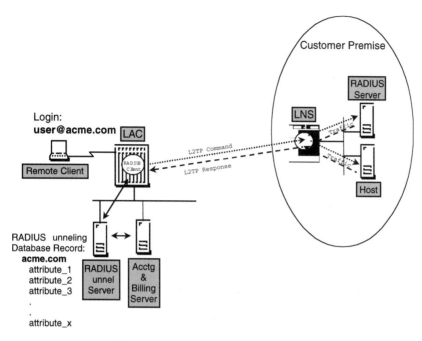

Figure 5.10 Compulsory Tunneling Example

1. User connects and logs in to the network.

2. The RAC sends a RADIUS packet to the RADIUS Tunnel Server containing the user's domain name (acme.com).

3. The RADIUS server performs a lookup on "acme.com" and, upon verifying the match, returns a set of attribute/value pairs to the RAC so that the RAC can learn all of the parameters required for tunnel establishment.

4. Based on the information received from the RADIUS server, the RAC goes about the task of initiating the tunnel.

5. Tunnel establishment completes, followed by completion of the PPP session negotiation between the user and the network or the user and the corporate LAN.

6. At the same time, the RADIUS Tunnel Server sends a "start" message to the accounting server.

RAC-initiated tunnels usually terminate at the customer premise in a server or home gateway of some kind (Hybrid Provider); however, we've also been acquainted with RAC tunnels terminating on the carrier side of the service demarcation (Pure Provider). In terms of commercial availability, tunnels of the Hybrid Provider variety will most likely be Layer 2 tunnels (such as L2F, PPTP, or L2TP) that terminate the PPP session on the customer premise. Pure Provider RAC-initiated tunneling solutions have usually been based on proprietary schemes such as BayDVS or ATMP that provide a nicely unique solution that features intricate protocol mappings in order to get the job done.

However, a new set of Pure Provider tunneling services are emerging that combine the best of the Pure Provider model with standards-based tunneling. This is good news for carriers who view managed CPE VPN services as a royal pain! The new services are made possible, by and large, by the new class of edge products that are emerging even as we write this book. If you are a Service Provider that is considering a Pure Provider model for your service architecture, we highly recommend taking a look at some of these products. Figure 5.11 depicts a typical remote access-based VPDN service.

RAC-based VPN Wholesaling

If you are a service provider that is looking for a slightly different twist on the traditional RAC-based VPN service, you could consider adding a wholesaling aspect to the service. The discussion that follows goes beyond simple remote access; however, we felt like this was the best place to describe it. We hope you agree.

Remote access equipment is fundamentally a shared resource. Through the course of a day, many users dial in, connect, disconnect, and dial back in to the network. The transience of dial connections allows the Service Provider to reap economies of scale from the RAC infrastructure that are not possible with dedicated access. Even with the economies of scale, however, many Service Providers have decided that supplying (building, supporting, maintaining, etc.) the physical access infrastructure is just not worth it. These providers (AOL is a good example) are quite content to focus their efforts on providing Internet content. Their model is, quite simply, to outsource the physical access infrastructure (i.e., the modem ports) to a larger provider. The larger provider, called the *wholesaler*, allocates a portion of its dial network to the content provider, who we will call the *wholesale subscriber*. This has been, and will continue to be, a successful model for Internet and other information access. The new twist to this, of course, is VPN services.

Dial VPN wholesaling is a *two-tiered* approach to offering dial VPN services. In a single-tiered system, the service provider deploys the RAC

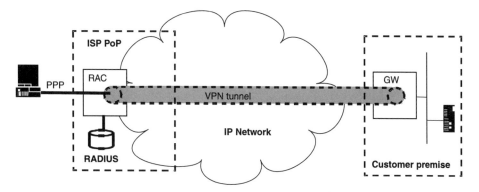

Figure 5.11 Typical Single-tiered Provider-based Dial VPN Model

infrastructure *and* offers the VPN service. As shown in Figure 5.11, there is no wholesaler in a single-tiered service.

With the two-tiered approach, the *wholesaler* implements and maintains both the RAC infrastructure and the technology used to implement the VPN service; however, the *wholesale subscriber* is actually the VPN Service Provider (as far as its own customers are concerned). Table 5.1 summarizes this hierarchy.

In the end, you *could* say that the two tiered VPN approach *virtualizes* the ISP PoP within the wholesaler's *physical* PoP.

Figure 5.12 graphically describes this. Let's first assume that the service uses a Hybrid Provider tunneling model based on L2TP, with the VPN tunnel terminating at the customer premise in a gateway functioning as the L2TP LNS.

Figure 5.12 shows two scenarios for two-tiered VPN service deployment. In Scenario 1, the wholesaler initiates the L2TP tunnel in its own

Table 5.1 Summary of Port Wholesaling Hierarchy Roles

	Buys	**Sells**	**Customer**
Wholesaler	Equipment to deploy service from manufacturer	Wholesale VPN services, ports	Wholesale subscriber (ISP)
Wholesale Subscriber (ISP)	Wholesale services from wholesaler	VPN services	Enterprise organization
Enterprise Organization	VPN services from wholesale subscriber (ISP)	Nothing	End users

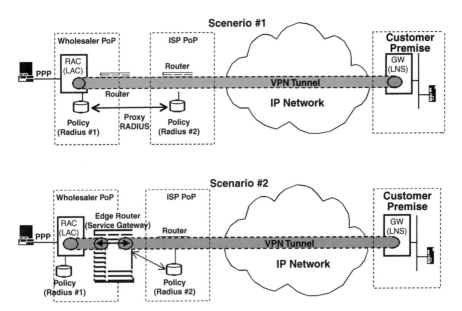

Figure 5.12 Two Scenarios for Two-tiered Wholesale VPN Services

RAC using a *proxy RADIUS* functionality to acquire the appropriate tunnel attribute values from the ISP RADIUS server. Still another RADIUS server, or another mechanism such as a token, performs user-level authentication at the customer premise. With proxy RADIUS, one RADIUS server queries a second RADIUS server on behalf of the requesting RADIUS client. Here's a brief description of how the process might initiate in Scenario 1:

1. User dials in to the wholesaler's RAC.

2. RADIUS client (in wholesaler's RAC) sends Authentication Request to RADIUS 1.

3. RADIUS 1 looks up user/domain information in RADIUS database, matching contents of Authentication Request packet against its records. Based on domain information, RADIUS 1 identifies user as a "tunneling" client.

4. Database record for user also indicates a RADIUS proxy function and lists the address of RADIUS 2 as the actual server where tunnel authentication shall take place.

5. RADIUS 1 issues the RADIUS authentication query to RADIUS 2 using the domain name only as the identifier.

6. RADIUS 2 authenticates the domain name, starts an accounting record, and responds to RADIUS 1 with all necessary tunnel attributes contained in the response.

7. RADIUS 1 starts its own accounting record and begins L2TP tunnel registration per the values contained in the attributes received from RADIUS 2 and its own policy records for the wholesale subscriber (ISP).

In theory, Scenario 1 would work fine; however, it may be challenging to both the wholesaler and the ISP in terms of the amount of specialized RADIUS work required to enable the intricacies (management, accounting, etc.) of the service to work properly. Another possible issue is security of the RADIUS infrastructure. Proxy RADIUS works fine within a single organization or between two trusted parties; however, in certain cases, the wholesaler and the ISP may be competitors as well as partners (particularly in the age of deregulation!). The ISP may not be comfortable giving its vendor access to potentially confidential customer records. Scenario 2 presents a possible alternative.

In Scenario 2, the wholesaler has deployed an edge router device that functions as a "service gateway" for its wholesale subscribers. One of the services possible with this device is outsourced VPN service. In this scenario, the wholesaler provisions virtual L2TP "instances" in the service gateway that function on behalf of its VPN wholesale customer, the ISP.

Also in Scenario 2, note the presence of two distinct tunnels "mapped" together within the service gateway. Here's how the process would initiate:

1. User dials in to the wholesaler's RAC. RADIUS client in wholesaler's RAC sends Authentication Request to RADIUS 1.

2. RADIUS 1 looks up domain or dialed number information in RADIUS database. Based on results, RADIUS 1 identifies user as a "tunneling" client and sends all pertinent information to the RAC in a RADIUS response. RADIUS 1 starts accounting record.

3. Based on attribute/value information received from RADIUS 1, RAC builds L2TP tunnel to the correct service gateway.

4. Service gateway/LNS strips off the L2TP header and hands the packet over to the service gateway's policy mechanism.

5. Using this mechanism, the service gateway examines the packet and, based on its destination IP address, sends a RADIUS re-

quest to the wholesale subscriber's (ISP) Policy/RADIUS server (RADIUS 2).

6. RADIUS 2 looks up customer information in its own database and responds to the service gateway with a RADIUS packet containing all required information to build a tunnel between the service gateway (LAC) and the home network LNS. RADIUS 2 starts the accounting record.

7. Service gateway encapsulates packet in another L2TP packet (LAC function of the service gateway) destined for the "home" network.

8. User is authenticated by mechanism (RADIUS, token, other) on "home" network.

One advantage of this scenario is that the service gateway's LAC is specifically tied to its subscriber's Authentication, Policy, and Billing/Accounting systems (without giving the wholesaler actual access to the customer records!). A second advantage is that the wholesaler can dedicate many instances of these service "elements" to each of its wholesale subscribers. The "new breed" edge devices used for these services scale to support upwards of 100,000 subscribers simultaneously and offer functionality far beyond what is available with a simply proxy-based service. We covered these devices in depth earlier in the chapter. The down side? Well, the up-front investment in equipment by the wholesaler is much greater than a two-tiered service built on proxy functionality. However, the cost is negated (to a large extent) by the additional revenues that all of these wholesale services generate.

By outsourcing the modem shelves and the VPN technology elements to a wholesaler, the ISP can sell its customers a VPN service with specific service-level functionality without having to invest a single penny into remote access or VPN infrastructure. This is a win-win-win-win:

Win 1—The wholesaler generates new revenues and continues to drive economies of scale from the physical network it has built.

Win 2—The ISP also drives new service revenues while continuing to keep costs down.

Win 3—The customer saves a fortune in remote access costs and provides its users with secure simple access to the corporate LAN.

Win 4—We, the authors of this book, have helped generate Wins 1-3, making everybody happy!

To summarize, then, the use of Remote Access Concentrators in VPN services:

♦ Many of today's Remote Access Concentrators feature VPN protocol support.

♦ Remote Access Concentrators utilize compulsory tunneling to enable VPDN services.

♦ Remote Access Concentrators with built-in wholesaling capabilities work in conjunction with specialized service gateway products to build powerful two-tiered outsourced VPDN services.

Summary

This chapter gave an overview of the types of products and platforms used for VPN services. Some of these platforms and products are designed for enterprise deployment and some are designed for deployment within the Service Provider network. Some are software-based and some are hardware-based.

When choosing your preferred solution, make sure to go with a product or solution that fits all of your needs. In particular, keep in mind your needs for scalability and performance and look for a product that implements strong security (this is especially true when evaluating provider-offered services that by definition shield you from the actual functionality within the "cloud"). Standards are also very important. Proprietary schemes can lock you out of interoperating with business partners or other companies that become one in this era of mergers and acquisitions.

We hope we have given you some direction and a way to narrow down your choices so that the time it takes you to complete your evaluation is shorter.

CHAPTER

6

The Enterprise Environment for VPNs

"Life is cheap. It's the accessories that kill you." We were unable to find an attribution for this famous piece of conventional wisdom, but it certainly serves to introduce the topic of this chapter: auxiliary services that complement and enable VPNs. As we have seen from the preceding chapters, the protocol mechanisms that enable VPNs are relatively straightforward. However, in order to integrate into today's networking environment, the VPN must support current and emerging distributed computing support services. These are series of common functions like authorization, user directories, accounting, bandwidth management, and other network management functions that typically live in the enterprise network operations center and are seen as the glue that binds the various networked applications into a distributed sys-

169

tem. The following discussion gives an introduction to this environment and discusses deployment and implementation issues related to VPNs. As implied, in the opening, it is often these "accessories" that cause the most issues in many VPN deployments.

One topic some readers might expect to see in a chapter on the enterprise environment for VPNs is a discussion of network management issues. These are often the services that enterprises want outsourced to Service Providers. We have included most of management discussions in Chapter 7, The Service Provider Environment for VPNs, where we discuss basic technology issues as well as the special problems of managing lots of VPN devices.

Authentication Services

The first multiuser time-sharing systems required mechanisms that determined whether a users was authorized to use the system. Once "logged on," they acquired an identity that determined their access rights and priority to system resources. The rise of distributed computing added a number of complexities to the initially simple process:

- Users usually accessed a number of systems, each with its corresponding authorization mechanism, user identity, and password.

- Networks opened up the company's resources to new populations of people who could try to gain unauthorized access.

- The authentication dialog itself crossed unsecured transmission systems and needed to be protected from interference or interception.

Authentication in Layer 2 Tunneling Architectures

The Point-to-Point Protocol or PPP is designed to connect systems, routers, and bridges over simple point-to-point links. PPP provides three main services: encapsulation, link control procedures, and network control procedures. Included as part of the link control procedures is the authentication of the identity of the peers on the data link. Two methods are commonly implemented to support this authentication: the Password Authentication Protocol (PAP) and the Challenge Response Authentication Protocol (CHAP).

In Chapter 4, we talked about Layer 2 tunneling such as L2TP and PPTP. These protocols operate by encapsulating entire PPP frames in a tunnel header to provide a Virtual Private Network. This encapsulation includes not only the user data, but the link control procedures involved in the authentication of the VPN clients for purposes of authorizing them to use the tunnel and the computing resources reached through it.

The PAP protocol is the simplest. An ID/Password pair is sent repeatedly by the requested peer until acknowledged. Originally, PAP was designed for implementations that needed a clear text password to simulate a login. If the receiver has the ability to decrypt a password, it can be sent encrypted, but the username is sent in the clear.

The CHAP protocol can be used to periodically authenticate the identity of a peer, but is typically only done at link establishment. CHAP involves a three-way handshake. The authenticator sends a "challenge" to the peer, the peer calculates a response using a one-way hash function based on the password, and finally the authenticator receives the response and verifies it against its own calculated value of the hash. If they match, the peer is authenticated. CHAP is a much stronger authentication approach than PAP, since passwords are never transmitted over the Internet.

While the data payload may be encrypted (for example, in PPTP), the link control procedures generally occur in the clear, albeit within the tunnel header. This provides a standardized and well-understood mechanism for providing the authentication function, and provides broad interoperability between vendor implementation. However, moving the function from traditional point-to-point environment to that of the Internet opens up new threats that need to be analyzed.

Microsoft in particular has recognized some of these threats and has made a number of enhancements to PPTP, with more to come in the Windows 2000 next-generation operating system. A recent upgrade to dial-up networking (DUN) provided the MS-CHAP protocol that tightened up the security and key generation properties of CHAP. Nevertheless, there are still areas to improve. Both L2TP and PPTP are looking at methods to protect and secure their control channels (where authentication and tunnel setup occur).

In the following sections we discuss a number of emerging alternatives to text-based passwords. In general, the current PPP link control procedures (PAP, CHAP, and MS-CHAP) are not very good at supporting these alternatives. A new procedure, the Extensible Authentication Protocol or EAP will be available in Windows 2000. EAP will provide an extensible Application Programming Interface (API) that allows developers of different authorization services to interface with the PPP link control protocol. This will give Layer 2 tunneling protocols like PPTP and L2TP much more flexibility to implement different authentication systems.

Authentication in IPSec

Since IPSec is not a Layer 2 tunneling protocol, it is not required to use the authentication methods available in PPP. IPSec deals with the more general problem of "key management." The Layer 2 tunneling protocols are most often used in remote access applications. IPSec, on the other hand, is often used for LAN-to-LAN leased line replacement applications, host-to-host applications, and of course the remote access applications we have been discussing. As we have mentioned earlier, applications such as the ANX and ICSA certification are driving interoperability of the LAN-to-LAN application, using shared secrets or X.509 certificates. The same cannot be said about the remote access application. Mechanisms for end-user authentication, address assignment, or attribute negotiation (gateways, DNS servers, etc.), have not been standardized. As of this writing, IPSec dial clients distributed by most VPN vendors are proprietary, and one vendor's IPSec dial client will not interoperate with a VPN server from another vendor. This is particularly true when the clients require dynamic address assignment.

As described in Chapter 4, the IPSec protocol involves setting up a Security Association (SA) that protects the user's data as it passes over a shared network. How the keys for the security algorithms used in the IPSec security associations are established is the key management system. In order to be ICSA certified, IPSec implementations are required to support automated keying methods. While manual keying may be useful in smaller VPNs, most of the interest is directed towards the ISAKMP/OAKLEY or Internet Key Exchange (IKE). IKE manages the establishment and deletion of IPSec security associations by setting up a special ISAKMP Security Association to provide a secure channel to exchange the required parameters and authorization information. IKE can dynamically manage the encryption keys for the various IPSec security algorithms selected by the user. For example, it can renegotiate keys after a specific time interval or byte count. Changing the crypto keys regularly makes it much harder to mount a brute force decryption attack on the data.

As we will see, remote access users typically want to use a variety of authentication protocols including RADIUS, Token authentication, and X.509 certificates. The extent that any IPSec dial client supports these methods needs to be verified. Each vendor's VPN client has a different strategy for interfacing these methods to its client. Special care should be taken to understand the security implications of the vendor's choice. For instance, passing username in the clear to support a RADIUS authentication is a relatively weak approach and can obviate much of the security technology of IPSec.

Other keying methods such as the Simple Key Management for Internet Protocol (SKIP) or PHOTURIS are occasionally encountered in the market. IKE has been selected as the default automated key management protocol for IPSec. The Automotive Network eXchange (ANX) has also selected IKE as the required key management system. Thus we expect to see increased interoperability in IPSec implementations, especially in LAN-to-LAN applications.

IKE Main Mode and Aggressive Mode

Two sites (or companies) having public IP addresses on the Internet are able to establish a LAN-to-LAN style VPN connection with IPSec. Unlike remote access users, who may roam from city to city (and Internet Service Provider to Internet Service Provider), the addresses of the two sites stay relatively stable. Since the key generation algorithms required to create an IPSec security association are computationally intense (as many as 1 million 32-bit multiplies), a VPN server may not wish to negotiate with an unknown party. The server will typically verify an incoming IPSec connection request against a pre-configured database of public IP addresses for known branch offices. If the connection comes from a site it knows about, it will invest the resources to create the ISAKMP security association and proceed to further authenticate the remote branch office. This is known as the *main mode* option of the Internet Key Exchange.

Since remote access VPN users will often have a different public address each time they connect to the Internet, the VPN server has two choices for remote access. It could simply accept all *main mode* connection requests, spending the resources to create a security association in order to see authentication information. Alternatively, the remote client can send an ID payload (for example, its username) in the initial connect message. The VPN server can than verify this username against a preconfigured database before creating the security association and actually authenticating the user. This is called the *aggressive mode* option of IPSec.

As we have stated above, the main mode option of IKE is well standardized and tested by the ICSA. Aggressive mode is not currently tested and most versions are proprietary. There are a number of main mode client implementations available that enjoy good interoperability with many VPN servers, but these implementations typically must be configured like branch office connections coming from fixed IP addresses. Enterprises considering IPSec client software for remote access VPNs need to understand if the client supports dynamically assigned public addresses.

Remote Authentication Dial-In User Service (RADIUS)

Organizations typically have many applications requiring user authentication: access to timesharing machines, traditional dial-up, access to file and print services, and of course access to VPNs. Traditionally, three basic services are required to support these environments. The Authentication process determines who can access the resource; Authorization is the assignment of user parameters based on a predefined user profile and security clearance; and Accounting records what activities the user did typically for billing purposes. RADIUS is a protocol originally developed by Livingston Enterprises (now owned by Lucent) to perform these AAA services in a distributed manner—so that they need not be implemented separately for every application. RADIUS in now standardized by the Internet Engineering Taskforce (IETF) and is widely available in high-quality implementations with well-established multivendor interoperability. Many enterprises, both large and small, have deployed RADIUS servers to handle their AAA requirements.

Most VPN devices work well with RADIUS servers for the authentication and accounting functions. Usernames and passwords received by the VPN server from IKE, PAP, or CHAP processing are relayed to an enterprise RADIUS server for authentication. If the password matches that in the database, the tunnel gets established and an accounting START record is written for the user.

The authorization process is a little more complicated. Even in traditional remote access applications, problems of interoperability often come up. The basis for authorization in RADIUS is known as attribute exchange. There are two types of attributes:

◆ *Checklist Attributes*   The RADIUS client, that is, the VPN server or the Remote Access Concentrator, can send information in addition to the username and password that the RADIUS server can use in determining whether to authenticate the user. Common items include the Caller-ID (phone number) from where the user is dialing in or whether the line type is ISDN or analog. A user not dialing in from his or her home, for example, would be denied access even though the correct user name and password were entered.

♦ *Return Attributes*   The RADIUS server can send to the client attribute/value pairs for use during the connected session, in addition to the go/no-go authentication. They include items such as the network address for the client station, session time limits, data compression options, or address filtering rules, among many others.

This area of the RADIUS protocol is the least standardized among different vendors and devices. Exchange of attribute pairs between the RADIUS server and the access device is controlled by vendor dictionaries. Users who have made extensive use of these "vendor specific attributes" may find that applications related to these attributes are not available in the VPN, or if they are available, they are implemented through another mechanism. Generally, the industry has recognized the problem and is moving towards other more standardized and robust methods for the authorization portion of the RADIUS protocol. In particular, the LDAP protocol discussed below is emerging as the standard for user attribute storage across the enterprise.

RADIUS Proxy

Many RADIUS servers today have the ability to forward authentication requests on to a second RADIUS server. This capability is often used in VPNs, both as an authentication mechanism between the Service Provider and the customer, as well as between Service Providers to provide an Internet "roaming" capability.

Imagine that a large enterprise getting Internet accounts for its 70,000 employees. Rather than force users to remember two possibly different usernames and passwords (one for the Internet and one for the intranet), the Service Provider may want to proxy against the enterprise VPN server or RADIUS server.

Other Password Servers

Enterprises often have existing user databases that they may want to use in to authenticate their VPN users. Some very popular access methods found in companies today include:

♦ The Novell Directory Service/Bindery used in Novell IPX networks

♦ Windows NT Domains or HOSTS files used in Microsoft NT networks

♦ Sun Microsystems Network Information System (NIS+) used with UNIX systems

- ◆ Cisco Terminal Access Controller Access Control System (TACACS+) used with typically with Cisco equipment
- ◆ SQL or ODBC database files
- ◆ Kerberos from the MIT Athena project

The same pool of users may need to switch back and forth between traditional access methods and VPNs. Duplicating databases causes a lot of work for the network administrator. Many RADIUS servers today can use the methods listed above as authentication databases. In this way, newer VPN servers can talk to the RADIUS server, which in turn passes the actual authentication request to the backend server actually holding the user record. Below we see how a RADIUS server can also be an interface into newer nonpassword or token-based systems. In this way, newer VPN devices do not have to know how to interface with all of these legacy systems and users have a migration path.

One-time Password Systems

Password-based systems rely on information users know—their passwords! There are other "factors" that can also be used to authenticate the users, such as something they have—a card or key—or something unique about them such as their fingerprints or voiceprints. These systems are generally known as two-factor authentication systems and are often more secure than just a password alone. With two-factor systems, one of the biggest problems with authentication problems can be overcome: weak passwords. This doesn't solve all of the problems, especially in the case of VPN. Once the user enters the password information, this information is transmitted over a network, and key information can be intercepted and perhaps replayed at a later time.

Recently a number of systems have been commercialized to help with both these problems. Like a two-factor system, they require that users know something—their passwords—and have something—typically a calculator-like device or smart card. These devices will generate a new *one-time* password that the user enters to be authenticated. This password is used for only one session. The next time the user wishes access the system, the password will be different. Thus any password captured by a malicious party would be useless for access to any later session.

There are a number of variations on the one-time password concept. Simple systems are called *shared sequence systems*. In this type of system both the user and the authentication server have access to a list of pass-

Figure 6.1 One-time Password Token Cards: Safe Word for Secure Computing on the
Left and Security Dynamics SecurID Card on the Right

words that the user can cycle through for each access. In the case of the
token cards like the ones shown in Figure 6.1, the list may be based on a
mathematical function that is recalculated every minute or so. When the
user wishes logon, they use the password displayed on the screen at the
time. This code may be appended to the user's traditional password or
entered in a special field on an authentication screen depending on the
implementation.

Another type of system is called *challenge-response*. These require the
token cards with keypad as pictured in Figure 6.1. Here the authentication server sends down a challenge, which the user enters into the "calculator," and the result is then entered as part of the logon process. This
type of system can be even more secure since the user may have to enter a
password to enable the calculator.

These types of password systems have added relevance to VPNs. A
key issue for users is understanding what support their VPN equipment
has for one-time passwords. The authentication server piece of many of
the systems described above interfaces with network equipment via the
RADIUS protocol. So often if the VPN device supports RADIUS, it will
support the simpler one-time password systems. Even simple systems
often require special form and message exchange between the authentication server and the VPN client. The PAP and CHAP protocol discussed
that is used for password exchanges between many of the Layer 2 tunneling protocols will not support these messages. Challenge-response systems may not be supported at all and shared-sequence systems may have
reduced functionality. IPSec-based systems often have their own client
software and are not constrained to a particular authentication message
exchange approach. The user, however, needs to verify the level of sup-

port in any given product as well as the one-time password vendors that are supported for use with the VPN model.

Public Key Infrastructure

Public and Secret Key Cryptosystems

There are two broad categories of cryptosystems that enable parties to communicate securely: secret key systems and public key systems. In secret key systems, both parties prearrange a secret key that only they know, which is input into both the encryption and decryption algorithm. The big problem is how the sender and receiver can coordinate the exchange of the secret key. This problem is exacerbated when the number of people with which a party may wish to communicate is large and diverse. On the positive side, secret key systems are quick and easy to calculate for streams of data typically found in networking today. Some popular secret key cryptosystems include the Data Encryption Standard (DES) and Triple DES often used in IPSec and Rivest Cipher 4 or RC4 used in PPTP.

In the early 1970s Whitfield Diffie and Martin Hellman developed the magnificent concept of public key cryptography. Here each party to communications has two keys. A public key is published to world, and a mathematically related private key is kept secret. When Alice wants to a message to Bob, she will look up Bob's public key and use it to encrypt her message. The public key and private keys are related such that only Bob's private key can decrypt the message. In this way anybody who can look up Bob's public key can send him a message but only Bob can read it.

Public key algorithms tend to be a little more difficult to calculate. So in VPNs and other applications, public key encryption is often used as an "digital envelope" to facilitate the sharing of secret key information. Diffie and Hellman have also looked at the problem of how users can securely exchange a secret key. The Diffie-Hellman algorithm that is the basis for the IKE key exchange uses two publicly known, mathematically related values that allow two parties to calculate a common secret key from separately generated random numbers.

Another wonderful characteristic of public key cryptography is it can easily be used to "digitally sign" a message to assure Bob that Alice is truly Alice and no one else. Alice can encrypt the message with her private key and attach it to the original message as a signature. When Bob receives it, he can look up Alice's public key and use that to decrypt the message. If the message Bob decrypted with Alice's public key is the same as the original message decrypted with his private key, Bob can be sure it came from Alice, since only Alice has access to her private key. The digital signature is based on both the document and the private key of the sender.

Rather than attach an encrypted copy of the whole message, a better approach would be to encrypt just a summary or "digest" of the message. The mathematical function that takes an arbitrary length input string and creates (a typically small) fixed length output is called a *hash*. A good hash is easy to compute for a given input, but it is difficult or impossible to reconstitute the original message from the hash. In addition, two different input strings should not generate the same hash. Two common hash functions found in VPNs are Message Digest 5 (MD5) and Secure Hash Algorithm 1 (SHA-1). An overview of these algorithms is shown in Figure 6.2.

In summary, public key cryptography has broad application for:

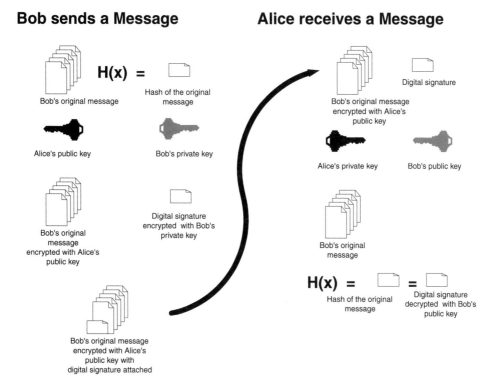

Figure 6.2 **Sending a Digitally Signed Message with Public Key Encryption**

♦ Secure communications between individuals via encryption

♦ Access control

♦ Identification and authentication

♦ Data integrity

♦ Nonrepudiation (users who sign messages cannot later deny they sent them)

These features can be used to securely enable a broad range of applications: VPNs, remote access, electronic commerce, secure E-mail, and conferencing. The list can go on and on.

Public Key Infrastructure Standards

We saw above how useful public key cryptography can be. But to put public key technology into production is a significant management task. Some questions we may ask include:

♦ How do public keys get generated?

♦ In what formats are they stored?

♦ How do users find public keys of others?

♦ How can I revoke a key after I have issued it?

♦ What should be the lifetime of a public key?

♦ How should applications such as VPNs use public keys?

Standards for protocols, data formats, and procedures to deploy manageable public cryptography within enterprises and the Internet community at large is known as the Public Key Infrastructure or PKI. Many of these standards are still evolving, and like many standards they are largely application driven. Electronic commerce using Secure Socket Layer (SSL) and Secure Electronic Transactions (SET), security-enhanced E-mail, and of course VPNs are leading the way.

Two key standards bodies are active in promoting standards for the Public Key Infrastructure: one driven by RSA—the Public Key Cryptography Standard or PKCS—and the other a working group in the Internet Engineering Task Force (IETF) called the Public Key Infrastructure Working Group, whose specifications use the PKIX acronym. One of the cornerstone standards of the PKI was originally part of the OSI protocol X.500 mail standards developed by the International Telecommunications Union (ITU-T). The X.509 standard is used for binding a user identity with a public key value. This is the X.509 "certificate" that is the basic currency of the public key infrastructure. Once public key certificates are generated, they will typically be stored in a publicly accessible directory. A scalable, robust directory service is the foundation for the widespread usability of a public key infrastructure. The obvious choice for this directory is the Lightweight Directory Access Protocol or LDAP. LDAP is discussed in detail in the next section. Even the American Bar Association (ABA) is joining the standards fray on this one by issuing special guidelines on digital signatures. An overview of the standards promulgated by these groups is shown in Figure 6.3.

Vendors are also key drivers shaping the deployment of the Public Key Infrastructure. To the extent that they can offer complete, functional, and cost-effective solutions, enterprises will be more inclined to implement them. Two vendors have taken early leads in this area: VeriSign, a spin-off from RSA Laboratories, and Entrust, a spin-off of Northern Telecom. Netscape also has bundled many certificate management functions in its SuiteSpot server, and Microsoft has announced plans to ship a certificate server on NT Server.

Key PKI Vendors

RSA Data Security.

A Security Dynamics Company

PKCS #1-14
PKCS #7 defines a general syntax for messages
PKCS #10 describes syntax for certification requests.
PKCS #12 Cert Wallet

Guidelines on Digital Signiture

I E T F

PKIX
Part I: X.509 Certificate and CRL Profile
Part 2: Operational Protocols
Part 3: Certificate Management Protocols
Part 4: Certificate Practice and Policy Statements

x.509

" version
" serial number
" signature algorithm ID
" issuer name
" validity period
" subject (user) name
" subject public key information
" issuer unique identifier (version 2 and 3 only)
" subject unique identifier (version 2 and 3 only)
" extensions (version 3 only)
" signature on the above fields

Figure 6.3 Key Players and Standards in the Public Key Infrastructure

Operational Overview of the Public Key Infrastructure

Since this is a book on VPNs, let's walk through an example of how a remote access VPN client would use a Public Key Infrastructure for VPN authentication.

Initialization

- The *principal* or VPN user runs PKI software on his or her client to generate a public/private key pair.

Registration

- The principal presents himself or herself to a *certificate authority (CA)*. Depending on the application, the principal may need to supply proof of identity. Occasionally, the certificate authority may generate the public/private keys on behalf of the application.

Certification

- The certificate authority generates an X.509 certificate with the agreed-upon validity period and signs it with its own private key.
- The PKI client requests the import of the X.509 certificate.
- The CA publishes the Client Certificate in a publicly accessible user certificate store (typically an LDAP directory).

Operation

- The VPN client signs a tunnel connection request with its private key and sends it to the VPN server along with a copy of its X.509 certificate.
- The VPN server uses the public key of the certificate authority to validate the VPN client's X.509 certificate.
- If the request was valid, the VPN server checks a special Certificate Revocation List published in the certificate directory to insure that the client's certificate has not been revoked by the Certificate Authority (for example, when an employee is fired).
- The VPN server checks to see if the certificate is still valid and that its expiration date has not passed.
- The VPN uses the VPN client's public key in the certificate to verify the validity of the tunnel connection request.
- The VPN server may have to validate itself to the VPN client using the same process.

Deployment Considerations for the Public Key Infrastructure

The above overview of the use of X.509 certificates for VPN authentication is somewhat skeletal. We didn't discuss many of the key deployment issues that an enterprise may face when considering deploying a Public Key Infrastructure in their organizations. Some of the thornier ones include:

- Trust Issues
  - Certifying the certificate authority
  - Cross certification of other certificate authorities
  - Operation security for the certificate authority
- Other Key Management Issues
  - Updating expired keys
  - Recovery of lost keys
  - Archiving keys for used on long-duration transactions (like contracts)
  - Frequency of revocation list publication

These issues are somewhat beyond the scope of this book and we refer readers to some of the resources in our bibliography for a more in-depth discussion of these and other issues. We believe that implementation of the Public Key Infrastructure is possible today but is not a project to be taken lightly. As standards are still evolving, wide-scale interoperability should not be expected.

An organization can also consider outsourcing its implementation of PKI. As noted above, there are a number of large management tasks associated with issuing and using certificates, and the enterprise may just not have the bandwidth for these tasks. Even before the creation of the Public Key Infrastructure, organizations have considered outsourcing the job of password management, as this has become a bigger and bigger job. In the VPN context, this can be a value-added service from the Service Provider and is discussed further in the next chapter. Outsourcing a Public Key Infrastructure deployment has the potential to touch many more applications and needs to be considered more carefully. Many of the issues around outsourcing are not technical—they relate to issue of liability, scope of responsibility, and trust. Nevertheless, outsourced PKI services are available today with more on the horizon. Again, the American Bar Association has entered the discussion to with guidelines on fiduciary responsibilities as well as other policies and practices around outsourced

PKI. These issues have further applicability when VPNs are used in the context of an extranet where two independent companies are using the certificate to authenticate or authorize electronic purchase orders, for example, versus when used as authentication for remote access within a single company.

The Lightweight Directory Protocol (LDAP)

In the discussion of Public Key Infrastructure, we mentioned that a directory service in which to store end-user certificates was an absolute requirement. In our discussions on the RADIUS protocol we pointed out that the RADIUS database is being increasingly used as a repository of used authorization attributes. These VPN specific requirements are just some of the applications of a more generalized directory service for the Internet. Most of us are familiar with the structure and operation of the Domain Name Service (DNS, which is discussed further below). LDAP provides a more generalized capability similar to both the White and Yellow Pages directories for the phone system.

As part of the Open Systems Integration (OSI) standardization effort started in the early 1980s, the X.500 Directory Access Protocol was developed to provide this function. Consistent with its desire to standardize everything in the universe, X.500 proposed a hierarchical Directory Information Tree (DIT). Below a fixed "root" directory were nodes for countries followed by entries for companies or other organizations such as states or agencies. Within these are entries for organizational units such as sales, marketing, or engineering, and finally, entries for individuals and other resources such as shared folders, printers, and VPN devices. Figure 6.4 shows the directory hierarchy for Babs Jansen in her new career in product development for Ace Industry. The *dn* or distinguished names defines her unique entry in the LDAP Directory Information Tree. The dn is made up of her first *cn* or common name entry, along with the hierarchy or organizational units, organization, and finally country. The entry gives a number of useful attributes such as her phone number and email address.

Figure 6.4 shows a Directory User Agent (such as a VPN server) using the LDAP protocol to request information about a person, for example, for the purpose of completing a remote access VPN request. The directory in the figure is modeled on the X.500 standard with multiple, perhaps replicated, Directory System Agents. Each holds a portion of the

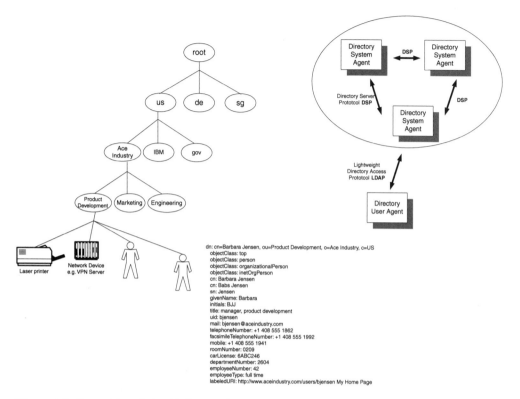

Figure 6.4 Overview of the Lightweight Directory Access Protocol

directory tree and the agents communicate to resolve the directory request. In most commercial LDAP servers this is rarely the case. While today most of these servers do offer replication capability, the directory tree is assumed to be an island, and an LDAP client needs to know which server contains the information it needs. A Lightweight Directory Interchange Format (LDIF) has been developed to allow interchange of data between servers. This can be used to offload directory data from an LDAP database internal to a VPN server to an external one on the net or to create a backup server to primary.

In looking at the contents of the directory entry above, perhaps the first question that arises is what kind of security protects this data. The LDAP V3 specification supports the use of the Secure Socket Layer (SSL). SSL can protect directory data by requiring authorization of clients, and it can also encrypt data passing between the client and server. SSL can be used in conjunction with X.509 certificates for enhanced authentication. But, as of this writing, there is no mechanism to insure that only data of direct interest to the authenticated client is visible. Note that only version 3 LDAP servers should be of interest to VPN applications, since the previous version did not support the syntax to store X.509 certificates.

Address management

In our discussion on authentication we looked at traditional the PPP initialization and compared this to what happens in tunneled connections. The same approach is useful in address management. Most of the issues in address management arise in the remote access VPN application since in the LAN-to-LAN application the tunnel endpoints will most likely need to be fixed in advanced. For remote access VPNs, it is often desirable that the user appears to the network in the same manner as if they had dialed in to a traditional remote access server with a modem.

The user needs to have an address assigned from the address space of the intranet into which they are dialing in order to function as a part of that network. Address assignment usually happens by one of four methods:

- The user's IP address is hard coded on their PC.
- The remote access server dynamically assigns the user an IP address from an internal address pool set up within the server.
- The RADIUS authentication server assigns the user an IP address as part of the authentication process. The address can be a fixed one associated with the individual user or drawn from a RADIUS managed address pool.
- The user can have an address dynamically assigned from an address pool on a external server, managed by the Dynamic Host Configuration Protocol (DHCP).

In VPN applications, methods assigning the address from an address pool are the most often used. Address space can be a precious commodity and preallocating IP addresses to individual users, whether or not they are currently connected, can use up a lot of addresses. The key challenge in assigning addresses from a pool typically involves putting them back when the user logs off. In the case where a user's PC crashes or experiences networking problems, the user's address may not be returned. This is known as pool "leakage." Over time this leakage can build up, emptying the pool that would cause subsequent users to be denied service. The Dynamic Host Configuration Protocol, DHCP, protects against this eventuality by using a system of "leases" that must be renewed periodically. If a client does not renew their lease, the address is returned to the pool rather than lost. On the other hand, many RADIUS address pools suffer from the problem of leakage.

Figure 6.5 shows the addressing environment in a typical remote access VPN environment. In this example, a VPN server has been added as a supplementary application to an existing Internet connection. An industry standard IP router (perhaps managed by the Internet Service Provider) connected the company to the public Internet. A firewall protects the company network from unauthorized access and provides Network Address Translation services for the company's private address. Network Address Translation and private address spaces are discussed further below. From its Internet Service Provider, the company received a block of public addresses between 142.19.2.16 and 142.19.2.31, accessible from anywhere on the Internet. The company has assigned public addresses to a Web server used to advertise the company's product on the Internet and to the firewall that will pass public E-mail to internal users and route Web traffic back and forth to internal surfers, among other things. The new public interface of the VPN server has also been placed on this segment in order to receive tunnel requests from users anywhere on the Internet.

The company's intranet was built before the company decided to connect to the Internet and was numbered from a "private" address space 10.0.0.0. This network is special on the Internet in that nobody owns it and routing information to it is not carried in the public network. The company has a great deal of flexibility to attach as many systems as it wants,

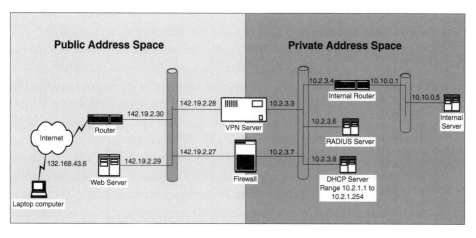

Figure 6.5 Typical Addressing Environment in a Remote Access VPN

subdivide (subnet) its network any way it wishes, and the whole issue of address management has been greatly simplified. However, in order to access systems on the public network from the internal network the company must implement Network Address Translation (NAT) on its firewall to map an internal user's private network address to a public one that is reachable on the Internet. This type of Network Address Translation is typically called "many-to-one," since one or a few public Internet addresses are mapped to serve a large community of internal users. Another kind of Network Address Translation, "mny-to-many," is discussed in conjunction with LAN-to-LAN applications.

We are now ready to examine how a remote VPN user will get assigned an IP address. In this section we will examine principally the case of end-to-end tunneling models such as IPSec and PPTP. Address assignment in hybrid models such as L2TP are a little different, although many of the same principles apply. We will examine these in more detail in the next chapter. When the user brings their computers up on the public network, it is assigned a publicly routable address using one of the four methods mentioned above. This address is typically known as the "outer address." This allows the PC to browse the World Wide Web and access many other applications on the public Internet. Of course, now the company's VPN server is also publicly accessible as well. The user launches their VPN client application (IPSec or PPTP) and connects to company's VPN server.

In the case of Layer 2 tunneling models, once the user is authenticated, the Network Control Protocol in PPP functions in the same way as when the user dials into a remote access concentrator. The VPN server manages the address assignment with client via the services (RADIUS, DHCP, etc.) mentioned above, using the standard operation of the PPP protocol. The client negotiates the "inner address," typically within the enterprise address block. Note that Network Address Translation is usually not needed, even if the enterprise uses a private address space. The inner packet that contains the source and destination addresses is tunneled inside of the outer packet that contains the user's public address and the public address of the enterprise VPN server.

In the case of IPSec remote access, the situation is less clear. Operation proceeds much as above with the user establishing a connection to the public network, then launching their IPSec application to create the tunnel. Address assignment protocol mechanisms haven't yet been standardized in IPSec, and although a number of proposals have been put forward, most vendor clients perform this function in a different noninteroperable manner. This is one of the main reasons why there isn't the same broad inter-operability of IPSec remote access clients as there is with the Layer 2 models. One approach that is common is to use the DHCP protocol to communicate with the client for address assignment, even if a RADIUS server or the VPN server ultimately assigns the address.

Once the client is assigned an IP address, it must be advertised to other devices within the enterprise intranet. Servers and other resources that the user may wish to communicate with have to know that the path back to the user is via the VPN server. This is typically a function of a routing protocol. Some VPN servers have the ability to advertise subnets reachable through them to other routers within the network. They can use protocols such as the Routing Information Protocol (RIP) or the Open Shortest Path First (OSPF). With other VPN servers these routes must be manually entered into a neighbor router for propagation throughout the intranet.

Name Services

We are hoping that most readers have a basic understanding of the Domain Name Service (DNS). This is the network server that translates user friendly names such as www.quote.com into a machine-accessible IP address. VPNs present some particular issues around naming that need to be discussed.

- How does a VPN client locate a name server?
- Which name server should a VPN client use?
- How can other network users find the VPN client by name?

DNS

Many of the issues around the assignment of name servers are the same as we discussed above for address assignment. In fact, the identical mechanisms are typically employed to send the DNS server addresses to VPN remote access clients as part of the tunnel initialization sequence. Once the VPN client has the DNS server address, name resolution can usually proceed as normal.

Figure 6.6 shows a company implementing a VPN with two extranet trading partners and illustrates some of the DNS issues that can arise in certain VPN networks.

Extranet partner A in the figure is a small office with only two or three users requiring VPN access. The partners only want to access the

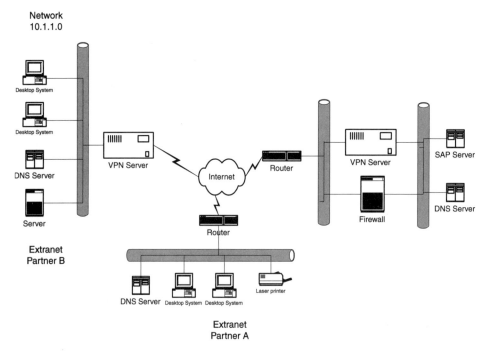

Figure 6.6 DNS Issues in VPNs

SAP application but want to continue using their local computing resources (like printers) and accessing the Internet. This user can run VPN
clients on the PCs and implement *split tunneling*. That is to say, their
VPN client will only send packets destined to the partner's SAP server
into the tunnel. All other packets will not be tunneled and be forwarded
as usual. Which name server should the client use? Different VPN implementations handle this question differently. Some will use the tunnel assigned DNS for all resolutions while others will try the local DNS first. If
no response is returned, then they will try the tunneled DNS.

Extranet partner B has a bigger office with servers desiring access to
the VPN. In this case, a branch office VPN is implemented with a VPN
server at the site. Note also that Extranet partner B also has a private address space in the 10.0.0.0 network. How will servers at the main company access resources at Extranet partner B by name, since the local
name server cannot resolve addresses in the 10.0.0.0 network? Here,
named resources at Extranet partner B may need to be manually entered
into the name server at the main company.

In traditional dial-up networks, clients always requested information from servers in the company intranet. This is changing. New classes of applications that push data to the dial-in client are appearing, along with applications such as desktop video conferencing, where clients may want to locate each other. This is not an easy task in remote access environments, where clients are assigned addresses from a pool and the client address can change from one day to the next. A new class of DNS servers is emerging that integrates the DHCP address assignment servers with the naming function. These have particular applicability in VPN environments. When a dial-in or VPN client requests an IP address via DHCP, the server will not only allocate an address for the PC but will also dynamically update the DNS record for the particular PC with assigned address. If I want to have a videoconference with the PC called BRUCESPC, I can now resolve the dynamic address through DNS.

Microsoft Networking and Windows Internet Naming Service (WINS)

Networking services for Windows-based desktops were available well before the immense popularity of TCP/IP networking, the Internet, or VPNs. Originally, the protocols were simple and enabled file and print sharing over a LAN using a special transport protocol called NETBEUI and an Application Programming Interface (API) called NETBIOS. Windows users have become attached to such Microsoft networking applications as browsing a network neighborhood and accessing file shares on a server.

Microsoft LAN Manager doesn't have a "name service" per se. The Microsoft name for name service is "browse services." The Microsoft name for name servers is "browse master" or "master browser"—these terms are used interchangeably. These contain entries of resources that can be shared called "shares." No one computer is fixed as the browse master. When your computer logs on to your network, it finds a master browser by broadcasting for one. When browse lists get too large, you can break the network up into "workgroups." A workgroup is a group of workstations that share a browse list.

When Microsoft implemented its TCP/IP networking stack, it wanted its TCP/IP modules to work like the already existing LAN Manager system, and LAN Manager used a naming system based on its NetBIOS application program interface. In order to make NetBIOS applications like net use, net view, as well as application programs written to this API work, Microsoft developed NetBIOS on TCP/IP or NBT. One of the key functions required of NBT is to resolve NetBIOS names to TCP/IP address.

There are a number of methods that a client can use to resolve a NetBIOS name to an IP address. It can use a text-based configurations file called HOSTS. If that is not present, it will contact the DNS server specified in your IP configuration. If the name is not present there, it will finally turn to a UDP broadcast as a last resort. However, the best alternative is to use a special Microsoft Windows Internet Name Server or WINS.

Using VPNs with Microsoft Networking

Most VPNs are designed to pass only IP or IPX traffic, accessing NETBIOS applications through a tunnel can provide some special challenges. To continue using Microsoft networking, a VPN user must insure that his or her PC is running NETBIOS over TCP, typically by removing the NETBEUI adapter. If the intranet is using the Microsoft Windows Internet Name Server (WINS), the VPN server will need to push the address of the WINS servers to remote access clients. Like the IP address, IP gateway, and DNS servers, this is usually part of the tunnel initialization process. WINS servers are designed to cache name to address mappings for a long time. VPN users receiving changing IP addresses from an address pool may have to adjust the WINS cache expiration value.

Beyond this, every VPN device will have different handling capabilities for NBT depending on the implementation approach taken. If the intranet makes heavy use of NETBIOS applications, it is important to review the operations of tunnels with these protocols with the VPN vendor.

Quality of Service

Despite most people's intuitive understanding of Quality of Service issues based on everyday experiences with airlines or on the roads, QoS, like VPN, remains a subject steeped in controversy and emotion. Many of the protocol mechanisms needed to implement various flavors of QoS are not fully standardized. Neither a standard industry practice nor even a clear definition of terminology has been developed. QoS is very much a work in progress at this writing, and thus we approach the subject with a little trepidation. Is there a good taxonomy for the variety of mechanisms and approaches to QoS? What is the best vantage point to examine QoS issues: Service Providers, end users, or equipment manufacturers?

For our taxonomy we will offer a simple one, dividing QoS mechanisms into two broad categories:

- ◆ Fixed QoS mechanisms requiring outside intervention to preprovision network resources
- ◆ Triggered QoS mechanisms done only on an as-needed basis, typically in congested periods

We will try to be neutral and represent all of the stakeholders' viewpoints. Before delving into these technical protocol mechanisms, we think it is important to recall some of the points made in the "Show me the money" chapter. To a large extent, VPNs are all about outsourcing. That is to say, delegating the job of managing network complexity to Service Providers for whom network complexity is their *raison d'etre*. Whatever protocol mechanisms may be available within a Service Provider to give better than "best-effort" service, they will only work to extent that the Service Provider network is well provisioned and well managed. There is no substitute for a good Service Provider. Another caveat is that the mechanisms discussed below vary widely from vendor to vendor. The following discussion presents some fundamental mechanisms. Individual implementation must be evaluated on a vendor by vendor basis.

Fixed Qos Mechanism: Entry Priority, Queueing, Shaping, and Preprovisioning

Many of the fixed QoS mechanisms represent mature technology available for years in network equipment such as routers. A short example can show how these may apply to VPNs. Figure 6.7 shows an enterprise VPN server connected to the Internet via a T1 leased line at 1.544 Mbps. The VPN server supports, say, 100 simultaneous connected users for the remote access VPN application out of a population of 500 employees with accounts.

Assume further that the CEO of the corporation is often traveling to visit customers and dials into the network via a modem. A great majority of the employees, however, live in neighborhoods served by broadband access, cable modems, or xDSL. The issues start to become clear:

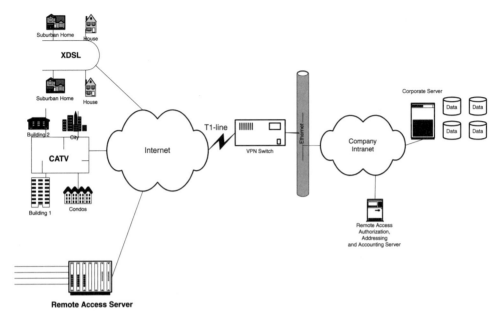

Figure 6.7 A VPN Implementation with the Probability of Congestion

◆ How does the VPN switch insure that multiple cable modem users with 3 Mbps access to the Internet don't swamp the VPN switch's T1 connection?

◆ How does the VPN switch insure that the cable modem users don't starve out the poor 56 Kbps dial-in modem users?

◆ How does the VPN switch insure that the CEO will always be able to access the network when there are potentially 500 users for 100 "ports," which may be all busy?

◆ How does the VPN switch insure that the CEO will always have good performance despite the presence of high-speed broadband users or a full switch?

Let's take a look at some of the mechanisms that can be used to insure that the VPN can insure "fair" access to the corporate intranet.

Entry Priority
Insuring that the CEO can always get into the VPN regardless of the number of other employees wanting access starts with categorizing users by their entry priority class. This is often done during the user authentication phase where IP addresses, DNS servers, and other attributes are

Table 6.1 Available Connection Slots per User Priority

Capacity	Priority	Available Connections
0–50%	ALL	100
51–75%	1,2,3	50
76–90%	1,2	30
91–100%	1	20

associated with the user. As the VPN connection slots get used up, typically by users logging in—although other metrics such as CPU utilization of the switch can also be taken into account—the switch will start to disallow connection requests from lower priority users. Table 6.1 shows an example of four entry priority classes on a switch supporting 200 total connections.

In this example, the switch will accept connections from any user up to 100 users connected. After that, in order to be connected the user must be in priority class 1, 2, or 3. Once 180 users are connected, only users in the priority class 1 can be admitted to the system. In our example perhaps only the CEO (or the executive committee) would be put in priority class 1.

Queuing Mechanisms

In our example above, the VPN switch was connected via a T1 (1.544 Mbps) to the Internet, and via a 10 Mbps Ethernet to the company intranet. Some users are connected to the Internet via high-speed (typically 1 to 3 Mbps) broadband services. Depending on traffic patterns, these interfaces may not be able to process all the data coming in or out of them. Most network devices (VPN switches or network switches and routers) provide memory to store packets, called *queues,* waiting for processing during these traffic bursts.

The way that packets are put in to queues and subsequently chosen for processing is call the *queuing algorithm.* During times of congestion, where many packets need to be buffered for processing, the choice of the queuing algorithm can have a large impact on the user's perception of performance. Imagine our CEO wanting to send a short E-mail confirming the big merger, while all of the field engineers are downloading the new product software over their cable modems. If the VPN switch implemented first-in, first-out (FIFO) queuing, the simplest and most common queuing algorithm, the mail message could take a long time to deliver.

As above, if we can associate users into particular service classes, we can be smarter about managing queues to provide better service to more important users. A pure-priority based queuing algorithm, where high-priority traffic is always serviced before lower-priority traffic generally isn't the best choice. Imagine that it was our CEO with the cable modem downloading files. A pure priority-based queuing algorithm could completely starve out the other users until the CEO was finished. Generally, VPN switches and other network devices implement sort of class based queuing. In this algorithm, a separate queue is implemented for each service class. On each "rotation" through the queues, a specific number of packets are serviced from each class, alleviating the starvation problem discussed above. A discipline called Weighted Fair Queuing also takes into account the traffic volume of the various flows and is popular on network equipment.

During particularly intense traffic bursts, buffer space provided for queues can completely fill up, causing packets to be dropped. In one sense, this is desired behavior, since dropped packets signal to TCP/IP endstations that they are transmitting too fast. However, if all the packets are simply dropped off the end of the queue in a traffic burst, this is likely to affect all of the applications at the same time. They all slow down their transmission rate, then proceed to slowly build it up again, however, in lock step. This causes a cyclical "feast or famine" pattern on the network that is not very efficient. A method called Random Early Detect (RED) is a method of randomly selecting packets to drop out of queues as they start to build up. Weighted Fair Queuing with Random Early Discard is often found on network equipment such as VPN switches.

IP over Virtual Circuits, Class of Service, Committed Information Rates, and Traffic Shaping

In Chapter 2 we discussed the traditional telecommunications services of Frame Relay and ATM with their capability of defining virtual circuits with varying traffic management capabilities. Frame Relay virtual circuits had a committed information rate (CIR) that was guaranteed through the network, independent of the speed of the line connecting the user. ATM virtual circuits can be provisioned to provide a number of traffic handling classes of service, including Constant Bit Rate (CBR); Variable Bit Rate, Real Time and Non Real Time (VBR-rt and VBR-nrt); as well as a best effort or Unspecified Bit Rate (UBR). Similar to Frame Relay's CIR, ATM circuits can provide similar committed information rates measured as Peak Cell Rate (or PCR). These telecommunication services are discussed here again, because they are oftentimes packaged as VPNs in managed network services. In addition, many of the QoS features found in these services are being deployed in more general IP contexts, for VPNs, Voice and Video over IP, and other services that desire Quality of Service through a service provider network.

It is interesting to note that, to a large extent, the Service Provider's capability to effectively provide the promised characteristics of these telecommunications services depends largely on the provisioning and management of their network. Often the Service Provider will offer the subscriber a Service Level Agreement (SLA) stating the agreed to levels of service. Service subscribers might want to use a queuing mechanism called *traffic shaping* to insure that they never present more than their committed information rate to the network, thus subjecting their packets to discard. When bursts of traffic arrive, they are placed in an output queue within the VPN server or network device. Protocol mechanisms such as the *leaky bucket* or *token bucket* insure that no more traffic than is specified in the CIR enters the service provider network. We will see below that traffic shaping is critical to the correct operation and provisioning of emerging implementations of Differentiated Services signaled Quality of Service.

Many proposals have been discussed relating to the mapping of various traffic flows onto specific circuit paths within the service provider network that can deliver appropriate Quality of Service based on the path characteristics: ATM Class of Service, path length, or transmission medium (satellite versus fiber optics, for example). We will briefly introduce some of these proposals in the next chapters when we discuss traffic engineering in the Service Provider cloud and the Multi-Protocol Label Switching protocol (MPLS).

Triggered Quality of Service Mechanisms: IntServ and DiffServ

A key difference between the fixed methods discussed above and the triggered methods discussed here are their interdomain nature. Above, a VPN customer could queue or shape packets into the Service Provider network, but once they left the customer premises, little interaction occurred between the customer and the Service Provider. With IntServ and DiffServ, the end user actively signals packet-handling requests into the service provider network. Today, all traffic in the public Internet classified as "best effort." The two triggered Quality of Service mechanisms discussed below attempt to make a fundamental paradigm shift in the thus far egalitarian world of Internet packet handling. Providing better than best effort is seen as a critical requirement mostly for future Voice over IP applications and the increasing "packetization" of the voice network, even more than VPNs.

This area of technology is very much one that is emerging in the industry; there is still much controversy over definitions, models, and implementation timeframes. Even worse, this subject has a high degree of complexity, covering multiple protocols, business models and even interworking between the different models. At this writing, none of the major ISPs or carriers has a commercial differentiated service offering based on the mechanisms discussed below. Network equipment manufacturers are starting to release their implementations, but multivendor interworking still seems to be a way off. Nevertheless, Service Providers are offering service-level agreements based on other mechanisms such as network engineering.

IntServ and the ReSerVation Protocol (RSVP)

IntServ and its associated Reservation Protocol (RSVP) are discussed here mostly for historical purposes. Development within the IETF is on hold, and as a Quality of Service mechanism, RSVP is generally felt to be incapable of scaling to provide a generally available service for the public Internet. RSVP may have new life as a signaling protocol for other initiatives such as traffic engineering with Multi-Protocol Label Switching. At one time RSVP was thought to be the answer to service guarantees through the network, mostly because it envisions a "circuit like" end-to-end reservation of resources through the IP backbone on a per application basis—much like the voice network. With further consideration, it became evident that the resources required to manage the state associated with the potentially millions of individual sessions would be impractical.

With the IntServ model of specific session bandwidth allocation, an end system uses the resource reservation protocol (RSVP) to request the allocation of a set of resources through the network. An admission control management system within the network decides whether the request can be granted based on the current utilization of the network and the business service agreement that has been negotiated with the network operator. If the request can be granted, the RSVP protocol sets up state information in *all* of the systems along the end-to-end path. A packet scheduler shapes the traffic in the flow to match the level of resources committed to the flow. Note that if the underlying path of the traffic was to change, the resource reservations would have to be negotiated over the new path, which may or may not be available.

Differentiated Services

The Differentiated Services approach for implementing Quality of Service has addressed many of the issues that prevented the wide-scale deployment of the IntServ model. Instead of signaling behavior at every hop in the network, a small bit field in each packet (the Type of Service or TOS field) is used to mark a packet in the network for a particular Per Hop Behavior at each router or switch in the network. In this design, individual flows are aggregated into particular service classes that can then get special treatment in the network cloud. DiffServ allows the main forwarding path through the network to be simple and evolve separately from more complex policy, admission, and management issues that are pushed to the edge of the network. An overview of the Differentiated Services Architecture is shown in Figure 6.8.

The following sections discuss each of the major components of the DiffServ architecture:

◆ The bandwidth broker

◆ Emerging service classes

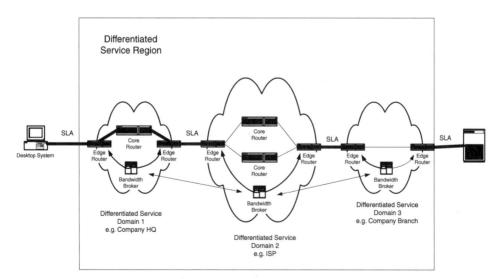

Figure 6.8 Overview of the Differentiated Services Architecture

◆ The DiffServ edge router
◆ The Diffserv Core node

The Bandwidth Broker

Within the enterprise network, decisions need to be made about which packets will take part in the defined aggregates. A network server called the *bandwidth broker* manages these decisions. How the bandwidth broker manages these decisions is called policy management. Policies can give priority to specific applications or users, perhaps taking into account such dynamic factors as the date, time of day, or even the dynamic state of the network domain.

We have seen earlier how the LDAP-accessible databases are the ideal storage location for this type of profile information. Once the policies are made, they need to be communicated to the edge routers actually implementing the policies. New policy protocols are emerging to accomplish this function. The most prominent one today is the Common Open Policy Service or COPS. Other protocols suggested for this function are the DIAMETER protocol (originally conceived as enhancements to the RADIUS protocol, hence the name) and even the Simple Network Management Protocol, SNMP.

Policies sent to edge routers can include traffic designated by any combination of fields in the packet header: source and destination address, protocol identifier, or port number, as a policy for setting the TOS field to the appropriate value. Ultimately bandwidth brokers will be able to communicate dynamic state information across domain boundaries as shown in Figure 6.8, but this is not expected in most early implementations. Static Service Level agreements between domains will likely be established and subsequently managed individually by bandwidth broker for its respective domain.

Emerging Service Classes

The TOS octet, is often referred to as the DS (Differentiated Services) byte, differentiates the packet for special treatment through the network. Historically, all traffic in the Internet has been best effort. When congestion occurs in the network, all packets have an equal probability of being dropped. Our discussion of Differentiated Services begs the question: What other kinds of services can be offered? This question is not addressed by the DiffServ architecture and although additional dis-

Figure 6.9 The Format of the Differentiated Services Byte

cussions in the IETF are starting to address this question, it remains controversial at this writing.

Two concepts have emerged with broad consensus: Expedited Forwarding, and Assured Service. Figure 6.9 shows new structure for the DS byte. The first bit indicates whether the traffic conforms to some prearranged profile.

The next field indicates the type of Differentiated Service requested or the Per Hop Behavior. Two behaviors are widely agreed upon. They are the Default, that is, best effort, coded as 00000, and Expedited Forwarding or EF, with a proposed code of 11100.

Expedited Forwarding, sometimes called Premium Service, is as close to a dedicated line–type service as this model will offer. It is typically implemented, although not prescribed, as a strict priority queue at core router output interfaces, but it must not starve best effort traffic. Note that in order to offer the Expedited Forwarding service, the network must not be underprovisioned, accepting more traffic than its capacity. Traffic shapers and policers at the edge routers help insure that this is the case. These are further discussed in the next section, but it is important to note that network engineering still plays an important role in the effectiveness of Differentiated Services.

Another traffic profile that is gaining widespread acceptance is the concept of assured service. The user may not need the strict performance guarantees of a premium service, but may want to get some sort of "better than best effort" service. With assured service the Service Provider customer agrees to some sort of traffic profile, relating to burst rate or time of day, for example. Although the user's traffic is not given any queuing priority in the forwarding path, should the network become congested and packets need to be dropped, assure services specifies that the user's conforming "in-profile" traffic be dropped last, after other best-effort traffic has been dropped. This allows the user to get better than the default treatment and may be acceptable for many applications. Here again, the effectiveness of assured service depends on the network engineering in the Service Provider network and how much bandwidth is left over for other than the premium traffic.

The DiffServ Edge Router

There are two borders to consider for the DiffServ Edge function. The first is the one between a particular host or system wanting differentiated services (which may or may not have protocol support for the services) and the first differentiated services device in the enterprise network. The second is located at the border of the enterprise network and the Service Provider. DiffServ-capable edge routers implement the most complex parts of the architecture at these borders where the scale of traffic is lower. The following functions generally need to be implemented:

- ◆ *The General Classifier*   The company business policy of giving expedited service to a particular user of a particular application at a particular time of day usually is translated by the bandwidth broker into a transport-level signature based on fields in packet header. The router inspects incoming traffic and classifies it with the appropriate class of service defined by the policy or Service Level Agreement.

- ◆ *The DiffServ Byte Marker*   Actually sets the value of the TOS byte.

- ◆ *The DiffServ Byte Classifier*   Sorts the classified traffic into output queues based on the value of the TOS byte.

- ◆ *Traffic Shapers*   As discussed above, shapers can be configured with a predetermined flow rate and burst size and force conformance to that flow rate. Traffic shaping is critical to the operation of DiffServ. It is critical for the technical operation Expedited Services that the network not be over subscribed. The Service Provider can make a commercial agreement with the enterprise customer to accept a certain flow and burst rate. The customer can put this policy in the bandwidth broker for loading into the edge router as a policy. The customer may need to shape both its Expedited Forwarding packets as well as its best-effort packets (in order to achieve the assured service)

- ◆ *Traffic Policers*   Service Providers are a suspicious bunch and don't just take it on faith that customers are complying with their Service Level Agreements. The Service Provider loads a customer Service Level Agreement into its bandwidth broker, which is sent down to the edge router supporting that customer as a policy. A traffic policer on the circuit insures that traffic from the customer meets the profile. If it does, it is classified and queued for forwarding. If it doesn't, the packet may be dropped or reclassified (for example, clearing the IN bit). Traffic policers use the same type of token bucket algorithms as traffic shapers and are relatively straightforward to implement.

The DiffServ Core Router

Once the packet has been classified and shaped into the core of the network, most of the hard work has been done. The core router is responsible for implementing the Per Hop Behavior, which typically involves relative simple queuing mechanisms such as Priority Queuing or Weighted Fair Queuing, as discussed above. Theoretically because the Expedited Forwarding traffic has been shaped, there will be no congestion for these packets, as shown in Figure 6.10. The best-effort traffic can use the bandwidth that expedited forwarding leaves behind. If there is more best-effort traffic than the output is able to handle, the best-effort traffic will be dropped. Assured-service traffic should have priority over simple best-effort traffic.

In period 1, Figure 6.10 shows that the entire line capacity is consumed by priority traffic. All of the best-effort traffic is dropped. In periods 2 and 3, not only is the priority traffic lower, there is enough capacity to pass all of the best-effort packets. In period 4, the priority traffic takes 70% of the line capacity, and the remaining 30% is filled with best-effort packets. These include as much of assured service as can be carried as a first priority. If the assured service was greater than 30% of the line utilization, all of the simple best effort traffic would have to dropped.

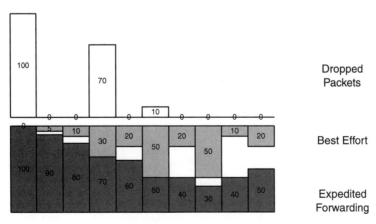

Figure 6.10 Line Utilization in DiffServ Trunks

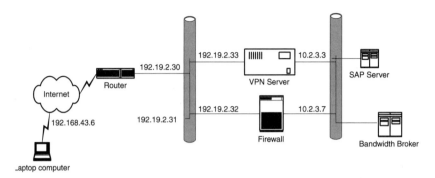

Figure 6.11 A VPN Server in a DiffServ Environment

DiffServ and VPNs

The previous discussion presented an introduction to the DiffServ architecture; here we make some observations about the implications of using DiffServ with VPNs. There are three models we wish to consider:

♦ The VPN server as non-QoS enabled device behind a DiffServ-enabled edge device

♦ The VPN server as a DiffServ classifier behind a DiffServ-enabled edge device

♦ The VPN server as a full DiffServ edge device

Let's use Figure 6.11 to discuss each of the cases. In the first case, the VPN server is not DiffServ aware at all. The policy manager (i.e., the bandwidth broker) in this enterprise may instruct the edge router to the Internet to classify and mark all IPSec packets as expedited. This will be a simple rule to implement since all of the packets will be coming from or going to the IP address of the VPN server. Note in this case that all of the packets within the tunnel get expedited service irrespective of their applications or source/destination.

An intermediate model will allow the VPN server to function as a DiffServ Byte Marker. In this case, the VPN server does not have to do the classification itself, but merely respect the classification that may have been done by a host itself or another DiffServ classifier at the edge of the network.

Figure 6.12 shows the VPN server copying the TOS byte from the original packet into the TOS byte associated with the new tunnel header. With this approach the VPN tunnels can have a variety of traffic going through them, each with a different classification. Thus, a Voice over IP or

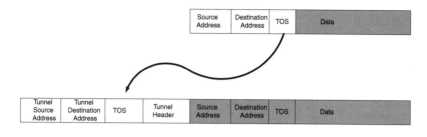

Orignal Packet as Data

Figure 6.12 Copying the Internal TOS Byte to the Tunnel Header

Enterprise Resource Planning application such as SAP can have expedited service through the tunnel, while E-mail passes as best effort or assured.

Finally, we can imagine the VPN server connecting directly to the Internet and performing the full VPN edge node function: interpreting the COPS protocol for the receipt of policy information, along with all of the classifying, shaping, and policing activity discussed previously. At the current writing, no commercial VPN product implements all of these functions but they are expected to make their appearance over the next year.

Summary

After reading this chapter, you should start to see VPNs as much more than a set of tunneling protocols. They represent the integration of a tremendous amount of technology from a number of different disciplines. The key challenge for people implementing VPNS, whether they are employees of the enterprise or work for a Service Provider, is clearly integrating the VPN service into the complex infrastructure environment of the user. This chapter has endeavored to give an insight into the key structural areas that need to be addressed when implementing VPNs in the enterprise. As we have seen in discussing this technology, some of the issues are tactical and are directly related to the implementation of the VPN service, while others are strategic and impact application and infrastructure issues well beyond the VPN. We hope that the information in this chapter has given you some tools and insights for analysis and good decision making that will help build not just good VPNs but good networks!

The Service Provider Environment for VPNs

"Double, double toil and trouble; Fire burn, and cauldron bubble. Fillet of a fenny snake, In the cauldron boil and bake; Eye of newt and toe of frog, Wool of bat and tongue of dog, Adder's fork and blind-worm's sting, Lizard's leg and owlet's wing, For a charm of powerful trouble, Like a hell-broth boil and bubble."

This chapter opens with the witches' spell from Act IV of Shakespeare's *Macbeth*. While VPN protocols are more or less straightforward, constructing the infrastructure to deploy a large-scale VPN service remains somewhat of a black art. In addition to the infrastructure for VPN protocols, systems for provisioning, management, and billing are required. Most VPNs are targeted toward business customers, many with mission-critical applications, and these systems must exhibit a fair degree of security and resiliency. Although VPN protocols use the sophisticated security technology discussed earlier, a poorly designed deployment can make for "powerful trouble."

We will examine these issues by taking an inside look at an example of a large-scale VPN deployment and, on the way, consider the design choices and supplementary systems deployed in the network. There is no standard practice here, and one size does not fit all. Often, system requirements need to be tightly coupled to vendor implementations. The goal of this chapter is to provide insight into these systems and to explore some of the most commonly encountered approaches.

A Large-scale L2TP Deployment

L2TP is a relatively new protocol, and most of the commercial services are still in pilot. There are a number of commercial installations of the older L2F protocols in operation. The issues involved in deploying L2TP and L2F are very similar. L2TP and L2F implement the hybrid service model as discussed in Chapter 4. L2TP enabled remote access concentrators in Service Provider Points of Presence (PoPs) function as L2TP Access Concentrators or LACs. These form tunnels with L2TP Network Servers (LNS, typically implemented on the customer site as Customer Premises Equipment (CPE). In contrast, end-to-end models do not require protocol support in the Service Provider network and are consequently simpler to deploy. We concentrate on hybrid models here because they are harder to analyze and deploy, however, many of the same issues regarding provisioning and management apply equally to the end-to-end models.

Figure 7.1 shows the various elements of a large scale L2TP implementation. On the left side (*a*) we see the various tunnel-enabled Service Provider Points of Presence. A large Service Provider can have multiple PoPs in a given city and provide service to many cities. Nowadays, carrier class remote access equipment has greatly increased in density, but within each PoP there may be a number of independent remote access concentrators providing dial-up connections for both standard Internet access and tunneling. In each city there is a pool of VPN dial-in clients (*b*) from each of the companies subscribing to the VPN accessing the service. The tunnel enabled remote access concentrators to connect into the Service Provider's backbone facilities and route tunnel connections through the infrastructure to an egress router (*c*) at the Service Provider edge. This router contains the circuits connecting the subscribing companies to the VPN service. The tunnel connection is routed from the L2TP access concentrator through this access router to the L2TP enabled CPE (*d*).

Figure 7.1 shows two different provisioning models. VPN customers can receive their dial connections integrated with their standard Internet connectivity, or they can connect to the VPN via a dedicated circuit used only for tunneling. In Chapter 5 we discussed the variety of devices available to implement the VPN server on the customer premises.

Supporting the VPN implementation within the service provider infrastructure is one or more Network Operations Centers (*e*) that contain the required tunnel management (VPN provisioning systems), along with various billing and management systems that support the Service Provider operations. In addition to supporting the VPN service, the network management and billing systems also support other services in the Provider's portfolio. Here, any VPN specific functions typically need to integrate with existing tools and processes.

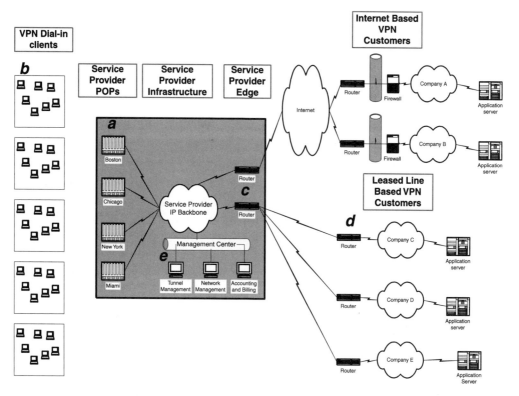

Figure 7.1 A Large-scale L2TP Deployment

CPE Considerations

Many Service Providers and customers are attracted by the capability to combine the VPN modem outsourcing application with general Internet service as a unified package. This is possible, but care needs to be given to the placement of the VPN termination point. Company A in Figure 7.1, for example, has an existing Internet connection consisting of a small access router behind a firewall. Although the access router (often provided by the Service Provider) may have the capability of running the L2TP termination point, this may not be a good idea. Once the tunnels are terminated, the dial clients appear as ordinary IP traffic, in this case, in front of the firewall. The in-place Internet firewall would need to be programmed to allow legitimate dial users to access the intranet while keeping out any wily hackers. This is easier said than done. Basing this on whether the IP source address is with the intranet address space is not a good idea, since it is very easy for an outsider to set its source IP address to anything.

A better solution is to put the L2TP network server behind the firewall and open up the firewall to pass only the L2TP protocol directly to the LNS. This would also have the advantage of offloading the L2TP and PPP protocol state machine from the often low-powered Internet access router. Standard Internet routers, because of their architecture, have very limited performance and capacity to handle significant numbers of tunneled users.

Another CPE management task that needs to be considered is how to handle L2TP access concentrator authentication. There are two issues here. The first concerns the possible number of LACs requiring registration. As we mentioned above, a large L2TP deployment can involve literally hundreds of LACs and their associated passwords. Keeping this database up to date on each subscriber's LNS can be a daunting task, especially if there are many adds, moves, and changes. Second, the tunnel authentication protocol is typically CHAP, which can be a little weak for industrial duty on the Internet. As we discussed in the last chapter, the LAC id passes in the clear and the CHAP password hash is not very strong. If the L2TP network server doesn't check the authorization, any rogue LAC from the Internet or even another L2TP subscriber could attach to a company's LNS. With L2TP there aren't as many speed bumps to prevent a hacker from attempting a password guessing attack. A middle ground may be to filter tunnel requests not originating from the service provider's address space at the CPE access router or firewall. But this provides only the slimmest of additional protection. Note that proposals to strengthen L2TP tunnel authentication with IPSec do not address the issue of registering the 100s of LACs that may be involved in a large deployment.

Protecting the Service Provider Facilities

Service Providers tend to wall off access to their infrastructure from commercial traffic. Internet subscribers typically can't address the remote access concentrators or management and billing systems. With L2TP, subscriber equipment needs to route packets into this infrastructure to the tunnel endpoints at the LAC. This requires that at least some of the internal Service Provider infrastructure is reachable from the outside world. Some thought needs to be given to protecting this infrastructure from malicious intent. Here again, the numbers of LACs and LNSs make it cumbersome to put specific access lists on every LAC. A more general traffic filter may be put at the gateway router (at *c* in Figure 7.1) to prohibit all but L2TP traffic from entering the Service Provider infrastructure. If possible, this would also prohibit external traffic from accessing and billing provisioning or management systems. Clearly, the Service Provider would not send any interior routing protocols down this circuit.

Sizing the Dial VPN Access Circuit

Dial VPN services replace modems and channelized access circuits with access from the Internet. As we discussed in Chapter 2, channelized circuits support 24 (or 32) users. The multiplexing capability of the tunnels can allow many more users to access their intranets, depending on their access speeds to the service (28.8 Kbps modem versus a 1 Mbps xDSL link) and their workloads (light application and E-mail access versus intensive download activity). Even with light application workloads, where throughput requirements are low, there may be response time requirements that need to be met. When dial VPN traffic is combined with the existing corporate Internet workload, this analysis becomes more complicated. The ebbs and flows of this traffic as well as the relative priority of Internet traffic versus the dial traffic need to be considered.

The Service Provider needs to decide to what extent it will be involved in the dial VPN performance management for the subscribers. This could be offered as a for-fee service, including regular performance reporting, analysis, and recommendations.

One approach to this issue is to simply offer the dial VPN services through a Service Provider link dedicated to this application alone (as shown in the bottom part of Figure 7.1). The exchange of 5 to 6 channelized T1 circuits for a single Service Provider link can still be extremely cost-effective for the VPN customer. And it can greatly simplify the security concerns raised in the above paragraphs. Using a dedicated link for dial VPNs can also make for shorter sales cycles for the Service Provider, because adding supplementary Internet applications through a company's existing Internet infrastructure may require much more corporate analysis and oversight.

Tunnel Management Systems

With basic Internet service, a dial-in user name and password is sent to an authentication server to determine whether the user is authorized to use the service and to generate a billing start record to register the time and traffic sent over the network. For the most part, the authentication service is implemented with RADIUS authentication and accounting protocols. The user can also append a *domain name* to the user name (Bruce@ISPB.com) to signal a RADIUS roaming request. Here the authentication is not done by the Service Provider accepting the call, but forwarded to a second RADIUS server indicated by the domain name.

For the most part, L2TP access concentrators have integrated the tunnel management server with the user authentication process. In L2TP, when the RADIUS server receives a qualified user name (with an @ or other delimiter), it will check to see if the appended domain is in a database of VPN customers. The tunnel management system returns the public IP address of the LNS and writes a billing start record for the VPN user. Since the tunnel management system see the tunnel requests for all users, it knows globally how many users are logged into a given domain (regardless of which LAC they originally dialed), as well as how many users are logged in to modem ports, both tunneled and not. This information represents system utilization statistics used in provisioning system capacity and, more importantly, drives the billing process for the services rendered.

It is important to note that not all RADIUS servers currently support the tunnel management capability. This can be a problem for some Service Providers if they have built customized provisioning and billing procedures around a particular RADIUS implementation. RADIUS implementations tend to vary greatly in the provisioning models (command line interface versus GUI), their support for back end database capabilities, and support of alternative authentication methods (such as Cisco's TACACS or UNIX-style password files). Thus, it is important that a Service Provider closely investigate what tunnel management systems are supported with vendor L2TP access concentrators, as well as the capabilities of their installed servers. It is not always that easy to simply turn on latent support for tunneling protocols in existing equipment.

Above, we mentioned that a user's desire to create a tunnel was signaled by a qualified user name with an appended domain name. Some users do not wish to change their dial-up procedures. They wish to continue using their simple user names and signal the tunnel request via the number dialed. Many remote access concentrators pass the Dialed Number Information String (DNIS) to the authentication server. Some RADIUS implementations will check this string against their tunnel databases and create tunnels based on this information. Thus a user dialing 555 1212 will always signal a tunnel request to Company A.

Another important issue to consider related to tunnel management systems is the failover capabilities of these systems. Clearly, if the tunnel management system is unavailable due to a disk head or other system crash, the entire VPN implementation comes to a halt. Most remote access concentrators provide for secondary and even tertiary RADIUS servers, and Service Providers have developed procedures to protect the standard Internet subscribers from these events. In implementing a VPN, the task still remains to insure that tunnel management entries are synchronized across the multiple RADIUS servers.

We are going to leave the specific discussion of L2TP issues for the moment since the following issues affect all VPN deployments, including L2TP.

Modem Provisioning and Dial Number Planning

Internet Service Providers are evaluated on the availability of their access systems. Failed logon attempts due to busy signals or no-answers are verified and published. Business-class Service Providers need to be sure they provide a highly available service. This is especially so for VPN services where the user may want formal SLAs, holding the Service Provider to specific levels of availability. For ordinary Internet service, queuing models and trend analysis techniques are well established to guide the Service Provider in calculating the number of access lines and

Table 7.1 Port Requirement Analysis for a Service Provider

	Company A	Company B	Company C	Internet Service	Totals
Total Dial Clients	1000	50	200	3000	**4250**
Boston	700	50	50	2000	**2800**
Miami	100	0	150	500	**750**
Chicago	200	0	0	500	**700**
Typical Port Usage	300	30	20	800	**1150**
Boston	120	30	2	500	**652**
Miami	90	0	18	125	**233**
Chicago	90	0	0	175	**265**
Peak Port Usage	500	35	100	2000	**2635**
Boston	300	35	10	1450	**1785**
Miami	90	0	90	250	**430**
Chicago	110	0	0	300	**410**
Reserved Ports	150	30	15	525	**720**
Boston	50	30	2	300	**382**
Miami	50	0	13	75	**138**
Chicago	50	0	0	150	**180**

modems required (despite the fact that these techniques are often unused). This analysis can be complicated when the VPN application is also included. Consider Table 7.1 analyzing port requirements for a simplified VPN service.

The question we now need to answer is how many modems to provision in each city. This equipment, along with the channelized circuits into it, represents large expenditures. Overprovisioning can eat into profit, while underprovisioning can cause customer dissatisfaction and trigger SLA violation penalty payments. The overall subscriber base is constantly changing as new customers come on line and existing customers change their profiles. The overall provision strategy is also tied closely to the pricing and billing strategy of the Service Provider.

In this made-up example, an Internet Service Provider offers general Internet access and dial VPN service in three cities: Boston, Miami, and Chicago. At this point, it has three customers for the dial VPN service. Company A is a large manufacturer, with say 2000 employees, headquartered in Boston. Of the 2000 employees, 1000 require occasional access to the dial VPN service, 700 in Boston, 100 in Miami, and 200 in Chicago. These users don't have heavy dial requirements. They only use the service when visiting other locations or traveling, typically to get their

E-mail or to look up a part number. On a typical day, 300 users are logged on, with the distribution given above. At the end of the month, however, utilization peaks to 500 users. The dial VPN usage is not considered mission critical, so Company A wants to save money by requesting that only 150 ports be permanently reserved for their dedicated use.

Company B is a small company of 50 employees that only operates in Boston. Thirty of its employees telework from home. Being connected is critical to their business operation, and they want all of these ports permanently available for their use. Occasionally, other members of the staff will want to visit customers and need to dial in, but the peak usage is only 35 ports.

Company C is headquartered in Miami, with operations in Boston. Typically usage is very low, but when crunch time comes, the staff in Miami works on the network.

The Service Provider's Internet business has about 3000 subscribers. During the day, when the VPN customers are most active, there are typically about 800 users logged on. During the "family hours" from 5:00 PM to 9:00 PM this can rise to 2000 users. The service provider doesn't want to starve the Internet customers servicing the VPN clients, and wants to reserve at least 525 ports for standard Internet Service.

Dial Plans and Hunt Groups

We mentioned in the Tunnel Management System section that the TMS could control the number of users logged in globally to a domain. In our example above, we may ask the VPN customer to commit to a peak number of ports it wishes to use (for example, 500 for company A). When the 501st subscriber tries to dial in, the Service Provider can configure the Tunnel Management system to drop the call. This helps, but it doesn't tell us how to distribute the 500 modems in each of the three cities. Imagine a crisis erupting in the Boston headquarters and 500 users dialing in to the Service Provider's Boston PoP. How could we honor our SLA to provide at least 50 ports to that customer in both Miami and Chicago? What if this sudden influx of Company A's users then prevented Companies B's and C's users from accessing their contracted reserved ports? The problem here is that the Tunnel Management System can't see the breakdown of users at a single PoP. One tool the Service Provider has at its disposal is organizing its dial lines into specific *hunt groups*.

When a user subscribes to a VPN service he or she is given a (typically local) access number to dial. Access numbers don't terminate at a single

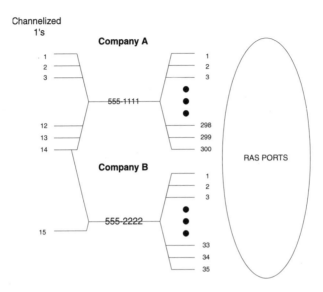

Figure 7.2 Hunt Groups Configured to Peak Usage

modem the way that a traditional voice call would, but step through a series of access channels. In this way, hundreds of users can dial the same number and still get connected to the Internet services. Simply giving each company's VPN users a different calling number mapped to a hunt group provisioned to subscribed peak requirement still would not be satisfying. It requires the Service Provider to provision access ports and channels to peak requirements as shown in Figure 7.2. Thus, Company A would require 300 ports and 14 channelized T1 circuits. Company B would require an additional channelized T1 line and 35 ports. There usually is quite a bit of flexibility in configuring hunt groups. The T1 channels do not necessarily have to be contiguous as shown in the figure.

If Company A was not using its peak capacity, say at night, the access lines and remote access ports would be unavailable for other applications or general Internet service.

Figure 7.3 illustrates a better approach, provisioning to the typical port requirements by sizing the hunt groups the lower number of ports and creating a separately sized *contention pool.*

Once subscribers exhaust their original hunt groups, their calls are serviced from the contention circuits. With this approach, each customer group is guaranteed its reserve requirements as well as its "typical" requirements. The VPN customer should realize that his or her peak requirements might not always be met. Further, if some customer groups

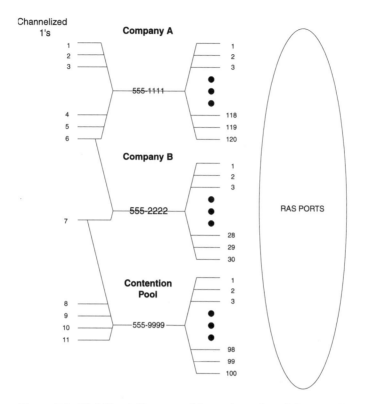

Figure 7.3 Dial Hunt Groups with an Associated Contention Pool

consistently exceed their contracted typical usage levels, this could prevent other customers from bursting above their typical usage profile and cause some dissatisfaction. The technical implementation of hunt groups should therefore be supported with good business practices, billing procedures, and trend analysis to help accurately track customer requirements. Some of these methods are discussed further below.

In the example of the Boston PoP from the Table 7.1, the total ports required for typical use is 652. The Service Provider might decide to provision 2000 additional ports in order to provide excellent Internet service as well as provide a buffer zone to take on new customers and the changing needs of its corporate customer base. This figure is close to the peak port usage because there is usually a lag time to bring new telecommunications and remote access equipment into service.

Implementing hunt groups and contention pools requires that the Service Provider have good support and relations with the carrier delivering calls into the PoP. These services are more or less traditional and have been used for Call Centers and 800 number processing for a while. However, the Service Provider might want more dynamism than is normally required for these traditional applications. Many of the advanced dialing plan services, such as the Dialed Number Information String (DNIS) and number translation and routing, use features of the Integrated Digital Services Network (ISDN). To use these features, the Service Provider would need to provision Primary Rate Interfaces (PRI) circuits into the PoP rather than traditional channelized T1/E1 circuits. All of these features may not be available everywhere.

Signaling System 7

The discussion of dialing plans, hunt groups, and number translation presumed an "arms-length" relationship between the Service Provider and the telecommunications carrier delivering the dialed data calls. Deregulation in the telecommunications industry along with advances within the telephone network have opened up new possibilities for closer integration of the Service Provider facilities with that of the carrier.

This initiative is called the Intelligent Network and is supported by a data communications protocol called Signaling System 7 (SS7), sometimes called Common Channel Interoffice Signaling system 7 (CCIS7). SS7 was originally developed in the 1970s to provide an "out-of-band" signaling capability to control call setup and routing, as well as to be a platform for advanced services such as Caller ID and 800 number translations. It also put a stop to a growing fraud problem that was inherent in the older in-band signaling methods and created some of the technical infrastructure that supported increased deregulation in the industry.

Increasingly, remote access concentrator vendors are integrating SS7 capabilities into their larger access concentrators. This capability allows the Service Provider to signal call handling information directly into the carrier network, based on application programs running in their own infrastructure. Rather than preprovisioning hunt groups to a particular size, the Service Provider can dynamically decide which calls to accept based on overall network conditions.

There are other advantages to an SS7 implementation. One advanced traffic management capability is the ability to reroute data calls from PoPs that are busy to those that have excess capacity. This lessens the requirement that Service Providers precisely calculate demand for each PoP and enables them to balance the call load over all of their PoPs should conditions warrant. SS7 can also provide large savings on telecommunication services when used in larger points of presence. Normal Primary Rate ISDN circuits have 23 B channels that are used for voice or data calls and a 64 Kb/s data (D) channel that is used to for signaling, controlling the calls on these channels. In a large PoP with 100s of PRIs, every circuit would normally require its own D channel. With SS7 all of these hundreds of D channels (several T1s worth) could be freed for data calls.

At this writing SS7 is still an emerging capability. Security and reliability requirements make carriers cautious in licensing Service Providers to attach to their signaling infrastructure. In addition, there are a wide variety of SS7 implementations around the globe, with varying capabilities and interoperability with vendor remote access equipment. Over time, the applications are becoming more compelling for both the Service Provider and the carrier. As more data equipment proves itself in trials and small deployments, we expect SS7 connected remote access concentrators to be the norm.

Pricing Models and Billing Services

Pricing and billing services for dial VPN service are closely intertwined with the provisioning strategy we discussed above. Further, it impacts many network planning and design functions. In addition to billing and pricing for basic VPN transport services, these functions also need to take into account any value-added services that may have been packaged with the offering and any Service Level Agreements that may have been included.

The TeleManagement Forum (*www.tmforum.org*) has proposed the framework shown in Figure 7.4 to integrate many of these aspects. In this section, we will principally be concerned with the shaded sections pertaining to the billing process, but we will discuss many of the other processes shown in later sections.

Usage and Performance Data Collection

There is not really that much to say about usage data collection for dial VPNs. Almost all remote access concentrators write RADIUS accounting records, indicating the start and stop time of the call, a byte count of traffic sent over the network, along with the identity (user name, domain name, and perhaps the called and calling numbers). In our L2TP example, this would be written by the Tunnel Management System as it brings up and tears down each user session. Note that a sec-

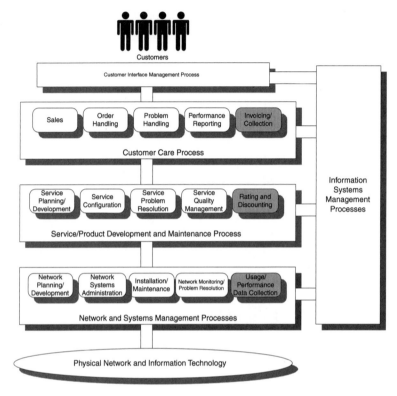

Figure 7.4 The Network Management Forum Business Process Model

ond RADIUS account record is generated in the customer premises when the particular user is actually authenticated at the VPN termination point. Thus, the Service Provider and the customer have matching sets of billing records with which to do reconciliation of bills. RADIUS servers do differ somewhat in their operational models. Some will write the start record, then will periodically write intermediate records that record at least partial usage should the server itself crash. They also differ in how they store the records for later processing of the actual bills. Most of the popular billing packages accept RADIUS accounting files directly. The Service Provider needs to devise operational procedures for periodically downloading these files and perhaps archiving them for use in resolution of potential discrepancies or as input to various trending and analysis programs.

Note that Service Providers are likely to offer both straight Internet access services as well as the VPN service. In the case of the hybrid tunneling protocols (L2TP and L2F) there will be different types of billing records generated for each type of access. In the end-to-end models, the Service Provider may not know if the user is actually using a VPN client or not. While it may be possible to offer the subscriber a premium business-class access service with bundled support service, they typically will not be able to differentiate between VPN and non-VPN service. In most broadband access networks such as xDSL or cable modems, the service is "always on." The infrastructure is more like a local area network and start and stop records are also not generated. Here again, pricing models need to be adjusted for the capabilities of the infrastructure.

Rating and Discounting

The Service Provider will typically prepare bills on a regular basis, usually every month. This involves matching the detailed usage records either against standard pricing packages or the VPN customer's custom billing plan. This is a process known as "guiding." Once this has occurred, the individual calls for a given customer can be priced and an invoice generated. Then the detailed usage records are priced or "rated." Once this is done, any supplementary services such as help desk access, reporting packages, or onsite trouble services are similarly guided and rated, and the user's invoice is prepared.

There is a great deal of variation in the industry for the different models used to determine how VPN services are priced. For standard Internet access services, the industry has largely moved to a flat pricing model of unlimited access for a monthly fee. Here, service level guarantees are minimal and processing of individual usage records is not required to generate the billing records. For end-to-end VPNs that use basic Internet access service, this might be a practical model. If valued-added services are also delivered, these are rated separately and added to the basic transport service to produce the monthly bill.

Alternatively, the Service Provider may offer a business class service with bundled valued-added services. These are currently the most common found in the industry today. Here, a fixed hourly rate, currently between $1.50 and $3.00, depending on the bundled services, is calculated against the actual usage records. As discussed in the provisioning section, the Service Provider might want to support its provisioning approach in its pricing methodology. Figure 7.5 below shows the average daily dial VPN usage for a given point of presence. The SLA could specify port usage "tiers." A minimum number of reserved ports that are always avail-

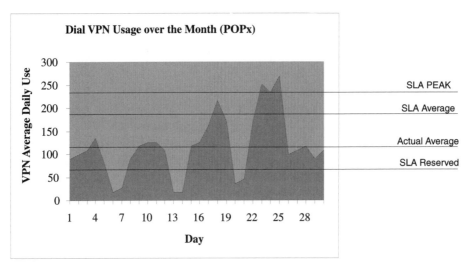

Figure 7.5 Dial VPN Usage over the Month at a Point of Presence

able for this customer's use, an average port usage level, and a peak usage level.

Dial VPN access up to the contracted average usage could be charged a lower or flat rate. Calls above the average but less than the peak could be charged at a higher rate, and calls above the contracted peak could be charged another rate, or not answered. The billing invoices give the customer detailed information on its usage patterns. This allows the customer to buy the right amount of service as well as negotiate volume discounts. It would also encourage customers to work with the Service Provider to understand the actual requirements needed for good service.

At this writing, VPN services are still relatively new, and few Service Providers offer this form of tiered pricing. As dial VPNs and their associated SLAs become more popular, it may become desirable to move from traditional, less sophisticated provisioning and billing methods.

Invoicing and Collection

Most Service Providers will already have a strategy in place for the invoicing and collection of other service offerings. Printing, stuffing envelopes, mailing, and collections are often outsourced to third parties. There are, however, a number of updates that might need to take place to support the rollout of the VPN application. This effort needs to be integrated with other aspects of the customer care processes of the Network Management Forum Business Process model, such as sales and account establishment, as well as the problem handling and resolution process. All of these functions may have supporting application systems themselves, which may need updating in preparation for the VPN service rollout.

The monthly billing cycle will typically offer a vehicle for delivering subscribed performance and usage reports, provide an opportunity for the customer to reevaluate service level selections, and discuss overall service satisfaction.

Network Management

The Service Provider infrastructure used for VPNs overlays and integrates very nicely with that already in place to provide basic Internet access services. This is one of the primary advantages of the VPN service. Most of the configuration, fault, and performance management tools for the basic infrastructure are transparently adaptable to the VPN application. Infrastructure security and accounting does need special attention, as discussed above. Much of what we want to talk about in this section concerns managing the tunnel endpoint or the VPN customer premises equipment.

Managing the VPN endpoint has two aspects that need to be considered. We will talk about the standard management of the VPN device as a network element and also about the management of the logical VPN definitions. Since the VPN server is often implemented as a managed network service, this adds additional complexity to this analysis. Often, there must be two different management planes to the VPN server—the view of the Service Provider and the view of the customer. These must be configured so that one set of managers cannot interfere or undermine the activities of the other. The Service Provider may also be responsible for hundreds of VPN servers across its customer base. Consideration needs to be given to tools and procedures to manage these "farms" of VPN systems. VPN devices need to be deployed into a broad range of environments. In a small company, the VPN server may be deployed without an extensive management infrastructure. In a large company, the VPN server might need to interface with complex multilayered structured management frameworks.

Figure 7.6 gives an overview of the most common VPN management interfaces and protocols.

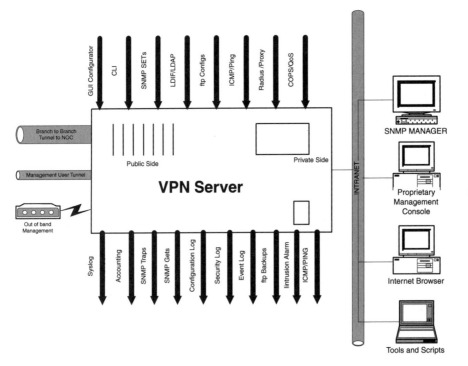

Figure 7.6 VPN Management Interfaces and Protocols

The CPE Native User Interface

There are two broad models for a network element interface: a Command Line Interface (CLI) and a Graphical User Interface (GUI). GUIs come in two flavors. Some are proprietary, usually separately purchased systems, that provide much of the added-value configuration logic on the management system. Other GUI-based systems put all of the application logic on the VPN server and use a web browser to provide presentation, possibly enhanced with Java-based applets. CLIs are often bundled with scripting capabilities like PERL or TKL that allow Service Providers to develop script files for many of the repetitive troubleshooting, provisioning, or statistics-gathering jobs. They can also be triggered in response to real-time events as discussed further below. Most VPN devices require both interface options. While learning the features of the product, a GUI with rich online help can be a real boon to users. Service Providers, however, want the speed and flexibility of the CLI interface.

One management model that is commonly found in VPNs is called *split horizon* or *role-based management*. Here the VPN customer may want to maintain control of provisioning users, looking at reports and statistics, and possibly closing branch office or user tunnels. The Service Provider takes charge of basic protocol operation of the switch, along with system configuration and troubleshooting. Some VPN servers allow the partitioning of management activities based on a user profile. The granularity of this profile varies from implementation to implementation.

In simple end-user configurations, a management console is located on the VPN customer's premises and the management activities are easily accomplished with a minimum of security problems. The Service Provider usually doesn't have staff at the customer location, so the VPN server needs to provide a mechanism for remote management. Since the VPN server is connected to the Internet, it is not wise just to make the management interfaces available from the public side, say via telnet or HTTP. The security risk should be obvious.

There are two solutions the remote management problem: in-band and out-of-band solutions. An in-band solution uses the communications capability of the server to provide a secured management channel. Here for instance, the Service Provider might tunnel into a special account set up on the server. If there were many resources in the Service Provider Network Operations Center (NOC) needing to access management interfaces on the customer VPN server, perhaps a special LAN-to-LAN tunnel could be set up between the Service Provider's NOC and the customer server for this purpose as shown in Figure 7.7. This is a simple extension of the extranet concept we told you was a driving application for VPNs. Clearly, care needs to be taken to ensure that NOC traffic doesn't leak onto the customer's intranet, and customer traffic cannot enter into the NOC. There is another issue that needs to be considered in managing VPN services through tunneled interfaces. Since the management traffic streams are typically directed towards the enterprise, they will often have nonpublic source addresses. If these addresses overlap those of other VPN customers, Network Address Translation (NAT) technology will have to be employed in the tunnel as described in Chapter 4.

There is a problem with the above approach. If a fault occurs that interrupts communications to the VPN server, how does the Service Provider diagnose and fix it? One approach to this is to provide out-of-band management capability on the VPN server. This usually entails putting a modem on the console or other serial port that allows the Service Provider to directly dial into the box to do troubleshooting. Here again the dial-in could provide GUI-based or command line access, or both, to the VPN server.

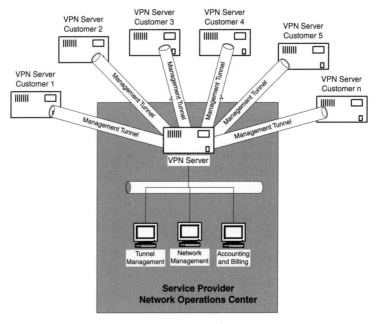

Figure 7.7 Service Provider Network Operations Center with Management Tunnels

The Event Logging Systems

Once the VPN server is connected to the network and operational, a tremendous number of events start to occur. First, there is a flurry of configuration activities. These are followed by a few connection tests, which may require some debugging efforts. Once the VPN is provisioned, users start their production access. Users and configurations may need to be added, deleted, or modified. Wily hackers may try to attack your system from the Internet. These events take place too quickly to be sent to a user interface, and if an operator isn't paying attention the events may be missed. VPN servers usually have an extensive logging system to write these events to files for later analysis. Alternatively, the event information can be written out on the network to a standardized event collector called a *syslog daemon*. A syslog capability can be very useful in a Service Provider environment since it can direct event streams to multiple listeners. This way, the Service Provider could have a centralized event log mechanism in the Network Operations Center, which collects logged information from all of the VPN servers being managed, and the customer could receive a stream as well.

There are usually a number of categories of logs that can be kept. The *general event log* is a real-time capture of everything that happens on the switch, often kept in memory for performance reasons. This log is mainly useful in debugging. A user calls the help desk complaining that its VPN client is not connecting. The help desk agent can watch this event log while the user tries his or her access and follow the connection process step by step. The problem may be a security setting mismatch, a mistyped password, or a connection timeout; the problem will show up in the log file.

Some of the events that are logged to this file should be recorded to disk and kept for later analysis or troubleshooting. These include specific security events, and configuration changes. It is often these events that are written to the syslog stream rather than the more general event log. The *configuration log* provides a detailed trace of who made changes to the switch configuration and when. This can be an invaluable troubleshooting tool as many problems have been traced to configuration changes.

Some events are of an urgent nature and typically require action right away. One example of this is an attempt to tamper with the hardware operation of the VPN server. Some of the security standards with which VPN servers have to comply (FIPS 140, for example) specify that there be a special *hardware-based intrusion alarm* that will physically signal any attempt to open the VPN server box. If this alarm is ignored, the box will usually need to provide *tamper evidence* to indicate that some attempt was made to open or otherwise physically alter the VPN server. Often this is done with a special type of sealing tape that provides irreparable evidence of tampering.

Other events that require attention include a whole variety of *security alarms* and any important *network or system failures* that dramatically affect the capability of the server. These are usually signaled to special management stations via the Simple Network Management Protocol SNMP discussed in the next section.

The Simple Network Management Protocol (SNMP)

The SNMP protocol, originally developed in the 1980s, was designed to be a "quick and dirty" fix to the problem of managing the growing numbers of devices making up networks. While not perfect, the SNMP protocol has evolved to become the foundation of most element management systems in use today. Most VPN deployments will use

SNMP for at least some of the most basic management functions. As we will see below, SNMP management systems are often at the core of more sophisticated management framework systems that automate many of the key functions that assure the overall health of a VPN deployment.

The SNMP model proposed a manager/agent paradigm shown in Figure 7.8.

♦ The *agent process* usually resides in the managed element and performs such operations such as setting operational parameters and recording statistics on actual performance. The agent can be paired with multiple managers in a concept called a SNMP community. SNMP communities an have an associated password, and read or read/write access for limited security

♦ A database of management information known as a *Management Information Base (MIB)* organized in a tree structure is associated with both the manager and the agent. It represents the operations and functions of the managed elements.

♦ The *SNMP manager* uses a simple set of commands to request specific information or set values in the Management Information Base and then listens to the responses. The agent can also asynchronously notify the manager of events via messages known as *trap*s. SNMP utilizes a simple connectionless communication protocol using the User Datagram Protocol UDP to implement its functions.

Many of the Service Provider VPN offerings highlight management services as a key part of the overall value proposition. It is clear that these devices must offer SNMP services. SNMP provides the means to integrate into the Service Provider's network operations centers and input

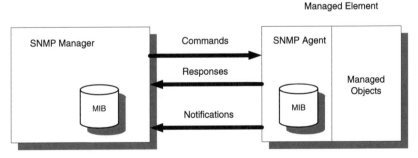

Figure 7.8 SNMP Architectural Overview

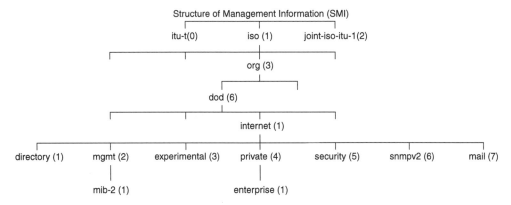

Figure 7.9 SNMP Structure of Management Information

into many of the existing network management processes. Some issues to keep mind concerning SNMP implementations are:

♦ What kinds of SNMP MIBs are available

♦ What kinds of SNMP traps are generated

♦ What information is provided with the SNMP traps

♦ Whether the frequency of SNMP traps be controlled

We mentioned previously that the Management Information Base or MIB contained a tree-structured database of information concerning both the static and dynamic operations of the device. Some MIBs have been well standardized, while some functions in the VPN space have no standard representation and may need to be represented in a private MIB. The standardized Structure of Management Information (SMI) is shown in Figure 7.9.

MIB-2 is a standard Management Information Base that most devices should support. It is composed of eleven different subgroups for areas such as general system information, interface type and statistics, configuration and operations for the TCP/IP protocol suite, and the SNMP protocol itself. Below each of these categories are actual structured data fields, containing identifiers, statistics, and other information that might be of use for network management.

As an example, the system group could contain a text description of the device, the unique vendor object identifier, and a counter for how long the system has been up and running. It could also contain the contact name for the node, a user-friendly name for the node (perhaps its DNS name), the physical location of the node, and the set of services this node typically pro-

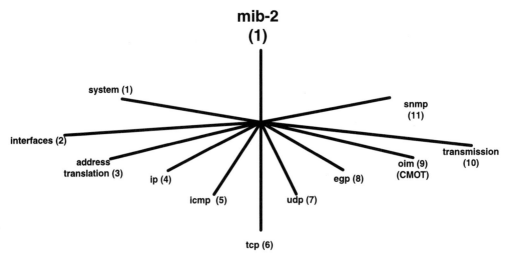

Figure 7.10 The MIB-2 SNMP Group

vides. The interface group contains an indexed entry for each interface on the node, telling its type (e.g., Ethernet, Token Ring, FDDI) and its Maximum Transmission Unit (MTU) size. It gives an estimate of its bandwidth, its physical address, and the administrative and operational status of the interfaces, as well as a whole series of counters detailing the traffic that has passed through the interface and any errors that may have occurred.

Note that in the MIB-2 structure (Figure 7.10) there is no place for much of the information used to describe tunneling protocols or their operational parameters and performance. There has been much discussion about a so-called VPN MIB, but as of this writing it hasn't been standardized (there is some drafts for IPSec MIBs). SNMP does provide the capability to add MIBs that haven't been standardized to the tree, under the "private.enterprise" branch shown in Figure 7.9. Some vendors do provide a VPN MIB at this location that is available for browsing from any of a number of MIB browser programs.

Like the MIB, a number of standardized SNMP traps have been defined for events such as cold starts, warm starts, link up, and link down, and authorization failure. In the VPN application, most of the key notifications will likely be vendor and application specific. Some of these include intrusion detection, security and authorization events, as well as hardware-related events such as fan or power supply failures. These traps are directed to a standard SNMP management station. Depending on the capabilities of the station, a whole range of activities could be triggered. Some of the more popular ones include paging the system manager, sounding an audible alarm, or invoking a command procedure to start up a backup procedure.

Network Management Frameworks

From the discussion above we can see that SNMP provides a relatively primitive capability for managing devices. There are a number of management "framework" products that are currently being sold that layer on top of the SNMP foundation to make it more useful for required network management tasks. Some of the more popular ones include Hewlett-Packard's Openview™, Tivoli System's TME 10 Netview™, and Sun Microsystem's Solstice™ suite of tools. Network equipment vendors usually have some suite of multivendor, SNMP-based management tools that are sold with their equipment.

Automatic mapping of the network topology and connectivity of the network is one of the most popular applications in these frameworks. This is often the screen you see displayed in many Service Providers' Network Operations Centers (NOCs) and often form the basic navigation tool for the network management system. As SNMP traps occur, indicating alarms or failures, icons representing the various devices turn red or yellow to indicate their status. SNMP pollers may be working in the background continually comparing network traffic levels on network interfaces with the speed of the lines. Bottlenecks in the network show up in yellow or red. By clicking on the offending device, the network manager can drill down and investigate the causes of the problem. Often this means spawning the actual management application for the particular device in question.

The network management framework may be a collector of SNMP traps from many systems. When a major network problem occurs, a flurry of traps from many different systems can sometime obscure the real problem. Some management systems offer event correlation that sorts through events to isolate the cause of the incident. Once this is determined, the management framework could invoke an appropriate prewritten script file that implements a backup plan or notifies key personnel by page or phone that a problem is occurring. The syslog streams from a group of devices may also be directed to the management system. This would allow the network manager to compare logs of a number of devices at the time of a particular event to see detailed information pertaining to what happened on each device.

Most of the discussion above centered on the fault management. The management framework can also play a key role in performance management. These systems will often plot historical trend information and give the network operator some insight into the various traffic patterns on the network. The system can be configured to trigger alarms if various key circuits are congested. These thresholds are often set much lower in order to provide sufficient headroom to guarantee business-class performance. The ability to poll the various VPN services in the network for performance and utilization information allows the Service Provider to provide a number of network planning and performance-oriented services to the customer. This information may be critical in meeting any obligations that have been agreed to in SLAs.

ICMP and PING

The Packet Internet Groper (PING), and its underlying protocol, the Internet Control Message Protocol (ICMP), is still among the most useful tools available to network managers. This tradition has carried over into the VPN space. The first thing a Service Provider will want to verify after the installation of a VPN server will be, "Is my server reachable on the network?" PING puts a sequence number, timestamp, and checksum on each packet. Therefore, PING can tell you if the network is dropping, duplicating, or corrupting packets and also the round trip latency of each packet. PING allows you to vary the size and content of the payload, which can help diagnose packet fragmentation and data sensitivity issues.

Both PING and ICMP have also been integrated into a number of tools within the frameworks mentioned above and offered as separate systems for applications in SLAs or performance management. Another popular application that is useful in the VPN environment is TRACE-ROUTE. TRACEROUTE uses the same ICMP messages as PING but successively increases the Time-To-Live parameter to build up a trace of all the nodes a packet traverses from source to destination. In the VPN environment, TRACEROUTE is useful for determining where delays in the Internet path are occurring. Note, however, that a tunneled circuit will always appear as one hop.

However, PING and ICMP do have a down side, especially on the Internet. There have been a number of hacker attacks that use these facilities mostly to deny service to legitimate users. A PING flood is a series of successive PINGS that can clog up the Internet connection to a company's VPN server. The PING of Death was an attack to which some routers were susceptible. It involved very long PING messages. In response to these issues, some vendors disabled PING or at least implemented a form a rate limiting, where the VPN server would only respond to a certain number of PINGs. Some company and Service Provider firewalls are programmed not to pass ICMP messages. Service Providers will need to be aware that tools based on these protocols may often have different results in a VPN environment.

VPN Provisioning

In the L2TP example above, we discussed the issue of modem provisioning for a dial VPN. This is actually only one part of a larger provisioning activity that is involved bringing a VPN customer online. Most of these other activities are very similar to those related to provisioning other telecom services and are not discussed here. In VPNs however, a few new issues arise. In this section we will look at issues pertaining to VPN subscriber management, VPN topology provisioning, and VPN server configuration management.

VPN Subscriber Provisioning

In the end-to-end tunneling models we have been discussing, outsourcing the remote access function typically involves giving Internet access accounts to potentially thousands of new users. These users may have had existing dial-in accounts for traditional remote access, or the company may have a different authentication model based on LDAP or other technologies discussed in Chapter 6. There, we talked about the growing difficulty of managing passwords. Here, by giving users ISP accounts we are talking about doubling that effort!

There are two approaches to potentially avoid this situation and allow the user to keep track of a single password for dial access. The first involves authenticating the users for intranet access against the service provider RADIUS database, and the second involves authenticating users for Internet access against the enterprise authentication database.

As we have discussed earlier, the job of password management is not easy, and some customers would dearly like to outsource it. Normally, a VPN server will direct VPN authentication requests to a private-side RADIUS server on the customer network. Some VPN servers will allow these to be directed either out the public interface or into a management tunnel to be serviced by the same authentication server that authenticated the original ISP connection.

Despite all the problems with password management, many customers are not comfortable with the idea of moving their security perimeter into the Service Provider. What they would prefer is the inverse of the above situation. That is to say, give the Service Provider the capability to use the customer authentication database to authenticate the dial-in user for Internet access. This will often take the form of a RADIUS proxy request, where the ISP RADIUS server will pass on the authentication request based on a domain name attribute. Some VPN servers provide the capability to be a RADIUS server and process these authentication requests directly.

VPN Topology Provisioning

In LAN-to-LAN provisioning based on telecommunications technologies such as Frame Relay or ATM, provisioning of the VPN network topology follows the traditional provisioning approach associated with these technologies. When IP based tunneling is used, these well-known processes are no longer applicable. There is little standardization in the provisioning models used between VPN products from different manufacturers, so it is hard to generalize about techniques and tools a Service Provider can implement to add value to this process. In general, the VPN definitions describing which resources are available through LAN-to-LAN tunnels have been a customer activity. For reasons of security, most customers want to have careful control over which parts of their private intranets are visible at each end of the tunnel.

There are, however, some application domains, especially in the area of EDI-based extranets like the ANX, where some Service Providers may wish to be involved in provisioning and managing the dense meshes of customer connections required for the application. In these cases, the tools and processes offered by the VPN manufacturer not only serve to simplify the customer's own provisioning process, but enable the Service Provider to provide this service out of the Network Operations Center.

One aspect that complicates LAN-to-LAN provisioning for both the customer and service provider is the distribution and management of shared secrets for tunnel authentication. Here, the use of X.509 certificates for authentication and authorization can often help. In many LAN-to-LAN based VPN systems, the receipt of a digitally signed tunnel request with an X.509 certificate can obviate the need to distribute shared secrets to all of the extranet partners.

Some VPN servers have the capability to download the VPN topology definitions from a seed server or management console (such as may be found in the NOC). In this case the Service Provider would be responsible for keeping the VPN definitions up to date and periodically updating them to the various customers. Others can be provisioned via command files or by importing separately generated configuration files that the service provider could manage centrally.

For the most part, VPN topology provisioning, like that of subscriber management, is most often a customer responsibility. The Service Provider adds value to this process with other services such as performance and utilization reporting and making sure the VPN links are up and running and reliable.

VPN Configuration Management

Like network routers and other network elements, VPN devices depend on system software images and configuration databases to perform their function. Managing the upgrades and backups to these elements is often a function that customers want Service Providers to perform. Once the installation of the customer premises equipment is complete, the Service Provider may want to back up the configuration files pertaining to the operational parameters of the server, including IP addresses of the various interfaces and the various auxiliary servers that are used to provide the VPN service. In general, any sensitive information such as shared secrets will be stored in an encrypted form in these images and present a limited security issue. These files can then be backed up on a regular basis. Given that many of the problems associated with networks in general are due to badly implemented configuration changes, the ability to revert to a known good environment is a service often appreciated by customers.

System images and configuration files can often be saved and restored using standard file transfer facilities. Some VPN servers offer the ability to store configuration parameters in command files that can be executed against a reloaded image. Like other aspects of the configuration and management process discussed above, configuration backup and restore are most often directed to the intranet side of the VPN server and, for obvious reasons, are not available from the public or Internet side. In order to provide these configuration management services, the Service Provider will require a secure path to the server, either via an out-of-band connection, through a modem, or by the management tunnels described above.

Summary

This chapter was designed to give enterprise customers considering implementing VPN services a look behind the scenes at some of the key systems that go into rolling out the various varieties of managed network services. With this information, it is hoped that you will better be able to decide which added value services you might like to have in conjunction with the basic transport provided by the Service Provider.

For Service Providers, this chapter was designed to give insight into the various interfaces and functions of the various VPN approaches on the market, and to document how these systems integrate into existing service management environments. In general, larger service providers have large-scale Operational Support Systems (OSS), which encompass most of the elements we have discussed in this chapter. Our intent was to focus the spotlight only on elements particularly relevant to Virtual Private Networks. Understanding these frameworks is very helpful in planning and deployment for the VPN service, but is beyond the scope of these authors and this book.

The future holds the promise of increasing standardization of both processes and protocols used in the management of the Service Provider business. Hopefully, future discussions of this topic will seem less like the witches' brew described in the opening of the chapter.

A Look Ahead

"I never think of the future. It comes soon enough." This comment from Albert Einstein seems especially appropriate for the Internet era. Developments in networking and communications occur so rapidly that trying to predict the future is less important than trying to get less behind. The technologies discussed in this chapter are not some utopian vision of the future, but a discussion of technologies and services in their early stages of becoming products. Key topics we will cover in this chapter include:

♦ VPN technology in broadband (xDSL and cable TV) networks

♦ VPN technology in cellular telephony networks

♦ The use of multicasting protocols with VPNs

- ◆ New encryption and authenication methods
- ◆ The use of Multiprotocol Label Switching (MPLS) for traffic management within the Service Provider and as a possible VPN protocol
- ◆ IPv6 and VPNs

In some cases, such as with multicast protocols, products are already deployed in the general networking environment and are just starting to make their presence felt in VPNs. In other cases, such as with cellular telephony, xDSL, and cable modems, capability exists today but is hampered by the lack of widespread availability of infrastructure to support broad acceptance or understanding. Last, standards in the networking community can be slow to reach consensus. Once consensus is reached on the standards, implementation and deployment details need to be worked out. This is the case for protocols such as IPv6 and MPLS.

This chapter is designed to provide background and insight into these issues. Since most of these technologies are still somewhat immature, rates of adoption are bound to be somewhat speculative. Opinions on these questions are our own. We are hoping that this book will be printed on acid free paper in case any words have to be eaten down the line.

Cellular Telephony and VPNs

Take a look around lately, and you will notice that cellular telephones are increasingly popular. People drive while talking on the phone; they take calls on the sidewalk, on the bus, in the subway, and in restaurants, movies, concerts and plays. We are optimists and believe a certain etiquette will eventually develop as the cellular telephone gets more and more embedded in our lives. That said, who hasn't wanted to send a critical E-mail during a customer meeting or in an airport during a layover? Have you ever wished that you could spend an extra hour or two at the beach instead of rushing home to "dial-in"?

It is currently estimated that over 50% of wireline circuit switched traffic is used for data. Ultimately, the same usage will likely be reached for wireless communication. Data communications capability is available for cellular telephones today, but it is agonizingly slow. Data rates are usually no higher than 9600 bits per second. Most of the major cellular switching manufacturers are planning to deploy new technology in their networks enabling data rates in the 100 Kb/s per second range. Tunneling protocols play a key role in these plans.

A Short Introduction to Cellular Communications Standards

It has been very frustrating to experience cellular telephone usage in Europe. There, subscribers have almost unfettered mobility. Back in the United States, the cellular telephone system seems to be a patchwork of disconnected systems. The ability to "roam" outside of devilishly designed territories may be possible in and around one's own city, but don't expect your cell phone to work when you travel, say, to another state. Billing and service plans are even more confusing. Many of these troubles stem from a well-intentioned decision of the Federal Communications Commission (FCC) not to impose standards on second-generation digital cellular telephone systems. Further, many of the older first-generation analog systems are still operating.

In Europe, thirteen countries signed a Memorandum of Understanding (MOU) agreeing to build a pan-European digital cellular telephone network based on a 900 Megahertz (MHz) frequency band called the Global System for Mobile Communication (GSM). GSM quickly expanded to over 100 countries worldwide. New networks come on-line monthly. North America is now starting to build GSM systems, but operating at 1900 MHz. These use smaller cells, more applicable to dense cities. Since most of the addressing and identifiers are the same between the 900 MHz and the 1900 MHz systems, dual frequency phones can be used to access both systems. Subscribers can put the *Subscriber Identity Module cards (SIM-cards)* in phones from different systems and still receive their phone calls and messages.

A generic topology of most second-generation digital cellular telephone networks is shown in Figure 8.1. The territory in which a system operates is laid out in a pattern of cells each served by a radio antenna and associated base transceiver station, or BTS. These are sometimes more simply called base stations. A number of these base stations are connected by wirelines (but sometimes microwave) to a base station controller or BSC. Together, these components manage the radio interface over the air to the cell phone or mobile station (MS). This function includes cell hand-over and other tasks involved in Radio Resource Management (RR). Calls are set up and torn down under the control of the Mobile Switching Center (MSC), which interfaces into the wireline public switched telephone network. These functions are known as connection management (CM). Included in the connection management function is traffic monitoring for billing purposes and overall network management functions for the system.

The Mobile Switching Center keeps track of a mobile station's location with two databases: the Home Location Register (HLR) and the Visitor Location Register (VLR). The Home Location Register keeps user profile and billing information for subscribers originating in the territory served by the MSC. The Visitor Location Register keeps track of subscribers that "roam" into this territory. When a subscriber enters another territory, the Visitor Location Register finds the user's Home Location Register based on an identification code from the mobile station. These two registers then exchange information about the user's current location.

When a call comes in from the public switched telephone network, the Gateway Mobile Switching Center uses the dialed number to query the Home Location Register of the subscriber for the current location of

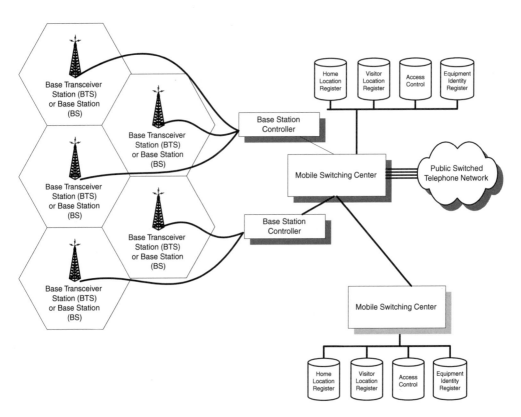

Figure 8.1 Overview of a Second-generation Cellular Telephone Network

the destination and switches the call to the MSC currently serving the subscriber.

The Access Control database keeps authentication and encryption information for the subscriber. Sometimes a separate Equipment Identity Register database contains identification information about the different equipment that subscribers are using to access the system. This information can be used, for example, to block calls originating from stolen equipment.

Data Operations in the Cellular Network

As we stated above, data communications over the cellular telephone network are already possible but are not very user friendly. They typically operate at frustratingly low speeds and often require special software and applications packages. These facilities could give access to Internet-based VPNs, but the result would likely be very unsatisfying. Most of the data communications approaches use the underlying circuit model of traditional telephony rather than the packet-oriented approaches used in data networking. The 200 MHz carrier used in most cellular system is divided into eight timeslots, each providing a single voice channel. When used for data, only 9600 (this may rise to 14.4 Kbps) bits per second can be squeezed into this spectrum. A proposal called High-speed Circuit Switched Data (HSCSD) is currently in early stages of rollout that will allow all eight slots to be available for data calls, but this also will be circuit-based. We feel that the best hope for future data services lies in the emerging General Packet Radio Services (GPRS) standard, which as its name implies, deploys a packet model between the mobile station and the cellular network.

More interesting to this discussion, the GPRS system employs tunneling protocols to shunt data between the number of serving GPRS support nodes (SGSN) providing wireless data services to a group of cells and a Gateway GPRS Support Node (GGSN) providing access to the Internet or other data networks. Eventually, the GGSN may provide tunneling services directly into VPN servers on enterprise intranets. Figure 8.2 shows how these components interface with existing digital cellular networks. The figure concentrates on the data paths and tunneling aspects of the systems. Not all of the control interfaces are shown.

With the GPRS system, a new type of cell phone puts data on a cellular frequency separate from the one used for voice. The phone uses a packet-based contention protocol between it and a limited number of

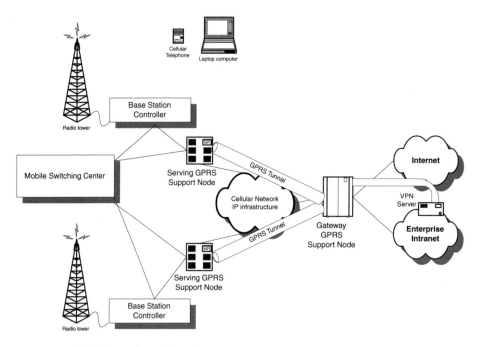

Figure 8.2 GPRS Topology Overview

other cellular data users. This way, it can simultaneously send and receive telephone calls as well as data. When the data arrives at the base station controller, the servicing GPRS service node (SGSN) encapsulates it in a special GPRS Tunneling Protocol (GTP), where it is shunted to a Gateway GPRS Service Node (GGSN) connected to the subscriber's Internet service or company intranet. If the company intranet is not directly connected to the GPRS, the data can be tunneled to an enterprise VPN server with traditional tunneling protocols such as L2TP or IPSec.

Since the GPRS doesn't use a circuit model for data transfer, it doesn't tie up resources when data is not being transferred and is expected to make mobile data communications much more cost effective. This will lead to a number of new usage models for cellular data. In conjunction with higher-speed access, simplifying the connection technology between the user's laptop and cell phone will enable even more flexibility. A proposed wireless protocol called Bluetooth can operate between these two devices without the need to set up a wired connection. Mobile users can, for instance, continuously receive E-mail to their laptops while traveling to and from the airport or while in business meetings without the need to connect the two devices or explicitly dial a connection.

VPN Applications in Broadband Access Networks

In Chapter 1 we discuss how a growing glut of newly installed fiber optics across the United States and even the oceans is transforming the Internet backbone. Many Internet users have not been able to benefit from this bandwidth because access technology to reach this backbone is still relatively slow. There are a number of forces that are chipping away at this situation. One is the exciting set of multimedia content becoming available. Another more potent force is the feeding frenzy let loose by telecommunications deregulation. Deregulation has opened the doors for the phone companies, Internet Service Providers, and cable television providers to compete for the Holy Grail of telecommunications: ownership of the converged information highway on-ramp into your home (the language of this writing mirrors the hype associated with phenomenon).

Below is a short introduction to two new broadband technologies for access, Digital Subscriber Line, in its many forms, known as xDSL, and high-speed data access over cable TV. The goal of this section is how VPN and tunneling technology can add value to this environment. VPNs present new revenue opportunities for broadband access providers to provide services directly to corporations. In the past, many operators of these technologies operated as their own Internet Service Provider, a method that all subscribers desiring data access were forced to use. A new concept called *Open Access* is being put forward as a way to offer consumer choice in this area. Our discussion is mostly oriented toward the still somewhat regulated public telecommunications environment, but there are significant opportunities for the technology discussed here in unregulated environments, such as hospital or university campuses and multitenant dwellings and office towers. The use of VPN technology in conjunction with broadband services can allow operators to offer corporate access services in addition to their consumer Internet access portfolios.

Digital Subscriber Line

Digital Subscriber Line (DSL) is a copper loop technology that uses the unused frequency spectrum on ordinary twisted pair copper wiring for high-speed (up to 7 Megabits per second) data transmission. This approach promises high-speed data connections to the Internet (and other data services) over existing telephone wiring, and thus is the telco contender for the converged access technology. There are several types of DSL technologies in the market place, collectively known as xDSL.

These standards are still immature and all regulatory issues have not been resolved. xDSL is still very much an emerging market.

Unlike the data over cable, the bandwidth on the xDSL circuit is dedicated to the individual subscriber and is not shared between other subscribers in the neighborhood. Data travels on the copper wiring in frequencies above the voice signal, which allows for simultaneous use of the telephone and data connection. The 7 Mbps of bandwidth offered by xDSL is enough to support a single television channel. The television tuner in this case would likely be located in the central office, and only the channel selected by the subscriber would be sent over the wire.

There are a number of variations on the operational and IP addressing aspects of xDSL implementations. A typical user will buy or lease an xDSL Remote Termination Unit (RTU) to connect his or her PC to a Network Access Provider. RTUs come in many varieties, depending on the application and the number of end stations supported. When the xDSL connection is used for simple Internet service, IP address assignment to the endstation is straightforward. If the user wants to be routed to his or her corporate network or a third-party outsourced Internet Service Provider, address assignment gets more complicated. Often the RTU in conjunction with the DSL card at the telco switching center supports complicated addressing schemes, proxy arps, multinetting, and so on, to route packets to different Internet Service Providers. These mechanisms are not standardized and vary greatly from vendor to vendor.

Data over Cable TV

One of the big technological transformations of the 1990s relates to the ongoing frequency shift in telecommunications. What traditionally ran over wires—voice communications—is being replaced more and more with cellular and other wireless technology. On the other hand, many of us grew up watching a television set with a "rabbit ears" style antenna to capture the signal from the airwaves. Now over 90% of homes in the United States are "passed" by cable TV networks. These networks (generally) provide a better quality picture and access to more channels. More importantly these can serve as a medium for high-speed data transport.

Cable modems typically attach via a 10BASET Ethernet connection to the user's PC. There are many possible configurations, but most often, a cable network operator uses one of the more than 100 6 MHz television carriers on its network for downstream transmission of Internet data. Different modulation schemes are available in cable modems to accomplish this, and for the most part, cable modems have been proprietary to the different vendor systems implemented for the network. A new standard called the Data Over Cable Service Interface Specification (DOCSIS) aims to standardize this access such that consumers will be able to buy their own modems for use with many services, rather than being required to lease one from the network provider. Depending on the modulation scheme, cable modems can give users on the particular channel up to 36 Mbps to share among themselves in a contention-based protocol. On some systems up to 2000 homes will be connected on this data channel. The upstream path is handled differently. It uses a cable frequency below the standard television channels and is often not symmetrical in bandwidth with the downstream data path.

Many of today's cable modem plants were implemented with only the one-way broadcast of television in mind. They use long coaxial cable runs with many amplifiers and splitters in the signaling path and are thus often subject to noise and interference. Cable modem companies are now rapidly upgrading their networks to new bidirectional Hybrid Fiber Coax (HFC) systems to be better prepared to offer two-way data and voice services. Data service is possible on the older one-way systems using a technique called Telco Return, where the generally slower downstream connection is via traditional dial-up and only the typically higher speed response goes over the cable system. These systems are not addressed in the discussion below.

Broadband Services Using Tunneling Technology

The following discussion presents an architecture that allows broadband access providers to *outsource* the ISP function to a number of partner Service Providers and provide data access services directly to corporations. As we mentioned above, mechanisms to support these applications are currently a hodgepodge of proprietary methods and nonstandard protocols. The discussion below presents a standard approach to these applications using tunneling technology. While not widely implemented at this point, this discussion brings together many of the protocols, provisioning, management, and auxiliary services discussed in this book.

The access provider installs and manages the physical plant and bills the customer for services (voice, video, and data) delivered over this plant. Data traffic from these customers arrive at the cable provider head end and is routed to an Internet Service Provider (or other data network) selected by the customer. Even though the customers are connected to a common access infrastructure (xDSL or cable), they appear as though they are connected only to their selected Internet Service Provider or company intranet. Figure 8.3 gives an overview of this solution. It requires three key technologies:

- Cable and XDSL access technology
- ATM/ SONET/ SWITCHING/ Quality of Service (QOS) technology for the head end
- VPN technology that insures connected clients are routed securely to their destination network

The approach described below does not require modifications to any of the component product sets and can be built today with off-the-shelf

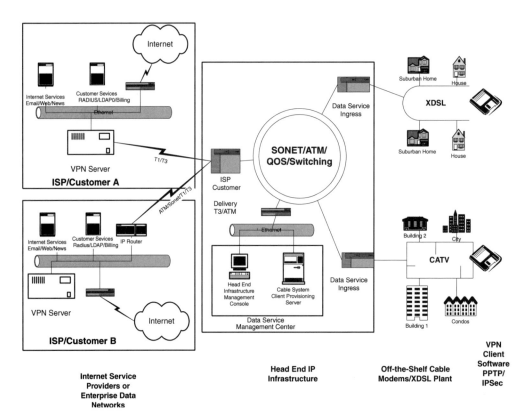

Figure 8.3 Use of Tunneling Technology to Outsource ISP and Remote Access Services to Broadband Subscribers

components. Although most of the cable modem and xDSL solutions sold today provide proprietary schemes for VPN management, very little of these mechanisms are used.

As described below, a simple addressing plan connects both subscribers and Internet Service Providers into a simple private internet onto which the VPN is then layered. The architecture discussed below handles subscriber routing in a straightforward manner by using tunneling to shunt the user packets to their destination data network.

Overview of the VPN Topology

In the tunnel operational environment, the broadband operator will create a standard IP infrastructure that supports high-speed IP circuits provisioned to the participating destination ISPs and data networks as well as address the end-user access plant. This network is a totally private network that has no other connections to the outside world. It exists only for the purpose of transporting IP packets between the end users and their selected data networks, thus it can use a private address space such as 10.0.0.0.

All destination ISP or enterprise networks are connected to the same private infrastructure. Participating data networks will have to have firewall connections coming in through these circuits to insure that only authorized users are entering the the networks via this path, as they would with other leased-line-based Internet access. This task is greatly facilitated by the tunneling approach. Packets entering these circuits should only be addressed to the VPN protocol server located in the target data network. They should only come into the proper TCP port number allocated for the tunneling protocol used (typically IPSec) and have the appropriate tunnel header format.

The connection between the broadband provider access network and the destination data networks is a standard IP connection. Any telecommunications technology can be used (ATM, SONET, HSSI, E3/T3, E1/T1, etc.), and any brand of router can be used on the cable network or destination data network. Some VPN servers can also terminate this connection directly for T3/T1 speeds and may incorporate integral firewall capability. End users' packets are only going to and from specific tunnel-server endpoints. This provides a convenient handle to implement QOS policies within the cable provider's network, insuring that no particular client or data network is using the cable provider infrastructure unfairly.

The VPN Provisioning Approach

Adding a user to an ISP environment usually requires a number of activities: creating mail accounts and reserving end user storage, setting up authorization and accounting profiles, and so on. These are largely automated in an activity known as the provisioning process. The point here is that the broadband access provider is not acting as a "jump station" where a user can connect first to one ISP and then to another arbitrarily. While the end user may be "registered" with multiple data networks or even ISPs, the provisioning process of establishing authorizations and resources is typically not that dynamic. A typical access provider may offer its subscribers a choice of three or four different ISPs that compete on service for the customer's business. Changing ISPs, however, is similar to the traditional model of first opening the new account, transferring any mail or web site, leaving a forwarding address for a certain period, and finally closing the first account.

When the user first subscribes to the broadband service, he or she receives a "modem" appropriate to the service and an IP address in the cable provider's address space (e.g., 10.0.0.0) appropriate to the technology of the cable, broadband, or xDSL. The only server visible to the subscriber on this network is the cable provider home page. It presents a menu of participating ISPs and data networks to which the user can register, along with cost, support services, and other terms and conditions associated with the service.

When a user selects an ISP or data network, an appropriate tunnel client (typically IPSec) is downloaded to the user's PC along with a script file configuring the client to point to the tunnel server address on the destination data network. Alternatively, the cable provider can distribute the tunnel client software to the end user upon subscription to the broadband network. Eventually, we can envision the client software distributed with the operating system (a built-in IPSec client for Windows) or integrated in to the modem itself. Integration into the modem can serve to offload the sometime heavy load of data encryption from slower PCs, but has the drawback of making the modem proprietary until the standards have been further solidified. Both of these approaches are clearly on the horizon, making this broadband VPN architecture very in tune with industry trends.

The cable provider would at this point signal the subscription to the destination data network, which initiates any provisioning activity required for the customer. Many mechanisms are available for this signaling: in-band, where the broadband provider and destination network provisioning servers can be members of a private VPN; or out-of-band, for instance, via E-mail. Depending on the activities required to provision the end user on the destination network, the user account may be available instantaneously or the end user may have to be notified at some later time (say via email) that the account is provisioned.

Operation of the VPN Client

Once the end user is provisioned with client software configured to point to a tunnel server on the destination data network, and the user's accounts and authorizations there are set up, the user is ready to connect to the destination network. As stated above, when the user powers on his or her machine, he or she gets attached to the cable provider's IP network and receive an IP address from servers on this network. The only resource on this network is the cable provider's home page. Since there is no gateway to the Internet or other destinations available, this network is of little interest to the user.

In order to attach to the selected destination network, the user must activate the configured tunnel client and start the session on the target destination network. The following steps occur:

♦ The user selects the particular target VPN server among those with which he or she may have been registered.

♦ The user fills in the authentication dialog box of the VPN client with the account and password information required on the destination data network.

♦ An encrypted tunnel is created between the user's PC and the tunnel server at the Internet Service Provider or enterprise.

♦ The user is authenticated against a RADIUS database on the destination network. A one-time password challenge may be issued via a Security Dynamics server. Other authentication methods such as X.509 certificates, can be used.

♦ A billing record may be generated via the RADIUS client to an accounting server.

♦ The tunnel client acts as a new network adapter on the user's PC, this adapter is allocated a second (real) address from the destination network's address space. This address can come from the either the destination network RADIUS database or a DHCP server.

♦ The user profile in the VPN server database provides traffic prioritization and filters that may be applied against the user's packets.

The key to the operation of the VPN is that with the VPN tunnel server, a second internal address is assigned to the user. The user appears to be part of the destination network address space. No address translation is required. This enables complete transparency to all applications the client may want to run.

Since the tunnel is encrypted between client and the destination tunnel network server, privacy is insured even on a shared media access plant. Since the user is required to activate the tunnel client and authenticate on the destination network, this gives a framework for additional security and accounting.

Limitations and Restrictions

The architecture described above uses off-the-shelf components to build a cable VPN that is simple to understand, scalable, and secure. The solution is standards-based and can be implemented with equipment from many vendors or retrofitted into an existing installed plant.

One question that does come up when a subscriber uses tunneling protocols to access an Internet Service Provider is, "What happens if the user wants to tunnel to an enterprise that is not connected to the access provider?" The requirements of tunneling basically stipulate the tunnel server and client have publicly reachable IP addresses. The IP addresses that clients receive in the discussion above have been non-routable 10.0.0.0 addresses. If the broadband access provider had a block of routable addresses, say from one of the attached ISPs, they could relatively simply allocate to these (typically business) customers, one of the routable addresses via their address allocation servers. These are often DHCP servers that allocate addresses based on subscriber MAC addresses.

Most of the limitations and restrictions of the solution stem from the need to install client software on the end-user PC.

- ♦ The client software is closely tied to the PC architecture and is currently only available for Windows-based clients.
- ♦ The client software interacts intimately with the Windows operating system, creating a new network adapter. Care needs to be taken that client installation procedures handle the diversity of PC environments.
- ♦ Certain older software packages bind directly with the adapter and installation of the client software may have adverse effects on these packages.

◆ The IPSec encryption is handled in software on the end-user PC. This load can be significant for many PCs. This is especially true during network intensive activities such as file downloading.

Once noted, these caveats are no more significant than those that occur with traditional ISP packages. The advantages have the ability to delight both broadband operators with the ability to offer their customers a choice of ISP networks or other corporate data networks in a secure and simple manner. The ISPs themselves should also be delighted with the opening up of such a large new customer base with such a small addition of equipment and complexity.

Multicasting Protocols in the VPN Environment

Some of the new applications available over the Internet involve collaboration between many parties. Examples of these include the ability to have multiparty videoconferences and whiteboarding sessions that can avoid the need to make a business trip. In addition, every network manager will be delighted to know that a whole new group of multiplayer games is also emerging.

In another new class of applications, a single sender "pushes" identical data to a possibly large group of subscribers. Some examples of these types of applications include: real-time data delivery of financial data, distance learning, multimedia video and audio broadcasts, and updating price files to retail stores.

In order to conserve bandwidth on the backbone, relieve network application hosts from making multiple copies of packets, and allow clients whose addresses are not known in advance to participate in these applications, a new class of protocols were developed known as *IP multicast*. Multicast applications send packets to special destinations in the Class D IP address range (224.0.0.0 to 239.255.255.255). Endstations register to enter or leave multicast groups by registering with multicast enabled routers via the Internet Group Management Protocol (IGMP). The multicast router then builds a tree-based topology to minimize the number of packet replications needed to reach all of the registered listeners. A multicast application running on a host simply sends a single packet with a multicast group destination address, and the multicast-enabled routers insure that the packet gets to every listener.

Depending on whether the listeners are "sparsely" or "densely" distributed throughout the network, a number of multicast routing protocols can be used. The Distance Vector Multicast Routing Protocol (DVMRP) used on the Internet multicast backbone (MBONE) and Multicast Open Shortest Path First (MOSPF) are common dense mode protocols. Core Based Trees (CBT) and Protocol Independent Multicast–Sparse Mode (PIM-SM) are common sparse mode protocols.

Despite some of the compelling applications discussed above, multicast protocols have had a relatively slow uptake. One reason is the number of overlapping protocol standards mentioned above. In additions, network managers are still leery of the possibility that multicast traffic will strain their network infrastructures and starve their mission-critical applications. Some of the push applications are being restrained by the fact that most multicast applications use the User Datagram Protocol (UDP) with the possibility of dropped or duplicated packets going unnoticed or with no built-in congestion control mechanisms.

Over time, as standards mature, we expect multicast applications to become a standard part of the enterprise repertory. Implementing multicast protocols in edge devices like VPN servers have some special considerations. Analysis is required for both the remote access and LAN-to-LAN applications.

Implementation Considerations for VPNs

The issues involved in secure multicasting include most of the same issues involved in VPNs: confidentiality, integrity, authentication, and nonrepudiation. Access control—that is to say, who can join a multicast group—takes on new implications from a security perspective, and one that presents many thorny problems in the security community. The IPSec committee in the IETF has formally tabled discussions of secure multicast to a later date, although much work on secure multicast is going on in research and military applications.

Almost all of this work uses IPSec as a foundation. ESP headers, AH headers, ISAKMP, and Diffie-Hellman all make their entrances in the expected places. Despite the recent push in the military to use more commercial off-the-shelf products, IPSec is often not suitable for military requirements. It is important to note that the multicast security associations are generally looked at as separate from those supporting unicast VPN tunnels. Major areas of research include *group* keys that are securely shared among the multicast user group for the multicast session, even though users may enter and leave the group at will. In conjunction with this effort are extensions to the Internet Group Management Protocol, and multicast routing protocols, particularly Core Based Trees (CBT), to support "secure joins." In this approach, stations are only permitted to join specific multicast groups permitted under explicit policy and authentication.

The discussion above represents an applications point of view of secure multicast. VPN users often look at IP VPNs as leased-line replacements. From this point of view multicast packets should travel over IPSec or other tunnels just as unicast packets. The VPN server should recognize the multicast packets on its private side interfaces. It should replicate them as required into the required security associations; once they are received on the other end of the tunnel, it should forward them on to other downstream branches of the multicast tree, if appropriate. In short, this means implementing the IGMP protocol and one or more of the abovementioned multicast routing protocols on the VPN server. There is also work on a standard called IGMP Relay, which will enable edge devices to offload much of the multicast routing to the core of the network. IGMP Relay may be particularly useful in VPN devices.

At this writing, we are not aware of any commercial products that have undertaken these efforts. Perhaps it is because the word is not in from the security community on definitive approaches to secure multicasting. Issues of performance and management can also be amplified with VPN technology. The same trepidation holding back many network managers from deploying multicast applications on their intranets may also be restraining demand for this feature in VPNs.

Multiprotocol Label Switching (MPLS)

Multiprotocol Label Switching is another one of those sizzling hot topics, that like VPNs have a lot of hype around it, proportional to the promise it hopes to deliver. Some of the chief applications of label switching are the following:

- Traffic management
- IP/ATM integration
- Advanced Quality of Service
- VPNs

In Chapter 2 we discussed the use of ATM switches in ISP networks. Service providers use this ATM switching fabric for many reasons. We saw how it is possible to provision many independent IP networks over their transmission facilities and offer these networks to customers as

VPNs. ATM networks give the ability to provision a "path" through a network of Layer 2 switches such that two IP routers can appear adjacent to each other when it might have otherwise required a number of routing hops between them. Each of these paths could be provisioned for a particular ATM Class of Service, for instance to minimize latency or packet loss. These features make up the foundation of early traffic engineering by Internet backbone operators. Their goal was to explicitly create paths through their transmission networks, then have the ability to direct certain streams of data down those paths.

As we have seen with the great number of ATM backbones found in Service Providers, this effort was somewhat successful. The method of *ad hoc* style of traffic engineering has been more and more fraying around the edges. The burden of provisioning and managing the overlay network of ATM PVCs is growing into a large headache for many Service Providers. And as transmission systems get faster, and faster—OC-48, OC-192 and higher—many question the ability for ATM technology to keep up. The cell tax gets more and more burdensome with the small 48-bit payload, and many question the ability of ASIC and circuit designers to effectively implement the packet assembly and disassembly functions at those high speeds.

MPLS promises to solve many of these problems. It is designed to give the flexibility and control of ATM switches without the need for actual switches. For networks that have a large investment in ATM cores, MPLS will help IP routers use that backbone more effectively, with less manual provisioning.

Multiprotocol Label Switching consists of two components, a forwarding component and a control component. The forwarding components use short fixed length labels to identify different data "streams." Instead of routing a packet based on its destination address (the longest matching prefix), MPLS switches do a direct lookup of the specific label to make the forwarding decisions. Labels can represent a wide range of forwarding granularities—individual hosts, protocol streams, and application groups. In addition, the labels can have special "semantics." That is to say, they might directly map to specific ATM VPI/VCI, Frame Relay DLCIs, or Ethernet Mac addresses, allowing the IP packets to more efficiently use these technologies.

The control component of MPLS involves creating the Label Switched Paths through the network over which the traffic will flow. This can be an automatic process, using a label distribution protocol, for example, in conjunction with topology information gained from tradi-

32 bits

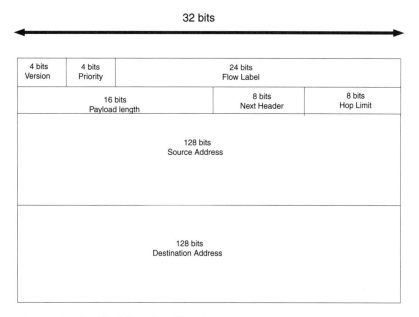

Figure 8.5 The IPv6 Routing Header

keys to understanding IPv6's features and implementation approaches is by examining its packet header layout shown in Figure 8.5. Note that the header is a fixed 40 bytes in length, and many of the fields found in the IPv4 header have been either renamed or moved out of the fixed header into optional extension headers. The fixed header size will enable much more efficient processing of packets by network routers versus the IPv4 variable header layout, which needs to be "parsed" to find key attributes. The IPv6 header also includes direct support for a flow label that will facilitate the label switching architectures discussed above. Among the optional extension headers are the Authentication Header and Encryption Header that are used to provide IPSec tunneling, authentication, and encryption features in IPv4. Thus, VPNs are a built-in component of IPv6 rather than an add-on.

Much of the focus of IPv6 has been on its new 128-bit addressing field. This larger address space will set the stage for IP networking to support the explosion of embedded and "hidden" networking that is looming on the future. Devices such as Personal Data Assistants (PDAs), automobiles, vending machines, and even common household appliances will require IP addresses in the future. The large address will also enable a more efficient hierarchical routing structure to support networking on a global scale. IPv6 addressing can take into account Top Level Aggregators (TLAs), Next

3 bits Address Type	13 bits TLA	32 bits NLA	16 bits SLA	64 bits Interface ID

Figure 8.6 A Typical IPv6 128-Bit Address Format

Level Aggregators (NLAs), and Site Level Aggregators (SLAs), that will permit network routers to route packets much like the telephone network does, with the TLA corresponding to the country code followed by the area code and prefix. Unlike the telephone network, the aggregators are not necessarily strictly geographical, since some large networks may cross over geographic boundaries. Further, Next Level aggregators may subdivide their fields to better reflect hierarchies of smaller Service Providers.

The new 64-bit Interface ID field allows a host on the network to simply autoconfigure its address, typically with the ID of its LAN cards. Once this is accomplished, a new Neighbor Discovery (ND) protocol allows the station to request its routing prefix from an upstream router. Note that, unlike the DHCP service described in Chapter 6, this approach does not require an addressing server to keep the state of allocated addresses or manage leases (although state-full address assignment via DHCP has been extended to IPv6 and can be used if desired). Autoconfiguration simplifies reconfiguration from node moves and changes and even facilitates an enterprise changing Internet Service Providers, if required.

Obviously, existing IPv4 Domain Name Servers will need to be updated to handle lookup and storage of the new 128-bit addresses. A new network of dual function IPv4/IPv6 name servers will have to be implemented to translate names to IPv6 addresses. These name servers can also be used in transition scenarios. If an IPv4 address was returned from a name lookup, a dual stack host would use IPv4 for the connection; if an IPv6 address was returned, it would use IPv6. Most applications use Application Programming Interfaces (APIs) to query name servers, but some applications that don't may require updates to work with the new 128-bit records. In a similar fashion, other network protocols such as BGP and SNMP will need enhancement to deal with the new environment.

Implications of IPv6 on VPNs

Happily, as edge devices, many VPN appliances (especially for the remote access application) will be the last worry facing the enterprise network manager. Key issues will involve insuring compatibility with authentication, naming, and address servers supporting the VPN application. Care will need to be taken that remote access clients will still be able to reach any dual-stack application hosts that may have been converted in a transition plan.

As stated above, the LAN-to-LAN application is supported directly in IPv6. Whether an enterprise can use this feature will largely depend on the IPv6 capability in the Service Provider backbone. At this writing, many Service Providers are participating in a trial IPv6 network call the 6Bone. Most likely, Internet Service Providers' plans for IPv6 rollouts will start with the cores of their network, moving slowly out to the subscriber edge. Most IPv4 VPN servers will require enhancements to enable the tunneling of IPv6 packets over the Service Provider backbone. While this is not a large technical issue, we are not aware of any VPN vendor providing the capability to provision IPv6 addresses in its VPN definitions.

The Advanced Encryption Standard (AES)

The Data Encryption Algorithm (DEA, the mathematical formula used in the Data Encryption Standard) was originally developed by IBM in the 1960s and formally standardized in 1976. DEA performs a transformation on a 64-bit block of data using a 56-bit key. Nowadays, the algorithm is typically implemented in software and to improve security, run three times (triple DES or 3DES). DES has held up pretty well over the last twenty years, but in 1998 a nationwide network of sometimes up to 14,000 small computers cracked 56-bit DES in about 140 hours. After trying 18 quadrillion keys, the message "Strong cryptography makes the world a safer place" won the $10,000 prize offered by RSA. Later, the Electronic Freedom Foundation cracked the code in only 56 hours using a machine built of custom chips for $250,000.

On January 2, 1997, the National Institute of Standards (NIST) began investigations for the next generation encryption algorithm to replace DES. Their initial requirements were:

♦ A standard that supports 128-, 192-, and 256-bit key sizes (preferably a block cipher)

♦ A standard that is royalty-free worldwide

♦ A standard that is more secure than Triple DES

♦ A standard that is more efficient than Triple DES

After a number of submission criteria and principles were developed, submissions were publicly solicited from around the world. After the first-round selections were closed and evaluations were made, fifteen algorithms made the first cut. These have subsequently been judged in round 2 on the basis of

♦ Security
♦ Cost (in terms of computation efficiency and memory requirements)
♦ Algorithm and implementation characteristics (flexibility, simplicity, and hardware/software suitability)

Round 2 Evaluations were completed in the summer of 1999. MARS from IBM, RC6 from RSA, Rijndael, Serpent, and Twofish will proceed to the Round 3 conference in New York in August 2000. It is expected that AES will become a Federal Information Processing Standard (FIPS) in 2001. Candidate algorithms as shown in Table 8.1.

Needless to say, this process is not without some controversy. The AES standard is supposed to last for twenty to thirty years. It is extremely hard to image what will be applications and operations environment in

Table 8.1 Candidates for NIST Advanced Encryption Standard

Country	Algorithm	Sponsor
Australia	LOKI97	Lawrie Brown, Josef Pieprzyk, Jennifer Seberry
Belgium	RIJNDAEL	Joan Daemen, Vincent Rijmen
Canada	CAST-256	Entrust Technologies
	DEAL	Outerbridge, Knudsen
Costa Rica	FROG	TecApro Internacional S.A.
France	DFC	Centre National pour la Recherche Scientifique (CNRS)
Germany	MAGENTA	Deutsche Telekom AG
Japan	E2	Nippon Telegraph and Telephone Corporation (NTT)
Korea	CRYPTON	Future System, Inc
USA	HPC	Rich Schroeppel
	MARS	IBM
	RC6	RSA Laboratories
	SAFER+	Cylink Corporation
	TWOFISH	Bruce Schneier, John Kelsey, Doug Whiting, David Wagner, Chris Hall, Niels Ferguson
UK, Israel, Norway	SERPENT	Ross Anderson, Eli Biham, Lars Knudsen

that timeframe. Other participants to the process gave lively discussion concerning the desire to have one winner versus two or three alternatives. What if a flaw in the winning protocol comes to light? Another interesting issue is discussed concerning the applicability of the algorithms to lightweight environments such as smart cards (8-bit processors and 256 bytes of memory). This would insure truly universal application in many environments. We will discuss smart cards further in the next section.

The implications for VPN products should be obvious. Networking products have shorter and shorter depreciation schedules. Many of the devices purchased today will be technically obsolete and fully depreciated in 2001 when the new standards start to be mandated in government and then enterprise environments. As the date grows nearer, users will need to take into account software and hardware upgrade strategies to integrate these new algorithms into their equipment. Alternatives to DES exist today, but are often hampered by licensing and royalty requirements. This situation should not be a problem with AES.

Biometric Authentication Methods

In Chapter 6 we discussed some of the problems of password-based authentication systems. The solutions proposed—two-factor systems using a token card with one-time passwords—increased security, but are still far from ideal. These systems require the user to carry and keep track of the token card! Using unique features of a user's body has existed as an identification method for a long time. From ancient China, where many important documents were signed with a thumbprint, to contemporary crime fighting, the unique characteristics of lines and ridges in a person's fingerprints have been used to ascertain identity. As the awareness and importance of authentication grows, the science of biometrics, that is to say, using the unique biological characteristics for purposes of identification, has gained increasing interest from the security community.

There are two main types of biometric identification systems. There are those that exploit unique physiological characteristics, such as the shape and proportion of the face, the abovementioned fingerprints, the unique geometry of a person's hand, and the unique characteristics found in the human eye—the pattern of a person's iris or retina. Another approach uses unique behavioral characteristics, including a person's signature, voice, or even the unique rhythm and speed of one's typing.

Within these systems, two different authentication approaches have been defined, one-to-one systems and one-to-many systems. In a one-to-one system, the digitized representation of the biometric for the user is stored in a database with the user identity. The user's biometric is then verified against this representation, which may be stored centrally, or locally, say on a smart card. In one-to-many verification, the user's biometric is matched against the whole database for a match, without *a priori* knowledge of the user identity.

Two metrics of performance are generally discussed with biometric authentication systems, the False Accept Rate (FAR), which is the probability the system would wrongly authenticate an impostor, and the False Reject Rate (FRR), which is the probability the system would wrongly reject a valid user.

At this writing the performance metrics of these systems haven't been sufficiently documented, and because of low volume, biometric scanners are still relatively expensive. It is also estimated that whatever the particular metric used, it will not work on 2 to 3% of the population, for one reason or another. Further, a number of social issues relating to privacy and intrusiveness of the process have been risen. These factors are being slowly addressed as the benefits over traditional password systems increase. There have already been a number of high-profile systems put into production, including a hand geometry system at Disney World in Florida, and an iris-scanning system used at the Winter Olympics in Japan. In the field of biometrics, the United States currently lags behind the trials in Europe and Asia. We believe that eventually we will see a more widespread deployment of one-to-one biometric systems for VPN authentication. Fingerprint systems look like an especially good candidate since they can easily be integrated with the mouse or other pointer device on the user's PC. They are commonly felt to be the least intrusive, inexpensive to implement, and fast and reliable.

Summary

"May you live in interesting times" is said by some to be a Chinese curse. Others say that it is a Chinese blessing. Still others say that the quotation is hardly Chinese at all! This situation sums up a lot of our feelings about VPNs. . . . Always a little controversy, definitely interesting, and a curse or blessing depending on the perspective with which one views the issues at the time. We hope you appreciated our personal selection of topics relating to the future of VPNs. Like this book in general, the material was not designed to be a totally exhaustive or completely tutorial treatment of these issues. It was designed to stimulating thinking and reflection. Another goal was to focus on topics that synthesize and integrate many of the themes discussed in earlier chapters. You may not have agreed with our spin on everything in this chapter, but if it has caused any sparks of insight or understanding our purpose was achieved.

The Light at the End of the Tunnel

This section is not the introduction to some new optical networking approach to VPNs, but some closing remarks about VPNs and their place in corporate networking. VPNs clearly go beyond simple protocol mechanisms, such as tunneling and encryption. More accurately, they represent the integration of technologies from all aspects of networking. Good implementations of VPNs require understanding and analysis at all levels of the ISO networking model—from applications to transport protocols and transmission systems. Each of the component technologies of VPNs—encryption, authentication, and management, to name just a few—is evolving in different directions and speeds. They somehow must come together cohesively to create a solution that works in the sometimes messy real world.

Of course there is always more. A complete discussion of all of the standards and protocols, along with their futures, would have to be delivered in volumes. We feel that our added value has been to distill and edit these technologies to provide a useful framework for understanding and to enable further inquiry by intelligent professionals, both in enterprise and Service Provider environments.

INDEX